GOOD IDEAS

Also by Michael Rosen

Selected Poems

Fighters for Life: Selected Poems

William Shakespeare, In His Time For Our Time

Michael Rosen's Sad Book, illustrated by Quentin Blake

The Penguin Book of Childhood

Alphabetical: How Every Letter Tells a Story

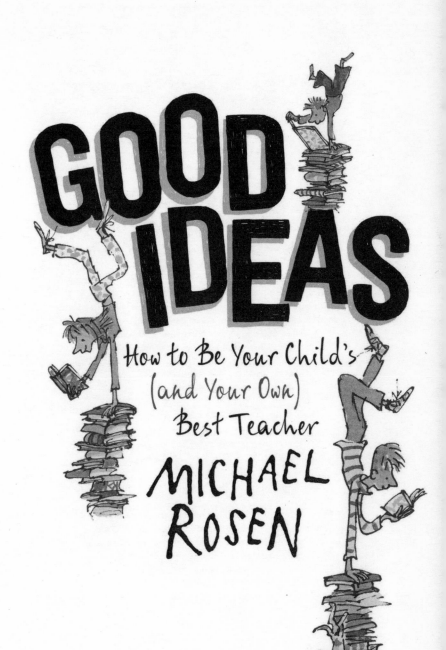

GOOD IDEAS

How to Be Your Child's
(and Your Own)
Best Teacher

MICHAEL ROSEN

JOHN MURRAY

First published in Great Britain in 2014 by John Murray (Publishers)
An Hachette UK Company

1

© Michael Rosen 2014
Illustrations feature *The Children's Book of Books* illustrations © Quentin Blake 1998

A CIP catalogue record for this title
is available from the British Library

Hardback ISBN 978-1-444-79642-1
Ebook ISBN 978-1-444-79643-8

Typeset in Sabon MT by Palimpsest Book Production Limited,
Falkirk, Stirlingshire
Printed and bound by Clays Ltd, St Ives plc

John Murray policy is to use papers that are natural,
renewable and recyclable products and made from wood
grown in sustainable forests. The logging and manufacturing
processes are expected to conform to the environmental
regulations of the country of origin.

John Murray (Publishers)
338 Euston Road
London NW1 3BH

www.johnmurray.co.uk

For Emma

CONTENTS

OUTDOORS

THE STREET

TRAVELLING AND HOLIDAYS

DAYS OUT, OUTINGS AND VISITS

FOOD FOR THOUGHT

INTRODUCTION

I am a very lucky person.

I had parents and an older brother who taught me two things that I have found incredibly useful:

1. Be curious. Endlessly curious. Go on asking questions. Never stop wondering why. Or how. Or when. Or where. Never stop wondering why or how one thing links to another. How something changed. How one thing turned into another. How something died out. How something else started up. Be curious, they said.

2. Anything out there, any knowledge, any culture, anything going on, can be yours, they said. You are entitled to find out about it, enjoy it, go there, do it, be it. There are no walls, nothing is too posh or too un-posh, nothing is too highbrow or lowbrow. Don't let anyone block you off from any of it. Don't block yourself off from any of it. Just give yourself a chance with any of it. Give it a go.

In a way all this is the opposite of what I often hear people say.

I once got into a taxi and the cabbie said that if he could have his time over again he would go and find all the really good facts and cram them into his head. I sympathize with where he was coming from. He was disappointed that there were things he didn't know or understand. What struck me as sad, though, is that he was a very knowledgeable person. He just didn't rate what he knew about London, how cars work, and stuff he had learned by growing up, living and being a parent. But then, if there was more stuff and more facts that he wanted to get hold of, the problem, I thought, is not that the facts aren't there. We're surrounded by facts every second of every day. The problem is being in the right frame of mind to know how to begin to know where to start.

I could put that another way. The problem is knowing *how to learn how to learn.*

OH NO! IT'S THE HOMEWORK

Many of us know what it feels like, sitting with our children doing homework together. All too often, it's a moment that is dull and tetchy, full of finger-prodding and hair-tearing. Sometimes children get fed up with parents talking about stuff in ways that don't make sense. Sometimes, parents get fed up with children who they think aren't trying, aren't concentrating or – fear of fears – aren't bright enough to get it.

And then the work itself: it can often seem to be full of exercises that go through stuff over and over again: lists of words; maths that repeats the same kind of sum but with different numbers; questions and answers in foreign languages in ways that aren't anything like any real bit of chat.

Whenever I talk to teachers about this, they tell me that they suspect that very little of it is much use to the children. If it's me working with one of my own children, I sit there trying to stay bright and smiley and keen. Perhaps too hard. I find myself wondering, Are we locked into some kind of conspiracy where none of the adults rates this stuff but we go ahead and do it – probably for not much better a reason than some vague memory that we did something similar ourselves? Of if we didn't, we should have. And if we had, we would have got on much better than we did, so, fingers crossed, so will my child . . .

I have some special anti-favourites: lists of words that are different but either sound or look nearly the same. Now, if words look very similar (e.g. 'breed' and 'bread') or sound very similar (e.g. 'reed' and 'read', or 'red' and 'read'), how does anyone learn the difference between these words simply by learning a list of them? The difference between these words only becomes clear in the talk or writing where they are needed. People don't eat 'breed and jam'. And that bit of bamboo stuck in the top of a saxophone is not a 'read'. By seeing and hearing words 'in context' over and over again, we get differences. All that lists do is help us keep them muddled.

WHAT CAN WE DO ABOUT THIS?

The idea behind this book is to remind you, your children, me and my children (as I write this, my two youngest children are nine and thirteen) of several things:

1. We live in a world surrounded by all the stuff that education is supposed to be about: machines, bodies, languages, cities, votes, mountains, energy, movement, plays, food, liquids, collisions, protests, stones, windows . . .

2. Of itself, none of this stuff is boring. In fact, we have to work very hard to make it boring.

3. The challenge, then, is to make this stuff not boring.

4. I have a hunch that the way to do this is not simply to try to make the stuff exciting.

5. The way to do it is to do with how we behave, how adults and children get along together.

6. That's all of us. In other words, this is not about what we adults do *to* children.

7. It's about how we do stuff *alongside* children.

8. It's not only about children's mindsets.

9. It has to be about ours too.

10. That's probably more than enough things.

MY KEY WORDS

I cannot promise that this book will not be annoying. I find it annoying when people try to squeeze years of knowledge and life experience into catchy abstract words or phrases like, 'be true to yourself'. Even so, I am not going to be able to avoid this entirely. What follows are several key words that are descriptions of the principles I work to when I think about learning. At any moment, I might ask myself, Is what's going on worthwhile? Is some kind of progress being made? I use these key words as yardsticks, or checks. If one or more of them is going on, I think that good things are happening.

INVESTIGATION

This is about asking your own questions and finding out how to answer them. Not all investigations are like this. Most people's experience of investigations is being told that we have to find out something. And then we're told how to do it. Quite often, you know that the person who sent you off to do the finding out knows the answer anyway. So in the back of your mind is the thought, Why am I bothering?

So, it's not just investigation I'm going for here. I'm going for: *investigations of things you really want to know.*

And learning new ways of doing it.

So, it's about making discoveries.

I could also call this 'being curious', or 'enquiry'.

INTERPRETATION

In the guidelines that teachers are given by examiners are the words 'retrieval' and 'inference'. A good deal of education is about telling children stuff and then asking them to 'retrieve' it. Rather cruelly, we used to call this 'regurgitating'.

So, I tell you that Billy has a blue hat. Then I ask you, 'What colour is Billy's hat?' You tell me it's blue. I give you a mark. If you don't tell me it's blue, you fail.

That's 'retrieval'.

The second process involves me telling you that it's raining. Then I ask you, 'Why is Billy wearing the hat?' If you answer, 'Because it is raining', you get two marks, because it's 'inference'. Now let's say you write that Billy's wearing the hat because he supports Chelsea. According to the sheet containing the OK answers, this is wrong. So you fail.

Now, the reason why you said, 'Because he supports Chelsea,' is that Chelsea Football Club wear blue kit. By saying, 'Because he supports Chelsea,' you *interpreted* the information I gave you. You 'retrieved' what was there, you did some 'inferring' and then you went one step further: you did some *interpreting*. For that, you fail.

My argument in this book is that:

a) you shouldn't fail
b) we all need space and time to interpret
c) when we discuss our interpretations, we pay very close attention to 'retrieving' and 'inferring'
d) the only real point in retrieving and inferring is so that we can make interpretations. We are not machines. We are thinking, feeling people who need to interpret the world so that we can act on it and change our lives and change the world.

I could also call this 'reflection' or 'figuring out'.

INVENTION

A good deal of education is spent showing children that this is the way the world is. In other words, it's presented as if it's complete and cannot be changed.

And yet:

a) it has changed
b) it's changing even as you are reading this
c) the child who is growing up will do some of the changing.

Sad to say, there are ways of discouraging children from thinking any of this – particularly the part to do with being involved in change themselves. The key way to discourage them is to prevent them from doing any inventing.

I believe that inventing is one of the best ways to find out how things work. If we make something, we find out what we can do with the stuff we're using – whether that's wood, glue, flour, eggs, clay, words, numbers, body movement or whatever. We find out 'what goes with what'. We find out what 'works' – especially if we share what we make with others around us.

I believe that some of our best thinking, talking and writing happen when we make things and do things.

I've called this 'invention' but I could also call it 'play', 'experiment', 'creativity', or simply 'making and doing things you want'.

CO-OPERATION

A good deal of our development is spent focusing on how 'individual' we are. We talk about 'personal development', 'self-expression', 'everyone is different'. It's not that these words and phrases are not true. My view is that they are not true enough.

What I mean is that at the heart of whatever we think is the 'individual' or the 'self' is something that is not the 'self'. We are made up of all our meetings and talkings with all the people we have known, met, listened to and talked to throughout our lives. It's not very individual at all. It's very social. Just take all the words on this page. It's me who's writing them and yet I borrowed every single word from many, many people who've spoken and written before me, some of whom I've met. They're 'mine' and yet they're co-owned.

This is crucial to how I am going to be talking about 'learning' and 'knowledge'.

Rather than talking about these as if it's a matter of a lone miser piling up bits of privately owned stuff, I will talk about how 'we' can learn more easily, how 'we' can get to know stuff, much more easily, if 'we' put at the centre of it *ways of learning that involve co-operation*. This might be through talking and listening. It might be through planning stuff together. It might be through doing things together. It might be through sharing things after we've done them.

This could also be called 'sharing', 'helping while being helped'.

I would add that we can never predict who will be able to help us, or who we can help. Education is mostly built in such a way that it keeps saying that some people are too clever to help you (they're in another stream), some people are too 'not-clever' to help you (they're also in another stream), some people are too young or too old (they're in another 'year-group'), some people are not able-bodied enough (they're in a 'special' school) and so on. These are the segregations carried out inside class-rooms, between classes and between schools. Outside school, we don't have to stick to these segregations.

THE LAYOUT OF THIS BOOK

Most people's education is chopped up and stored in towers of knowledge. We study 'subjects'. When we are at secondary school, we even go from room to room in order to study the different subjects in their towers. It's as if one subject has a home in one place and one subject has a home in another. So we separate out maths, geography, English, history and the rest.

Yet, it only takes a moment's thought to remember that the walls between these subjects are nowhere near as clear or as strong as they first appear. A lot of 'geography' is about how things came to be where they are. In other words it's 'history'. One of the ways you can figure out what a poet is doing in a poem is to listen to the rhythms of the lines. In other words, it's mathematical. When someone tries to explain a mathematical problem or feature, we sometimes ask them to try explaining it in another way. In other words, it's to do with language, which in my case here is English.

In the world outside classrooms, where this book lives, the walls between subjects are harder to make. When we're cooking, we can do physics, chemistry, biology, maths, English, geography, history all at the same time. Same goes for going on holiday, or walking round a museum.

This book chops up knowledge, learning and wisdom in a different way. It asks, 'Where is knowledge?' 'Where is the stuff we might want to know?' And so I'll be looking at the places where the stuff is, and what we can do in those places. As I go along, I will be bringing my key words with me: Investigation, Interpretation, Invention and Co-operation.

THE TOOLS

Our most important places to go for answers are the internet and books.

A word about the internet: if you are someone who can find out whatever you want from the internet, read no further. For those who find it maddening or mysterious, here are some tips.

INTRODUCTION

1. The best way to search is to use up to four or five of the main words used to describe whatever you're trying to find out. If there's a phrase that you know for certain will be in the answer to what you're looking for, you can put double quotes (" ") round the phrase like this: "leg before wicket" or "narrow gauge railway". So, for example, if you type in the words impact, climate, change, skin and cancer as five separate words, you'll get over 14 million hits, many of which are nothing to do with what you're trying to find out. If you type in "impact of climate change on skin cancer" you will get many fewer hits. You've hit your target more accurately and you will be able to get to what you want more easily. You can also play about with different phrases, e.g. "effect of climate change on skin cancer" or "climate change and cancer" and so on. In fact, thinking of it as 'play' or a game in which you're trying to catch something stops it being frustrating.

2. Google has some lesser-known facilities that are very useful. If you look along the menu across the top of the Google page, you'll see one that says, 'more'. If you 'pull' that one down, you'll see 'books'. If you click on that, you have a facility now that will look up your word or phrase in books. This may well lead you to a book you might want to read.

   There is also 'News'. This not only gives you up-to-date news, you can use it as a search engine in itself too, going back many years.

   Again, there is also 'Google Scholar' which you can find by typing 'Google Scholar' into the search engine. If you search in here, you will be taken to the most scholarly and academic articles in journals, magazines and books. Most of them, though, you will only be able to read in their entirety if you either pay or go through a library that subscribes. A big reference library will enable you to do this. Even so, this search engine takes you to the most accurate writing on any given subject.

For up-to-date information on tips for searching on Google, just Google the words 'google', 'search' and 'help'. What better example is there of the fact that 'finding out how to find out' is itself a kind of 'knowledge'!

3. If you live in the UK, you pay for libraries through your local taxes or council tax. One of the best ways to find out things with your children is at a library. It's the librarian's job to help you find whatever it is you're after. Watching a librarian doing this is a lesson in itself. In most libraries, there are computers that will enable you to get on to the internet. You can get ebooks for free if you have signed up to your local library. Libraries are of course great not just for 'finding out things' but also as a huge resource for stories, picture books, novels, poetry books and much more.

4. One of the most important things to do with children is to encourage them to browse. Browsing is the least rated, most important thing I know! Browsing is one of the key ways – if not *the* key way – in which we learn how to pick out what we want and need, and reject the stuff that we don't need. As we browse, without knowing we're doing it, we create a mind-map of where to go to get at the stuff. So, when we encourage very young children to browse through piles of books in a children's library, we're setting them up for many other kinds of browsing they may want to do later: in shops, on the internet, in archives, in offices or wherever. It's

a life-skill. People who don't know how to browse are often intimidated or even scared of shelves full of files and books. Thousands of hits on a Google search can seem like an impossible task.

When I see parents in a library or bookshop shortcutting their children's browsing, I always feel like intervening and saying, 'How will your child learn to use shelves and search engines if you don't let them make mistakes, ask for help, and find things that they weren't looking for?'

In other words, it's vital that we find places where children can browse. And that we make space and time for children to do it, without us standing over them.

Apart from anything else, browsing teaches us how and where to scan to find out things: book spines, labels on shelves, back covers, inside the front cover and so on. We learn how to pick out key words or phrases that tell us that this is what we need or want. In order to follow up our interests in a fun and easy way, we need to know how to find and juggle with key words and phrases. These are, just as we say, 'keys' to unlock the web-page, book, archive that we're after.

Browsing is crucial.

THE COMMANDMENTS

I carry in my head some guiding ideas – commandments if you like – that I try to stick to when it comes to working alongside my children. Like any commandments or resolutions, it's much easier to write them down than it is to stick to them. They are then 'best intentions'.

INTRODUCTION

1. I will try never to tell children to shut up.
2. I will try never to say to children that they are stupid.
3. I will try never to tell children that they are not good enough.
4. I will try not to make children anxious and worried about not understanding something, or not being able to do something.
5. I will try to give children real choices in matters to do with their interests, tastes, reading and the like.
6. I will try to involve children in decisions to do with their own lives.
7. I will try not to mock, diminish, denigrate or belittle anything that they do or care about.
8. I will try to take every question and query they make as serious and either do my best to answer it or – given the time – offer to help them find it out for themselves.
9. I will try to build children's confidence.
10. I will try to 'be there' – whether that means hanging out, mucking about, playing, going out, thinking up interesting things to do, or turning up for key events that matter to that particular child.
11. I will try to listen, not to dive in and finish sentences, not to speak for children when other people ask them questions.
12. I will try not to pretend that I find everything easy, or that I know everything, or that I always know what's right, or that I have never made mistakes.
13. I will try to apologize when I've got something wrong.
14. If children discover there is something that they're interested in, I will try to support it in any way they and I can think of.
15. I will try not to take over our children's interests or appear to know more about them than our children do.

THE POWER OF 'I DON'T KNOW'

I've seen David Attenborough tell a story about his own childhood that tallies with something that happened to me.

Attenborough says that when he was a boy he got interested in old bones. Anyone who goes for a walk in the countryside will come across old bones. He used to pick them up, bring them home and collect them. (By the way if you do this, you should a) pick them up with disposable gloves on and b) soak them in a bleach solution.)

At home he used to question his father about the bones, asking him things like: 'Which animal does this one come from?' Or, 'Which part of the body is this?' As Attenborough explains, his father was a GP and would have done a solid slog, first of zoology, then anatomy. In other words he would have studied skeletons of animals and then the human skeleton. But Attenborough senior didn't pick up the bone, turn it over and pronounce on it: 'This is the femur of a sheep,' or some such. He wanted to encourage young Attenborough to be interested and excited by the idea of finding out. He wanted him to get the hang of how to come to an opinion or judgement on a bit of old bone. Just looking at the bone himself, and telling the boy the name of an animal or part of a body wouldn't have done that. So instead, says David Attenborough, his father used to look at the bone and say, 'I don't know. I wonder if we can work it out . . .'

Then, he would dig out his old zoology and anatomy books, and together they would pore over these, comparing the pictures with the bones that David had found. Instead of sealing up and closing off young Attenborough's questions and queries, he encouraged them, and led him to a place where he could experience the fun of the hunt, the excitement of the discovery.

And, clearly, it worked.

Now for my version of this.

I studied English literature in the sixth form for two years (sixteen- to eighteen-year-olds). In the second year, we got a new teacher who arrived in our class and said that he had looked at the books that we were going to study. One of them, he said, was a long poem called *Comus* by John Milton. 'To tell you the truth,' he said to us, 'I don't understand it. You're going to have to help me with it.'

This seemed very odd. I think it was the first time I had ever heard a teacher say that there was something that they didn't understand. We had learned that the job of teachers is to know stuff and to tell it to us. That was because we didn't know that stuff. The job of the teacher was not only knowing the stuff, but also to know the exact, dead right way of telling it that would enable it to go in and stick. And here was a teacher who was admitting that the very thing he was supposed to teach was too hard for him! Surely this was a disaster. We would flap around for a year and end up failing our A-level in English literature and not get into university.

I went home and told my father. He laughed. 'Very good,' he said. 'Very good technique. I like the sound of that. Of course he understands it. He's just said that he doesn't understand it, in order to get you and your class to do some work on it yourselves, and not think that he has to spoon-feed you. Very clever. I like the sound of him.'

So, we spent a year trying to figure out *Comus* by John Milton. It was hard. And not terribly exciting. It's also quite hard to understand why Milton wrote it. This was all before the days of Wikipedia, of course, so what did we do to understand it? We sat in class and worked slowly through the poem, asking questions of each other and then trying to answer those questions. We used the notes at the back of the book. We went to the library and tried to find out things to do with Milton. As we worked our way through it, one day it would be one of us who came up with a good idea, sometimes someone else. Sometimes it was the teacher. We would each bring our different experiences to the table and share what we thought and what we knew. I remember it being a fascinating and uplifting experience – even though I didn't like the poem! What I really liked was the feeling of trying to figure out what a poem might mean – especially an old one, written hundreds of years ago, at a time that I was also learning about in history. It felt great *not* to be told what it meant, or what we ought to think about it. It felt great to be given the right to investigate it and make discoveries about it.

Many years later, I was at a school reunion – and there was the teacher, Mr Spearman, now a headteacher. He made a beeline for me and said, very kindly, how pleased he was to see me. Then, almost immediately, he went back to that time, some twenty years earlier when I was studying English literature with him. 'Do you know,' he said, 'I've never forgotten that year. I thought that it was a really good year. Do you remember, we were doing *Comus*?' I said that I did. 'And do you remember how I told you folks that I didn't understand it?' I said that I did remember all that and I was just about to tell him what my father had said, about what a good teaching technique it was, when he said, shaking his head, 'You know, Michael, I really had no idea what it was about at all, but working with you and the other students in that class – I got it!'

He hadn't been kidding.

So, what can we make of these two stories? For me, they tell me something very important about learning and knowledge. In the short term, of course you can tell children and young people things. If they ask you a factual question, say, and you know the answer, you can tell it to them. As we all know, they may or may not remember it. You can even tell them how you remember it, and perhaps you've got a special way (or think you do) of linking it to an image, some letters, a little rhyme or whatever. Perhaps you can pass on techniques of remembering things:

TECHNIQUES FOR REMEMBERING STUFF

1. Look at the page.
2. Stare at the thing on the page, trying to remember it.
3. Cover it up.
4. Say it out loud, or write it down.
5. Uncover the thing on the page.
6. Compare what you've just said out loud or written with the thing on the page.
7. If it's not the same, repeat the process from 1 to 6.

Or this:

If you are trying to learn a long sequence or passage of something – or perhaps it's a series of 'causes' and 'consequences' – the trick is to shorten it in stages. This means rewriting the passage several times, each time shorter than the previous one. I find that doing it in about four stages is best. In the end you should finish up with a handful of small phrases, numbered in order. What this does is help you remember what the real core meaning is for each item or point. Then at the end you have a set of trigger words or phrases that will trigger off your memory of how you shortened from the long version to the short. And you will also have learned off by heart most of the long version. The more you do this, the better you get at it, until in the end you can look at a passage and shorten it in your head.

Or this:

Let's say it's an account of something. Make each paragraph of the account into a 'room' in your mind. They can be rooms in a house or building you know. So what you do is attach a particular paragraph or part of the account to a particular room. These should be rooms in a building where you know how to get from one room to another. So, as you try to remember one paragraph at a time, think of yourself as being in that room. Then imagine yourself walking out of that room into the next room where the next paragraph is waiting for you . . . and so on. I've found that one useful for where the account is more like a story, rather than a causes and consequences thing.

Or this:

You remember the 'links'.

Any story or account will be like a staircase with each step linking to the next. Part of the problem about remembering something like this is remembering the right order. One reason for that is because we haven't thought through what links one step to the next. So we just try to remember it as if it's a list. Of course some lists are just lists and there is nothing to link one item on the list with another. In this kind of situation the other methods work. But if the items (or 'steps' as I'm calling them) are linked, then the trick is to put as much effort into remembering what the link is – why and how one 'step' is linked to the next – as you do into remembering the 'steps' themselves.

So what you do is write down what these links are. You try to figure out exactly why and how one step links to another. This makes the 'reasoning' of the thing you're learning 'explicit' or 'known to you'. Sometimes, you can do this by spotting link words like 'because', 'therefore', 'so', 'thus', 'although', 'consequences', 'conditions', 'causes', 'resulting in . . .' and the like. Once you've found the links, the 'steps' themselves will often slot into place. You get to see the whole passage or account like a staircase or ladder.

I did these sorts of things many, many times as I studied for the exams we did when I was sixteen (O-levels), eighteen (A-levels), and for my 'First MB' (a kind of foundation year for training to be a doctor) when I was nineteen, my preliminary exams when I was twenty and for my first degree, a BA in English Language and Literature when I was twenty-three. All I can say is that the techniques worked for me!

HOWEVER . . .

. . . what this sort of thing didn't teach me very often was how to find out things. It didn't teach me how to find things that I really wanted to learn about. It didn't take me down interesting side-alleys where I would find things that I didn't know I would be interested in until I found them.

I most certainly did get this from studying *Comus* by John Milton, in that particular way that year.

I also got something that's more to do with feelings than knowledge or learning: it was a confidence that I could investigate and discover things for myself. It's ironic, isn't it, that I got that feeling from someone who quite genuinely didn't understand something?

WAYS
AND
MEANS

TALK

Double-decker buses have the great advantage of giving people a chance to look out over the top of life. Life is all going on – down there. If you sit upstairs, you get a chance to do something you can't do in any other way: move through places viewing the world from high up. It's wonderful that we can see so much of it, in one look. And then by swivelling round, we can take in another huge chunk. And we can home in, like a camera, on something quite small. A dog peeing on a lamp-post, a cyclist's purple outfit . . .

All this seems to have an effect on children.

Again and again, when I'm sitting on the upper deck I hear streams of questions coming from children, asking about why that person over there is doing that, what that shop sells, what kind of car is that . . . and so on. What interests me is that sometimes the child gets no answers and the questions dry up. End of. Sometimes, the adult joins in, tries to answer, points out things, does a bit of wondering and thinking aloud themselves. Sometimes bits of family history come up.

I think these moments are treasures. It's at moments like these we talk about being part of the world; and part of the world becomes us. Talk is what makes that happen.

It's easy to downgrade talk. We have downgrading words for it or for the people who appear to do a lot of it: goss, chat, 'givin'

23

it all that', chatterbox. In fact, it's the opposite: it's a crucial way in which we get to understand everything and anything. Of course it's more than just talk – it's 'interpersonal communication' which includes gesture, touch, grunts, sighs, smiles, tears, eyebrow movements, nods, shrugs, sign languages and any other system we might choose or have to use depending on who we are.

For babies, children and young people it's essential. But it has to be 'interpersonal'. It has to be two-way. As adults we have to listen, we have to leave gaps and wait for children to ask questions or finish what they're saying; we have to make efforts not to interrupt, not to make corrections while the child is asking or telling. Sometimes, without making a big deal of it, it's worth 'echoing' (repeating the last thing the child says, but making it sound like a question):

CHILD: And that bus has got more than four wheels.
ADULT: More than four?
CHILD: Look, over there . . .

Talk is much more than a matter of 'communication' or 'exchanging information'. It does do all that, but it's also about feelings, indicating to each other that we care about each other, like or love each other. Sometimes a child asks questions more in order to get reassurance about that, rather than wanting to know the answer to a question. I've noticed that this seems to happen quite a lot around the age of six or seven. I've often felt that when it gets urgent and insistent, it must be pretty important. Yet it's hard to satisfy the child – especially when they don't listen to your answers!

CHILD: Why's the sky blue?
ME: Well, it's to do with water. You know the . . .

CHILD: Is Betty coming over tomorrow?

ME: She said she was but there's . . .

CHILD: We forgot to get the plug. You said we'd get the plug . . .

ME: We will get the plug, we haven't had . . .

CHILD: If you were a buffalo, would you like spaghetti?

And so on.

At moments like this, sticking with the flow is more important than 'exchanging information'!

What's also going on here is to do with how we think.

It's easy to buy the idea that talking and thinking are two separate things. Or that talking and thinking happen in some kind of neat order: first I think, then I speak. Or: someone else speaks, then I think. Or some such.

What really seems to go on is that through talking and listening, we create an 'inner talk'. This inner talk is a huge 'playlist' of the conversations we've had. In the playlist are the obvious things like: important memorable stuff I've been told; important memorable moments when I was in a great or awful or sad or exciting conversation; wow moments when someone said something that has never left me. But there are also the less obvious things like, say: how I am with people who I think are more important than me; or less important than me. In other words, how I've learned about my 'role' in life, whether I think I'm someone who has the right to speak. Or not.

Now that part of the playlist can be expanded into all the thousands of ways in which we 'get to know' or 'get to understand' almost everything to do with how I am with other people: am I someone who will or won't ask a question if I don't understand what's going on? Am I someone who will let myself wonder about things for a while, or am I someone who needs to get it all wrapped up very quickly? Am I someone who needs to be encouraged and rewarded by someone else or can I get along for a while without that? Am I someone who feels that there is a real me that is very different from the 'me' that others see? How much does it matter to me that that person over there thinks I'm a good person? What do I do when I think something is not fair for me? What do I do when I think something is not fair for others? And thousands more . . .

If we don't do a lot of talking when we're young, it is very hard to get much of this sorted. It's very hard to know who we are. It's very hard to know about other people. It's very hard to learn.

Again, there's the big question of how I learn to be able to string words together to explain what I mean, what I know, what I remember and what I understand. Putting things into words that I can speak is a crucial part of understanding any-thing and everything. We may well think we know and under-stand something, but until I put it into words and say them, I may well not have really understood it at all. Then, the moment I've put it into words in front of others, people can ask me questions about it, check it against what they know and under-stand. They can tell me something about what they know as a kind of parallel thing and we can make comparisons between what I said and they said. A great deal of conversation is like that. I tell you something that happened to me at the checkout at the supermarket. I gave them a £20 note but got change for £10. You tell me something similar happened to you. We talk about people at checkout counters. You say that you once worked on a checkout. Our conversation shifts to thinking about what it would be like to be the person who handed out the wrong change. We start talking about flexi-working and zero-hour contracts. We enlarge our knowledge and feelings about checkout counters. Next time I go to the checkout counter, that conversation is inside me. It's part of my inner talk. It shapes what I say and do when I'm standing there.

If I don't get practice at doing these things, it's likely to be difficult to put things into words, to take part in learning. But this isn't just a matter of learning 'techniques'. It's a matter of being in conversations when I was young, where I was encouraged to finish what I was saying, where I was listened to. That's because one of the key listeners to what any person is saying is the 'me'. I listen to myself. You listen to yourself. And while you're doing that, you're also watching and listening to the people around you. We get to know what 'works', what doesn't work.

In other words, I say one thing – and I find that people around me don't hear it or ignore it. Without knowing, I will probably junk that way of talking. I say another thing – and people perk up, they listen. Again, without knowing, I will return to that way of talking and see if it works again. This may be to do with the 'what I'm saying'. Or it may be to do with the 'how I'm saying it'. Or both.

And that little scenario gets more complicated if we think that when I said 'people' there, all these people are not the same. Some people matter to us more than others. People matter to us in different ways: one person might be someone I am desperate for approval from but not affection. Another person might be someone I am desperate for affection or love from. Unpleasant but true, another person might be someone I'm in competition with, or a person who wants to dominate me. Or I want to dominate them. Or someone I pity. Or who pities me. For all these different people and different situations, I will want my talk to work.

Meanwhile, all those people are doing similar things back to me!

This means that in talk (and the whole gamut of 'interpersonal communication'), we find ourselves. We find ourselves through trial and error, through listening to others, through listening to what we ourselves say.

This is why sometimes – but of course we mustn't overdo it – it's a very good idea to talk with our children about how we're talking. In fact, one of the ways you know that your children are getting older is that they do this talking about talk without you starting it off. They make comments about the way you speak. They mention our tone of voice, the words we use, our accents, the way we sound as if we're trying to say something important – or not important – the way we change how we speak when talking to that person . . . and so on. As they stop wanting to be a child, they want you to stop talking to them with that 'talking-to-a-child' voice.

Irritating though any of this can be, it's a crucial part of developing talk and developing 'inner talk'. It's all part of the sorting and shaping of our minds. And we have to get in there, listening and talking with them about it.

So, this is partly about what we usually call 'knowledge' – the kind you find in books of knowledge, in school homework and in worksheets. But it's also about a lot of other things we don't usually call knowledge: how we are with other people; how we think; how we feel about other people in general and how we feel about the particular people we know well; how we care or don't care about things; how we get through a day; how we think of ourselves.

I'd go one step further: the stuff we usually call 'knowledge' can't really be separated off from these other kinds of knowledge – call it what you will: 'interpersonal awareness', feelings, self-awareness, empathy, 'emotional literacy' and so on. We can often pretend that we can separate things off. We can pretend that we can go into the room called 'Knowledge' and do some learning about French verbs, and then come out and go into the room called 'How to be Kind' and do kindness; and then go into the room called 'Speaking Clearly' and learn how to do that. And we can pretend that all these rooms are separate from each other.

In actual fact, we will be learning, say, kindness (or unkindness) in a situation in which we are learning 'Knowledge' about the French verbs. When someone is being kind to us, we may well be learning something about where I am in the pecking order of life – and whether I'm happy with that or not. And in any of those situations, I will be learning whether I'm being 'heard' or not. And this is the crunch: the reason why I find French verbs difficult may well not be because 'French verbs are difficult' but because of some stuff in my 'inner talk' about kindness, or pecking order, or a view of myself as someone who can't ask questions, or who can't put into words what I feel and so on. In other words, through a particular way of having experienced talk – or lack of talk – I might have learned that I'm not good at doing French verbs things.

And that may well be nothing to do with anyone having mentioned French, verbs, or anything like that. Rather, that it was how the people I thought were important (probably parents) talked with me, or didn't talk with me, what they showed me about what part I could play in conversations. How they talked to me about the stuff that I thought, as a child, was important.

On the other hand, if I was given the freedom and respect in conversations where I was heard and encouraged and treated with kindness, I might well think that I have the right to know anything or learn anything. Or it may be that I learn that I have the right to make choices about what to learn and how

I learn it – because I have a strong sense of myself in relation to other people.

What's weird about all this is that we can do pretty nearly all of it, without having to read me trying to explain it! We will all talk to each other – if we're allowed to.

If we're allowed to.

And that's the bit that's not particularly easy.

Most of us live very busy, complicated, tiring lives. It is much easier to get children to do things where they don't talk to us. Or even to each other. We have invented an array of stuff that enables us not to talk to them: computer games, tablets, TV, iTunes and so on and so on. They ask for it. We give it to them. They use them. We're all happy.

I think we have to think all this through.

If I'm right about this learning through talk, learning how to do 'inner talk', learning how to learn, then we have to make very conscious efforts to make times when we just talk. I'm not going to pretend it's easy. Even as I am writing this, I am not talking to my youngest. He wants to talk to me because he wants to show me some comics he's been reading. In my mind, I'm thinking that his comics are not as important as me writing this. I have twenty reasons for thinking that this is more important than his comics: I'm an adult and all adults are important, especially this adult who is me; I am earning a living by doing my work, which is writing this; I am communicating important things to the world by writing this; I'm busy and being busy is what makes me important; oh yes; and comics are OK but it's just a few gags. And a few pictures . . . and so on and so on and so on. And it's all in order to justify not talking with my son.

It's also about not seeing the world from his point of view. From his point of view, after being in the world for nine years, his comics are among the most important things in his life. It's no use me thinking, Wouldn't it be great if algebra or *Hamlet* was one of the most important things in his life? This is important to him. And he wants to talk to me about it. He wants to talk to me about it because I'm his dad. And he wants me to love him, he wants me to show that I love him, and he wants me to like his stuff, he wants me to show that I rate what he does. He wants me to respect anything that he thinks of as important. He wants to matter to me. And the best way for me to show all that, is to show that I think if there is something that he thinks is important, I will take notice of it.

So we talk about the comics.

And I listen. I don't interrupt. I try to answer his questions. I don't get arsey if he doesn't wait for me to finish the answer. When he gets stuck halfway through explaining something, I don't finish the sentence. I notice that he keeps looking at my face, to see if I am really listening. Of am I doing that Dad-thing of pretending I'm listening while thinking of the bills I haven't paid? I ask a question myself. I make sure it's a question I really want to know the answer to. I make sure it's about something he hasn't already told me, because if it was about something that he had already told me, that would prove that I wasn't listening. And the whole thing would fall apart and he would get very cross. Very cross indeed.

So we have one of those conversations. In actual fact, he gets me very interested in his comics. That's what should happen . . . ideally. In the best of all situations. Which is not always.

But we can try. We have to.

WRITING AND READING

I'm a writer, so I'm bound to say that writing is really important. And that we must do all we can to help children write and enjoy writing.

So, this is me trying to back that up.

Everyday talk on the one hand and most of the writing we see in newspapers and books on the other are two very different ways of using language.

When we talk to each other, we change what we say and how we're saying it as we go along. One of the main ways we do this is by reacting to what the person we're talking to is looking like, what they do and what they say. If they look bored, I will maybe repeat myself, slip in a 'you know', raise my voice at the end of the sentence. If they look disapproving, I might change what I'm saying midstream and try to make it 'nicer', by slipping in a 'please', or turning single words into phrases by adding 'a bit' or 'quite' or 'almost' to make what I'm saying sound less in-your-face. I might be interrupted so I have to stop mid-flow. I might try talking over the interruption which might mean talking louder, or with more grabby words – possibly swear words.

You can't do this when you're writing. In other words, when you write, you don't have the help and guidance that a listener is giving you when you're talking. You may well have a sense of who you're writing for, but those people (or that person) are not there in front of you as you write. So you have to keep guessing what is the best way to write for them. Children and young people find this quite hard. It's not just a matter of learning off pat some good words or sentences. You have to learn the special kind of 'voice' that is the writing 'voice'.

When we talk to each other, we don't talk in complete sentences. We interrupt ourselves, tail off, repeat ourselves, correct ourselves, make what would be called mistakes if we were writing. Quite a lot of the time, we talk in shorter groups of words, without linking them with more than one or two neatly thought-out connecting words like 'although', 'therefore', 'insofar as'. We use a lot of 'ers' and 'ums' and 'you knows' – or 'fillers' like that.

When we write, we have time to think ahead. We can make sentences that have all sorts of provisos or conditions. We can do it a bit when we speak, but it's harder. By using words like 'although' and 'if' and 'should it be necessary', we can put the 'condition' or the 'proviso' in front of what we are getting to a moment later. This makes writing sound more measured and more thought-out than when we're speaking.

We can move from one time-frame to another by using words like 'when', 'after', 'however before that', 'eventually'. Again, we can do this when we talk, but in writing, when we put those time-frame words up front, our writing sounds more logical and thought-out.

We can easily comment on what it is we're actually writing. We can do this ahead of writing it by putting in words like, 'What I'm about to mention', or 'In the following, I will reveal'. The chances are that when we are actually writing phrases like that, we've actually written down the list of things we will 'reveal' before writing 'I will reveal'! That's because when we're writing, we can of course go back and insert, 'I will reveal'. If you think about it, this is very odd, but we do it as part of writing. Again, this is something that is quite hard to learn.

When we're talking, we use a lot of words like 'he', 'him', 'she', 'her', 'it', 'they' (they're called 'pronouns') and 'my', 'their', 'our' and the like (these tend to be called 'determiners' these days, though they used to be called 'pronouns' too). On their own, these kinds of words don't tell you who you're talking about. I might say, 'He gave it to her yesterday.' And usually, the people I'm with will know who the 'he' is, what the 'it' is, and who the 'her' is. If they don't, they will probably ask me, and I'll tell them. Though I may explain by pointing and then saying 'him', or 'this', or 'her over there'.

Now, as you can see, I can write that but it doesn't mean very much unless the writing all around explains who 'he' and 'her' are, and what 'it' is. When I'm with people, I may well not have to. Or if I have to I can explain with nods and pointing.

When I write, I have to do a special kind of explaining. This is to make the people, things and the relationship between them very clear for the person reading. Again, I can't learn how to do this simply from being told to do it or by having the grammar explained to me. I have to learn that special writing 'voice'.

As a very broad generalization – and it's easy to think of exceptions – when we speak we tend to avoid using too many 'abstract' words, unless we quickly give examples of what we mean straight after. Outside education, we tend not to have many conversations where we compare and contrast abstract ideas. We don't sit in casual conversation and talk about which is the more painful, 'envy' or 'shame'. We are much more likely to talk about someone who we think was being envious, or someone who did something that showed he had no shame.

In other words we 'embed' the abstract ideas of 'envy' or 'shame' in examples we have heard about.

Then again, there are many terms that crop up in education that we would not often use in everyday conversation away from the classroom. Or if we do, we might use one or two but not juggle one with the other. So, it's unlikely that we would get out of a car, look at a view and turn to the person we're with and ask them whether they think 'erosion' has affected the landscape more or less than 'movements in the earth's crust'. Or if we do, we might talk about how rain and frost and wind have, say, 'eaten away at that rock'. And we might say something about how 'all this got lifted up, once, you know'.

In writing, though, we might well read in school about such things in these very terms (erosion and movements in the earth's crust). They might well be in what we read but compressed and made abstract by, say, comparing 'erosion' with 'movements in the earth's crust'. This makes it 'general', meaning that it happens anywhere and everywhere all over the earth. We might be asked to write about that and so we have to take on that generalizing voice and think of 'erosion' as not just something that happened to that particular stone you picked up. We have to think beyond the 'specific' into something 'general', that can happen everywhere. This involves learning how to write with this particular kind of 'voice'. Yes, it is possible to talk that way, using a word like 'erosion' in this general sense. But it's unlikely that you will talk in that way unless you learn how to read and write like that first.

To be clear, this is not to do down the kinds of thought-out generalizations and abstract ideas that we all come up with through our everyday experience of personal life and work. I've heard some of the most profound ideas and wisdom, from, let's say, people without many years of formal education who've faced hardship and injustice, or, for that matter, from a man who had come to remove a wasps' nest. What I'm talking about is a particular way of using language that handles pairs or groups of abstractions, comparing and contrasting them.

So, writing (whether we do the writing or reading of it) has a special place in how we understand things and change things.

If we are interested in helping our children get hold of finding this writing 'voice', there are many ways of helping them.

First, though, some thoughts:

It won't be done in one way alone.

It's never a complete process that you begin and then finish. Learning how to write is a job that is never finished. We should think of it as something fascinatingly huge, full of difference and variation; something that we can think of as wonderful precisely because it is so varied.

We all make mistakes when we write. The more important question is whether we have time and help to 'edit' them. If we think mistakes are things to be ashamed of, we will end up being afraid of writing or, even worse, making others afraid of it.

We should think of all language as constantly changing. The way we talk probably changes faster than the way we write, but it changes all the same. This is not a snag or something to be cross or sad about. It's something exciting and interesting. What's more, the children you're trying to get interested in learning are themselves involved in the change. As indeed you are too.

Though I've talked about 'writing' as if it's one thing, in reality there are many ways of writing. Just think of the difference between the writing on advertising posters and an article in a newspaper. Think of the difference between the words in the lyric of a song and the write-up of a football match. Think of the difference between a recipe and a diary entry. Think of the writing you do when you text someone and the writing you do when you have to make a job application. This means that when we say that we learn how to write, what we really mean is that we learn how to write *in many different ways*. We learn when it's best to write in one way rather than another. We learn when it's a good idea to mix up some of these different ways.

There are ways of discussing how writing works. The moment we talk about how writing works, this is 'grammar'. Even by saying something as simple as, 'That's a short sentence' or, 'That sounds very "wordy"' we are talking grammar. Like anything that is very varied and complicated, there are hundreds of words or 'terms' to describe how writing works. It's a mistake to think that writing gets easier or better simply because we know some of those terms. It's a mistake to think that young children will find learning those terms as easy as older children do.

Using grammar terms like 'noun' or 'adverb' is a way of making the words we use abstract. We are trying to get children to see that there is something similar, say, about words like 'uncle', 'banana' , 'breakfast' and 'rage' (they're nouns), when we say, 'If my uncle doesn't have a banana for breakfast, he gets in a rage.' This is abstract because there isn't much that's similar in life about uncles, bananas, breakfasts and rages. They only become similar if we group them for reasons to do with what we get those words to do when we speak and write. This is summed up when we call them 'nouns'. That is abstract. When we say to a child these words are 'nouns', they will think that this has nothing to do with what uncles, bananas, break-fasts and rages feel like to them. That's what's difficult about talking about 'nouns'. And it gets more difficult when you say that this or that word is not a noun, it's something else. Or if you say: you use nouns to be 'subjects'. This is as complicated as, let's say, the effect of alcohol on the metabolism. In general, older children find 'abstract' thought easier than younger children. In general, older children find it easier to use abstract ideas than younger children do. Using abstract ideas is always made easier if you keep giving examples, working from a specific example to the abstract and back again. This gives you time to see the patterns of things.

An example of what I mean about patterns, abstractions and children: we do multiplication sums. We see the pattern. We feel the pattern in the rhythm and shape of the figures and the process to get the answer. We can see what happens when we say, '4 groups of 3 apples' or '5 groups of 4 cakes'. We see what's similar about doing those two sums. If we're learning 'multiplication', it doesn't matter that it's apples in one sum and cakes in the other. The process is the same. Even if the numbers are different, the process is the same. The teacher calls it 'multiplication'. That is the abstraction. Then she does 'division' and we get to see that the pattern is different. We might say at some point that 'multiplication is division, the other way round'. They're 'reversible'. This is even more abstract because we're juggling abstractions. Many young children will find that quite hard to get hold of at first. It will need plenty of going one way and coming back the other to 'get it'. All this is 'abstract thought' and it's at the heart of education and knowledge.

Talking about writing, reading and grammar is like this. Grammar in particular often involves juggling abstractions. And sometimes we get some of it. Sometimes we don't. Very, very few people get all of it. Even then, the very few who get all of it disagree with each other. It's a debate, a work-in-progress.

An example of that is when I said earlier that a certain kind of word used to be called a 'pronoun' but is often called a 'determiner' these days. There are many different ways of learning how to read and write. Knowing the terms may or may not help you. They're much more likely to help you as you get older, when you get the hang of juggling with abstractions.

Writing cannot be separated from reading. When we write, we read what we write. The stuff that we read is called 'writing'. We can learn something of how to write from reading. We can learn something of how to read from writing. We become 'reading writers' and 'writing readers'.

WHAT TO DO; HOW TO HELP

From the day our children are born (yes), to the day they tell us to stop, we should read to them. This does many things at the same time:

1. It gives them a thing to do, a place to go, that is separate from you, even as they remain attached to you. This means that they develop feelings and interests that are theirs while feeling safe and loved.

2. In the 'thing to do', the 'place to go' are other worlds: creatures, beings and people who have emotions, face challenges, make discoveries, go through changes, and – because we are talking about children's books here – usually everything comes out pretty OK.

3. Whatever it is that we're reading with our children usually sparks off questions, thoughts and comments. These are the

building blocks of learning. Every one of them is a vital treasure that we have to safeguard and respect. We do that by joining in the conversation, answering questions, staying interested, 'echoing' things that the child has said, saying, 'I don't know', or 'I wonder . . .', listening to what the child says.

4. If you have more than one thing to read with your child, you have the possibility of leaving to your child the choice of what to read. One school of thought says that your child will never 'develop' unless you tell them what to read. Another school of thought says that you should never choose for your child. A further school of thought says that you should persist in encouraging your child to choose but also occasionally throw in suggestions of your own. This can be enlarged and expanded by encouraging other people – siblings, relations, friends, librarians, TV commentators – to make suggestions. I think that in my lifetime the freedom of children has changed. When I was a boy in the 1940s and 1950s, I thought my parents knew everything. They certainly knew more about books than I did, so they chose. They filled my room with books that they had chosen. Once I could read, I chose the books I wanted from the books they gave me or that I had inherited from my brother. I used to go once a week to the library with either my father or mother and they usually encouraged me to choose my own there, though my father got more prescriptive about it when I was a young teen. 'Time you read some Thomas Hardy,' he said and I did. I never do that with my children. Instead, I keep putting them in front of shelves full of books, books of all kinds in libraries, bookshops, shops that sell comics and magazines, gift shops – wherever.

5. As I've said elsewhere, one of the most powerful agents of learning is 'browsing'. I believe we should do all we can to encourage children to browse. This means going to libraries, going to bookshops, going online with them to look for song lyrics, Wikipedia entries, helping them to collect books, recipes, football programmes, comics, magazines, newspaper articles and the like. This enables them to learn *how to sort* and *how to scan*. It enables them to build up interests within the 'safety' of something they really care about. You can't do this for them. Sorting stuff that has writing in it, whether books or any of the other items I've mentioned, also involves abstraction. In order to sort, you have to come up with a category. One of my children spent hours and hours sorting his comics. When I asked him what he was doing, he explained a complex sorting arrangement that involved: the comics that had the best 'Roger the Dodger' pages, the best comics that he had inherited from his older brothers, the best comics that he was getting each week and so on. This is high-level abstract thinking. And he was six! He had to be in charge. He had to be left alone to do that. He had to be safe in knowing that no one was going to tell him that he was being fussy or foolish or that comics are crap. It was his world, his stuff and he taught himself how to be confident about shunting them in and out of whatever category he thought was important. So he also learned something else very important: that categories are made by humans. They don't come flying out of the sky given by some great educational god answerable to no one. And this 'tool' or 'technique' or 'transferable skill' is a key method that can be applied to many different kinds of work in education and life. I cannot emphasize it enough.

6. When we are read to and when we read, we learn how the special writing 'voice' works. I've already talked about the differences between most talk and most writing – particularly the kind you meet in books. If, for a moment, we say that when we speak that's one kind of 'dialect' but writing comes in another kind of 'dialect', that would conjure up the image of, let's say, me talking with a London accent and dialect, trying to understand or even use the dialect of someone from Liverpool, or Sydney, Australia. These are different ways of using English, but in order to 'do' a dialect different from my own, I need to tune in and practise.

Now, it's not strictly accurate to say that talking and writing are different dialects but I gave it as an example of how we can learn different ways of using what is the same language. The word that linguists use is to call talking and writing different 'registers'. Whatever we call it, our job is to help children get writing. The simplest, most pleasurable way is for children to hear writing being read out loud. If you read to a child every night – quite apart from all that vitally important intellectual and emotional stuff I was talking about – you also give them the sound, shape, rhythm, pattern, words and structures of writing. As I've said, it's not just a matter of new or big or better words (or 'vocabulary', as some people call it). Much more important is the matter of the structures of writing that I described earlier.

The child is not speaking these structures as part of everyday life. Neither are you. You want the child to use these structures when they write. Teachers may well try to teach the structures. You as a parent don't have to do that. You can 'teach' the structures simply by reading out loud hundreds and hundreds of times while having great fun, laughing and crying over wonderful stories and poems or whatever. Teaching without teaching!

Then, as your child starts to read for themselves, they find these non-talk structures familiar. The writing-way of using language becomes familiar. They're not thrown by a sentence like, 'When Dozo walked into the room, he may or may not have been sure who was there, although last time he was upset simply by not being sure.' It may not be a great sentence, but with its 'when' and 'although' and 'by not being', it's just the kind of complicated structure that a child might come across. Getting what it means will be a hundred times less of a problem to the child who has been read to every night, than to the child who is not read to. The child who has been read to has learned what I could call 'hard-sentence-ese' before they've tried to read hard sentences for themselves.

Reading is one of the key ways in which we learn 'interpretation'. If we talk about what we read, almost certainly, we will very soon be getting into interpretation, which sounds as if it's something you do when you're sixteen or at college. Not in my book. Here's an example. When my youngest was about three, his favourite book was *Where the Wild Things Are*. He chose me or his mother to read it to him over and over again. So, consider the picture: he is sitting on a lap, hearing the story while looking at the pictures. Though we say that pictures in picture books 'illustrate' the story, it's truer to say that the pictures tell stories themselves. A child being read to is mashing up what they hear with what they see, transforming these different inputs (different stories) to make sense of it all. We will get glimpses of what a deep and complicated process this is by the things the child says or even by the kind of noises or movements they make.

Sometimes, picture books are extremely good at favouring

the child-viewer while making the adult who's reading seem behind the story. So, in a book like *Rosie's Walk* by Pat Hutchins, the adult reads a story about a hen crossing a farmyard. The child sees a story about a hen crossing the farmyard, who has no idea that a fox is trying to eat her. What's more, the fox keeps having pratfalls until in the end he gets chased off by a swarm of bees. The adult reading the story appears not to know about the fox either, because there is no mention of the fox in the words of the story. The child knows more about what's going on than the adult. Provided the adult keeps quiet and doesn't say, 'Oh, look at the fox,' the child gets the immense pleasure of doing the interpreting, and knowing more than the adult. Very young children will interpret the pictures, interpret the fact that you are a dozy grown-up who hasn't mentioned the fox, and tell you what to look out for.

This process is repeated hundreds of times in all sorts of different ways with picture books and comics. If we give the child time and space to point out things they will. Of course we can do that too. We also wonder and speculate about what this or that is there for. Some of the best books for that kind of wondering have been made by Anthony Browne.

Back with my son: we were reading *Where the Wild Things Are* over and over again. He was starting to join in. The book has a cunning way of not finishing the sentence on one page, so that you can't finish it without turning over the page. He was starting to fill in the word that was coming. We would point at the word on the page, so he started to make the connection between the word on the page and the sounds we were making – that is, saying the word out loud. This is one of the building blocks for learning how to read that millions of people have used down through the centuries.

He was also controlling the speed we turned the pages so

that he could sometimes move quickly over the pages where the 'Wild Things' and the boy in the story, Max, have a 'rumpus'. Sometimes he could move slowly over it. The rumpus doesn't have any words on the page so that the child can choose whether to talk about it (or anything else) when they're turning the pages.

Because he was choosing to hear the story over and over again, something other than 'wanting to know what happens next' was going on. We might wonder what that was. Was it just the pleasure of getting to know the story better and better? Off by heart, if you like? Was he in some way getting pleasure from getting to control the story? So, the very first time he heard and looked at the story, it was coming at him from 'outside', as it were, being read to by his parents and displayed in front of him as he sat on our laps. But as he heard it over and over again, we could say that there was a way in which he was telling the story. He was telling it to himself, and to us. Maybe it was two tellings at the same time: the one that was being performed by us and the one that was going on in his head, where he knew the words and story already. And let's not forget: this is a three-year-old telling the story in the writing language of an adult, 'writing-language', with those particular writing-language structures. This isn't the language that he or we spoke.

And could we also say that he was getting some kind of satisfaction of experiencing the naughtiness, danger and fear in the story, knowing each time, more and more certainly, that these are overcome? So, first time, perhaps he didn't know what would happen. Perhaps the Wild Things would eat the boy. Perhaps the boy would never get home. Perhaps if he did get home, his mother would still be angry with him. The great thing about hearing or reading a story over and over again is that you know that the danger is overcome. You probably get a special pleasure from a story at the moment where the bad guy or obstacle is overcome. The first time, it's partly the surprise. The next times it's the recognition and confirmation of that moment. The 'YESSS!' moment.

Now, in the book (in case you don't know) the boy's mother sends him to his room, because he's been naughty. We don't ever see the mother, and – this is important – we only know her by the word 'mother'. At the end of the story, Max gets home where he finds that some food has been left out for him in his room, and it's still hot. We aren't told where this comes from. So, whatever sense a child makes of that, it involves interpretation. You can't 'retrieve' it from the story. And the word 'inference' doesn't really cover the brain-work you have to do to figure it out. What's more, within the world of this story (perhaps all stories), there are no dead certain right answers. We might say, as an adult, that the most likely interpretation is that this comes from 'mother', but we don't see 'mother' making any hot food. There is room to interpret, say, that the food came into the room magically. After all, a forest grows in the room earlier in the book, so why not the food?

While Max is with the Wild Things, first of all he tames them, then he dances with them and then the story tells us that Max wants to be 'where someone loved him best of all'. If we stop for a moment and think about that phrase and a three-year-old – well, my three-year-old – it's quite a strange thing to hear. I can't think that it's a phrase he would have heard anywhere else. Adults and children tend not to talk to each other with a phrase like 'someone loved him best of all'. We might say, 'I love you' and 'do you love me best?' and the like. The 'someone' is quite distant and strange. And we don't usually talk about *being somewhere* where you are loved. That's quite an adult, dare I say, quite psychobabbly way of talking. As when people say, 'I need to be where I'm safe' or some such. So, we had read this phrase many, many times over and never stopped at it. He hadn't asked any questions about it. Neither of us had asked him anything about it. Then one day, while I was reading it to him, he said, 'Mummy'.

He didn't say anything else. Just 'Mummy'.

Now what was going on here? He was interpreting the phrase 'where someone loved him best of all' and putting it in his own words. In fact, the word 'mummy' doesn't appear in the book. It's the word 'mother'. 'Mummy' in his life was of course his mummy. So in order to say 'Mummy', he had to figure out that a mother-mummy person would be the most likely person to love Max best of all. She would be the 'someone'. Because he said 'Mummy' and not 'Max's mother', I think that what he did was mix up his own feelings for his mummy and what he imagined (interpretation) were Max's feelings. This is what some critics have called a 'transaction'. He has done some mixing and swapping between his own life and feelings and the situation – as he understands it – of the boy in the story. He thinks that Max would feel as he (my son) would feel, if he was in a situation like the one Max finds himself in.

Now all this is both very simple and very complicated. It's dead simple to get *Where the Wild Things Are* and read it. If a child wants you to read it again, you read it again. And if they ask you, you read it again and again and again and again. That's because important stuff is going on. Then, as proof that it's important, your child will say things. This reaction is a tip of an iceberg of interpretation. The child's reaction appears as a word and that word reveals that a huge amount of interpretation has gone on.

Now, I don't know the totality of what education is for or

what learning is for. But my own view is that a big part of it must be that it should give whoever is going through it the *power of interpretation*. This is not something that we as parents need to think that we have to put on the shelf for later when they're mature, or that it's something special and hard that only a clever sixteen-year-old can do. It's something that we can help happen by doing nothing more complicated than finding interesting picture books to share with our very young children.

I suggest that if we do this sort of thing over and over again – and believe me it's fun – we give our children a door through which they can walk into the world of interpretation with confidence.

Another story. My daughter came home with a worksheet from school. It was about a Greek myth. The heading said, 'Here is part of a myth from ancient Greece'. Then there was a re-telling of the Greek myth of Perseus and the Gorgons. Next to it was a black and white picture of a Hollywood-looking warrior with a sword and shield, appearing to fight against some female monsters with snakes instead of hair. On the back of this were some questions about the story. Very nearly all of them were 'retrieval' questions, like 'Who gave Perseus the bag?'

I have to say that it made me quite angry. I thought, Why only give the child 'part of' a Greek myth. Surely, this takes away the whole power and purpose of the myth. If it's a story worth giving to children, then give it all the power it's got. Not only was it just 'part of' the myth, the way it was told – very briefly, like a summary – gave you no idea why anyone in the story was behaving as they were. So you didn't know why Perseus had turned up to see the Gorgons, or why he was going to kill them, why a goddess had given him a bag, why he chopped off the head of one of the Gorgons, or why he was wearing winged sandals. If you read stories where you have no idea why anyone is doing anything, you don't care. And the quickest and easiest way to get children turned off and bored is to give them things they don't care about. This whole exercise was about getting children to do things that they wouldn't and couldn't care about.

So what to do?

When I was a boy, when I came home with stuff from school that my parents disagreed with, they made a fuss about it, in front of me. On the positive side, it taught me that anything and everything can be debated and argued with. On the negative side, it taught me at the time to be a bit disaffected, that this stuff I was being taught wasn't up to much. On balance, therefore, I think it was a mistake of my parents to make their views quite so obvious.

So, I hid how angry the 'Perseus and the Gorgons' worksheet made me. I thought, How can I turn this into something more positive? I found a book of re-tellings of the Greek myths: *The Orchard Book of Greek Myths*, re-told by Geraldine McCaughrean. Then, every night, we read these stories to our daughter. They are beautiful, simple, poetic re-tellings.

One night I was reading 'Persephone and the Pomegranate Seeds'. In the story, Persephone is abducted by Pluto, god of the Underworld. Her mother is distraught, hears where she is and pleads with the gods to have her back. Zeus, the king of the gods, explains that if she eats anything while she is in the Underworld, she can't return. So Persephone's mother pleads for Zeus to send his messenger to the Underworld to fetch her.

Meanwhile, in the Underworld, Pluto is tempting Persephone to eat something. This went on for days, until she was starving hungry, and she started to eat some pomegranate seeds.

At that moment, my daughter sat up straight and said, 'Oh, I didn't want her to do that!'

Obviously, she cared. She cared about Persephone. She cared that now it seemed as if she was doomed to stay in the Underworld and she would never see her mother again and her mother would never see her. We might say that the story was working. My daughter was involved in what was going on and whether things were fair or cruel or unjust.

So how do things work out? Because Persephone eats just six of twelve seeds (the messenger burst in before she got to eat the rest), Zeus decides that she should spend six months in the Underworld and six months on earth. And that's how we get six months of light and sun and six months of rain, frost and winter.

Meanwhile, Persephone changed her attitude to Pluto. In this re-telling we hear that Persephone 'learned to pity' Pluto.

My daughter asked me what that meant. What's 'pity'? So we talked for a bit about 'feeling sorry' for people. Had she ever felt sorry for someone? Well, it must have been a bit like that, we thought, with Persephone feeling sorry for Pluto because he said that he was lonely.

I'm relating this story of how my daughter reacted to 'Persephone and the Pomegranate Seeds' because it gives us a glimpse into how reading and talking about books and stories is so important. First of all, there is her involvement. She cares. She cares about Persephone. Those are her feelings. We can say her feelings are 'engaged'. But a story is also about ideas. Are people behaving in a right or wrong way? What would be a just solution to the problem? A story will give an outcome that we may or may not 'agree' with. Stories get us thinking about that. When my daughter asked about 'pity' we were moving from gut reactions to talking about ideas. 'Pity' is an abstraction.

As we know, talking about abstract concepts like 'pity' is hard for young children. (My daughter was about seven at the time.) Without examples, without a good reason to be interested, without a good reason to care about it, words like 'pity' just fly in one ear and out the other. But here, there were big reasons to care and there were the examples of the people in the story, and examples from her real life. Who had she ever felt sorry for?

So, stories are about feelings *and* ideas, and these feelings and ideas come attached to the beings, creatures and people who we care about. In fact, stories are one of the most powerful and pleasurable ways we know of dealing with wisdom – if we let them. Now, compare the tatty little worksheet of 'part of a myth' of 'Perseus and the Gorgons' with its silly little questions about 'who gave Perseus the bag?' and compare that with the power, beauty and wisdom of the whole stories and the conversations that just crop up when we share them with children!

And – excuse me if I'm repeating myself – if we make the space, ideas flow out of stories, sometimes at a very abstract and intellectual level. In those conversations during and after stories are the building blocks that enable children to think and learn. In those conversations is the stuff that makes the kinds of work schools ask children to do much, much easier.

In my experience, something else often happens when you share stories and talk about them. Children start to want to have a go themselves. I'll avoid the word 'magic' but it can feel magical, as if the power in the story and the conversation spark off a desire in the child to have a go themselves. My youngest got very interested in the 'Captain Underpants' books. These are very funny, clever, silly books, full of cartoons and jokes, with touches of *The Simpsons* in them. He and I read all of them and somewhere along the way he started itching to do one of his own. My job then was first to make sure he had plenty of paper, pencils, pens, and second to be around, if possible, when he wanted to brainstorm out loud, or talk through a problem where he felt that he was stuck. I am completely hopeless at drawing, so I also found a couple of books that help you draw cartoon figures. He found the author's website and read about how the author got into creating 'Captain Underpants'. Then, bit by bit over about three weeks, he produced his own cartoon. His grandmother helped him stick it together so that it was a book.

Along the way, there were times when it looked as if he might not finish it. I thought it was crucial not to nag or to turn it into a chore or even to try to chivvy him. At the same time, I thought that without encouragement it was just possible that he wouldn't get to the end. Part of me felt strongly that it was important that he did finish it off so that he would have a sense of what it means to go right through the whole process of making something: from vague, blurry ideas to actual stuff on paper, to editing and making it ready for others to read and look at.

Since then, he's made another one. He may or may not do more. Either way, these are thought-through and finished cartoons. He knows what it takes to do such a project and he's done it. Having ideas is what we all do. The problem, more often than not, is turning the ideas into the finished thing. And then once we have that thing – whatever it is – we can, if we want, share it.

In the sharing, we find out more about what's good or not so good about our work. We find out something of what it means. People point at this or that part of it, and say that they like this or that. That's what's happened to him and his two cartoon books. People smile or laugh. They puzzle over other parts. They ask to know more about the characters he's invented.

They wonder where he got his ideas from. He tells them about the cartoons he watches and reads and how his characters are mixtures of these. He is sometimes surprised about how ignorant we adults are of these cartoons. How can we not know about *Futurama* or *Adventure Time*?

So this is a world that he lives in. It's separate from us, but he can share some of it, if he wants to. Also, it's one that he's now contributing to. He's putting items that he's made into that world. I think we should help our children do this sort of thing as often as possible.

Finally, and perhaps this is obvious anyway, enjoyable reading generates more reading. If you like the feeling of reading, you read more. And the opposite is true: if you don't like the feeling of reading, you read less. With all my children, I've seen that there have been moments, usually around the age of six, when they've felt that the gap between the pleasure they got from stories they heard or watched on film and TV, and the pleasure they got (or didn't get) from the stories they were reading was so big that they didn't really see the point of reading. For some of them this lasted a few weeks. For others it lasted a year or so.

In practical terms, this meant that our job was to find books or reading matter of any kind that sustained their interest and pleasure and helped them become experienced enough readers to want to go on with it.

This meant getting rid of any ideas I might have as to what they 'should be' reading 'at this age'. It meant getting rid of any ideas about there being some kind of progression from 'easy' to 'not so easy' to 'hard'. I had to tell myself there is no virtue in reading a book that's hard just because it's hard. The virtue is in reading something you enjoy. Then reading something else you enjoy. Then something else. Then something else. The more you read of what you enjoy, the more you will read. This builds up the experience of how the written language works. It builds up the experience of how stories and non-fiction unfold and reveal what they reveal.

It is a great mistake to think that a film and a book tell the 'same' story. The only thing that's the same is some kind of core summary. Words on a page and moving images with speech on a screen make for two fundamentally different story-experiences. It's only through reading many, many books and stories – enabling a child reader to get pleasure from making sense of the words – that they will ever find reading easy.

So, whenever my children have reached that point where 'making sense of the words in books' started to seem like a drag, I've used every possible ruse to widen and broaden the reading-matter. I took it as a challenge. 'OK,' I said to myself, 'if you're saying that reading is a drag, let me see if I can find some stuff that you will find interesting.'

This means listening to what the child in question is interested in: fairies? football? castles? cartoons? aliens? dinosaurs? Then, it means thinking, 'What kind of stuff is there that puts any of that into words?' Quite often, it's books – stories, poems and non-fiction. Sometimes it's the kind of printed material you get when you go on a visit to a museum, a show, on a trail or wherever. Sometimes it's on the internet, on sites for children or for adults. It can be found in leaflets, programmes, catalogues, posters, newspapers and magazines.

And we should never think of the quick fix. It may be that some of the stuff we help them find – or that they find themselves – hangs about for a year or two. We need to make space for it to sit about being available. We need to make space for them to find the wish to browse through it and sort it.

This way, we give them the confidence to get anything they

want and need from a multimedia world. We say to them, sometimes without saying, you are entitled to have access to any kind of words wherever they are.

That feeling of entitlement about words is one of the most important platforms we can give children – whether that's for getting what they need from education or beyond.

TEACHING AND LEARNING

My father's first job was as a secondary school teacher of English. After that, he trained students to become teachers. A part of this was to go to the school where they were doing teaching practice and watch or 'observe' a lesson that they were teaching.

I used to love hearing the stories of these 'supervisions'. This tells me that our children quite often want to know what we do at work. They are intrigued – sometimes disturbed – by why and how we get so racked up about it. Where in the importance stakes does our work rate? What's good or bad about it? They wonder about the people we work with who they hear us talking about as if they were anything from dearly beloved allies to vicious enemies. Answering children's questions about any of this tells them that they are part of our world, and that they matter as much as the world 'out there' where we earn money.

Remembering my father's stories about students and schools reminded me that many of my teachers were once students and they too had had to teach a lesson while being watched by an experienced ex-teacher. Sometimes it happened to us too. We would be taught by a student, while at the back of the class their supervisor observed, took notes, or even came to talk to us. Thinking about this somehow unpacked or exposed the business of teaching and learning. I mean, in the situation where your teacher is a student and their supervisor is asking you questions in order to find out what the student has taught, who exactly is the teacher here, and who is the pupil? I recall thinking about how a teacher can be a teacher and a pupil at the same time. And, on occasions, a pupil can be a teacher. I know my father's work related directly to education but whatever work we do will relate in one way or another to what our children have to do and talking about it will offer an interesting angle on their own schoolwork or life.

One time, my father came home with a story that has intrigued and puzzled me ever since. He said that after he had supervised a student, he went and sat in the staffroom. After a bit, one of the teachers on the school staff walked in, flopped into a chair, sighed and said, 'Well, I've taught it to them. Whether they know it or not is another matter.'

My dad told the story in such a way that I knew he thought that what the teacher had said was nuts. But I couldn't see what was nuts about it. Surely, the teacher was saying that he had tried really hard to teach whatever it was, but he couldn't know for certain whether the pupils knew it. My dad said that's not the point. The point is, he said, the teacher thinks that there is a thing called 'teaching' which doesn't include 'learning'. It means, he said, that he can go on and on doing what he's always done, without ever knowing how or why the pupils are or are not learning. So I said, but that's what exams are for. No, no, no, said my dad, by then it's too late . . . and anyway, the exams will only test the kinds of things that tests can test: it's very hard for an exam to test whether you're good at finding out things; possible, but difficult – and an exam won't tell you *how* a pupil has learned something; it won't tell you why one pupil has learned something and another one hasn't. But none of that matters, I said, because all that matters is the mark you get at the end anyway. That's true, he said, unless you think of life beyond exams; unless you think of a time in life when there are no exams and you're at work or getting on with your life, trying to find out things, trying to solve problems that crop up. Then it really does matter that you know how to find out things and solve problems . . .

. . . and on and on we would go!

Back with the teacher, though: how can you do what my father was talking about – think of a kind of teaching that includes learning? I'm not going to claim I know the answer to that, but this book is in part me having a stab at it. At the heart of it is something to do with helping a child to become interested.

Whenever I think that I want to interest my children in something – let's say we're on an outing to see an old castle, and on the way round one of them asks me a question – I often think of this conversation with my dad, and the teacher in that staffroom. I ask myself, How can the next thing I say not be about me just teaching? How can it also be about their learning? I also teach adults doing a Masters degree. I ask myself the same question then, when we're studying a new topic, because at the end of the day, for those students and for my children, the fact that I know something or that I'm 'doing some teaching' is neither here nor there. What's important is: are they learning something? Are they getting to know something? Are they getting hold of some new ideas, new information, new ways of looking at the world and at themselves?

This means – whether as a parent or as a teacher – my job surely is more like 'enabling'? If it's analogous to anything, perhaps it's being more like a midwife. After all, it's not the midwife who gives birth. The midwife enables the mother to have the baby.

So, if our job as parents is enabling rather than teaching (in the old sense), what can we do that is more enabling? And what should I avoid on account of it being not-enabling, or what should I avoid on account of it being discouraging?

I guess my attempt at answering those questions is what the rest of this book is about!

CLUBS AND ACTIVITIES

Both in my own life and in the lives of my children, the clubs, associations, courses and workshops that take place out of school have been among the most important learning experiences of all. Perhaps, on second thoughts, *the* most important.

It's easy to see why – so long as the motivation for them rests with the child, so long as we as parents are not overly insistent that the child goes on doing the activity after they have repeatedly said that they don't want to or don't like it any more. It has to be voluntary. It has to have its own rewards – I mean for the child, not the parent. If we do the opposite, and chivvy and harass and nag our children into carrying on, we achieve the exact opposite of what we intend, the most obvious and frequent one of all being the music lessons that end up killing our children's interest in playing music.

The trick is to do it all with a lightness of touch, without investing too much expectation, too much over-expectation, too much interference. The ideal situation is where the child has a genuine sense that you've enabled this to happen (it proves you care), along with a genuine sense that this activity is their thing.

Whenever I think of encouraging our children to get involved with out-of-school activities, I think of how it was that I got into the things I did, and what I got out of them. Then I try (I try!) not to think that my own children should do the wonderful things that I did, because look at me, they made me what I am! Rather, I try to think about the feelings I had when I did these things, rather than what the actual activity was. It was my feelings about them that kept me going, so, I figure, what's important is to get to a point where those feelings of enthusiasm – passion even – kick in. That's the key, not whether the activity is the kind of thing I care most about. After all, I have to keep reminding myself, it's not about me, it's about the child.

When I was a boy, I had several out-of-school activities that meant a lot to me: Cubs, acting, hiking, rugby and a naturalists' club at the Natural History Museum. Between the ages of twelve and sixteen, I shlepped across the London suburbs to get to an acting club at a semi-professional theatre called the Questors Theatre. It was serious, demanding, challenging and quite emotional. It was entirely separate from school. No one from my school went there. No one from the theatre ever met anyone from school. Sometimes my parents came to see the end-of-term productions or public workshops, sometimes they didn't. I felt that this was something I was carving out for myself, and I can now see that it gave me a platform for the next activity I became obsessed with, which was going to cheap Saturday afternoon productions of West End and fringe plays. So, starting off watching the 'senior' Questors at work, I went on to booking many, many outings to the theatre, mostly on my own, when I was aged about fourteen and fifteen.

Hiking took me to youth hostels in England and Wales, and ultimately to hitch-hiking and camping all over France. I learned how to read maps, how to pace a day's hill-climbing, how to feed myself, keep dry, look after my feet . . . and much more. Again, this was what I was doing in my holidays from about fourteen onwards. Somehow the pace and rhythm of walking gave me enormous pleasure. And it was a mental and emotional space too. When I planned the trips, it involved massive amounts of thinking ahead and organization. Doing the trips themselves meant engaging with the world around me in strange places, often on quite difficult terrain. Afterwards, I would brood for hours on the memories of climbing hills and the exhilarating feeling of walking along high, exposed walkways where, I was told, Celts, Romans and Anglo-Saxons had walked before.

The Naturalists' Club at the Natural History Museum was a club organized for children as young as seven or eight and took place behind one of the old mahogany doors that used to be just off the main hall. When I was in my last two years at primary school (aged between nine and eleven) I would go with my best friend to the museum and we would draw the animals, or go on outings to Hampstead Heath in the pouring rain to spot birds and animals. Or on one occasion, I collected stones and pebbles while we were on holiday in Pembrokeshire and brought them in to the club. The organisers showed me how to mount the stones on a thick piece of card using – what was then very new! – PVC glue mixed in with cotton wool. Then we looked in various books to see if we could identify the stones.

The rugby came about because I used to go with my father to watch rugby internationals at Twickenham and we would watch it on TV, roaring and shouting as if we were at the match. My schools played football (soccer), which I wasn't much good at, but I could see that I might be OK at rugby, getting my head down, pushing and grabbing, rather than being skilled and dexterous with my feet. So I joined the local rugby club and played in their fifth team along with a bunch of mostly over-weight men, much older than me, who were mostly in it for the booze-ups on a Saturday night. Again, this was something that had nothing to do with anyone from school but started to offer me that fantasy space that regular sport gives you: the great goal or try or leap or sprint that you are going to do, the great achievement or awful mistake of last week's game, the envies and rivalries, the lost opportunities, the suspicions about others' motives . . . Part of my fantasy life was that I would end up playing for England.

When I was much younger, I had been in the Cubs for two or three years and loved the games, 'bob-a-jobbing' and badge-collecting involved. The woman who ran it, the 'Akela', was sweet and kind without being cloying in any way. She was rather brusque and distant and yet seemed to be very involved and knew us all and what we liked. I remember comparing her with my own mum and with our teachers at school. In my last year at primary school, we had a teacher who I suspect now was massively anxious about the status and reputation of the brand-new school we were in. We were 'founder pupils' and she was a founder teacher. It's not that she showed her anxiety – I'm only saying that now. What she showed was an extreme irritation, short temper, snappiness. She seemed at the time to have an extreme dislike of boys apart from two or three favourites. So she would call girls by their first names and all boys apart from her three favourites by our last names. My only point in saying this is that going to Cubs gave me a way of being able to be somewhere else, from where I could, as it were, look back at school. I wasn't just immersed in one place of learning and activity as if it were the one and only possible way. And I compared people; I compared Akela and my class teacher.

When I put those five out-of-school activities together and think about what they did for me, I can see that a huge amount of my emotions and thoughts went into them. They all mattered greatly to me. I wanted to do good things there. I wanted to learn things and above all I wanted to get better at whatever it was, in each of them, in all their different ways. They all 'used' my mind and body in ways that were different from school and different from each other. One moment I was being asked to think about the meaning and sound of words, the next how eight large sweaty blokes can all push together. One moment I was thinking about how to find and collect interesting things in 'nature', the next how to climb a hill before the rain comes down.

At the same time, I could relate all these back to school and education, showing how each of them in their different ways helped me with school subjects – and believe me they did. But that would be to diminish their importance. Each of them was a fascinating and wonderful 'place' to inhabit on their own account. They were places that were separate from my parents but also places that I could spend a good deal of time discussing and talking about with my parents – who, incidentally, had done quite similar things themselves when they were in their teens. I had something to tell them about. They had questions to ask me about the things I told them.

What's been important for me as a parent – and still is – is to use what I remember of the feelings connected with these activities, and see if gently, carefully, not too intrusively, we can discover if our own children might want to take up things that enthuse and excite them in a similar way.

Much more available now than when I was a boy are one-off workshops and short courses. The great advantage of these is that they can serve as tasters for children to see if they fancy these activities. I have run plenty of them myself over the last forty years and taken my children to plenty of different ones too. I'm bound to say this, aren't I, but they are very nearly all fantastic opportunities. It really is worth the effort of grabbing the leaflet from the library, leisure centre, arts centre or wherever to see what's on offer.

I said that there weren't many of these short courses when I was young but one I do remember. I found out that the Royal Shakespeare Company was running a day course around their production of *A Caucasian Chalk Circle* and wrote off to take part. I got in and went along, though they were a bit surprised that I was so young (sixteen, I think). We met the director of the production, who 'produced' us in one or two of the scenes. I remember being in a crowd scene shouting horrible things. We had a talk from the artistic director of the company about the author's (Bertolt Brecht) intentions and methods. This was over fifty years ago, and I'm remembering it now. One day's activity and it's stuck in my mind.

It was a powerful enough single day to have been a trigger to get me into writing, to get me into thinking that school wasn't the only place where I could learn and figure out what I wanted to do. Again, I hope very much that when my own children do one-off days with all their intensity, that it will spark off ideas and hopes in them, just as it did for me.

In saying 'hope', perhaps that's at least as important as anything else that happens in these out-of-school places. Without the pressure of exams, success-or-failure mindsets and the like, doing out-of-school stuff can fill you with a sense of exciting possibility and, yes, hope. There *is* something that can grab you, fascinate you. There *is* something that you can put a great chunk of yourself into. And maybe one day, you could be the kind of person who does more of it and be really good at it, or really interested in it. These are feelings that are like powerful motors inside us, encouraging us to want to find out more, know more and do more.

This kind of out-of-school activity was also part of my

political interests. Of course these change and vary over the years and between different people. The point of this book is not for me to be telling you either that you should be involved in politics or that you should be involved in my kind of politics. What I would say, though, is that through a combination of the home debates, school work in history and geography, my interests in the theatre, I became very interested in politics. This interest wasn't some kind of add-on – though there would have been nothing wrong with it if it had been. In my case, it flowed through almost everything else I did. What seemed to be the burning issue of the day was 'the Bomb'.

To get involved in that, or indeed anything similar, is to get involved with massive amounts of reading, writing, thinking, debating and – if you want to – graphic design, singing, dancing and a good deal else. It also meant getting involved with a way of thinking: talking about ideas and talking about them even as you felt as if you were part of making them. After all, in the case of the Bomb, the debates I was part of (aged from thirteen onwards), the action I was part of (marches and the like) were debated on TV, the radio and in all the newspapers.

This is very different from simply hearing about ideas, or even talking about ideas in a classroom. Apart from anything else, the events I was concerned with involved huge debates and disagreements. People said that they would or would not take part if this or that happened or did not happen. People not only argued about what our government was doing but also about the governments of the rest of the world and the United Nations. There were ideas whizzing around in the air that I had never heard before, never heard in school, would never hear in school. At the time, I didn't know whether they were nonsense or profound. I became very interested in trying to figure out if it mattered whether an idea came from the 'right' people, or whether the 'wrong' people could have the right idea. And then, moving on from that, whether a person or a group could have one 'right' idea alongside a load of 'wrong' ones.

I was figuring out how our personal, social and political allegiances work. Who do you go with? Can you change the world? Should you try? Or is the world OK as it is? If you try, who do you get in with?

Things that might seem clear at the weekend would sometimes get muddy back at school. I remember spending many hours arguing with people at school who hadn't taken part in or shared my experiences.

A good deal of this would apply to any young person getting caught up with political or social affairs, whether of my persuasion or others, whether those more to do with religion and charities. It's heady stuff. I don't regret a moment of it.

Again, I might say that it was all massively helpful for school. And it was. It was about debating topics, about figuring out how to express ideas in writing. It was also about speaking in public: putting my thoughts together in short, punchy ways that people could connect with. But it was also important for emotional reasons too: a sense that I could listen to people with very different ideas, analyse what they were saying and make up my mind. It's easy to see how much of this could feed into the kinds of work that go on in school.

There was something else exciting and exhilarating going on. Because of the particular politics I was involved with, there really was a way in which the world got bigger and more complicated. Taking part in meetings or marches meant working with people from all over the world, from all sorts of different backgrounds – many of which were nothing like mine. I have strong memories of standing outside an aircraft base next to two men who came from India – no rarity these days, of course. And they quizzed me about why I was there and what I believed in. And I quizzed them back. Why were they there? And they started talking about India and the 'third world' and 'development' and I had never heard anything like it. It was like a crash course in world economics, standing next to a barbed-wire fence.

As I say, I am not telling you this in order to make a specific political point. I am saying that our job as parents – as mine did – is to provide a safe context for our older children to get involved with this sort of thing if they choose to.

HOW TO HELP WITH HOMEWORK WHEN YOU DON'T KNOW MUCH ABOUT IT

I've often had the experience of my children asking me to help them with homework which I knew very little or nothing about. So, a child might say to you, 'I'm stuck with these chemical equations.'

One of the odd things about being a parent is that we keep thinking we have to know everything. After all, if we don't keep proving to our children we know everything, they'll run wild, not respect us and the family will fall apart. Or not.

Another way of thinking about it is to say to yourself, I don't know everything, I certainly don't know about chemical equations but I do know how to find out things when I don't know about them. This might also work for my child.

So, when one of my children comes to me with something that I don't remember from school, or never knew, or, if I did know it, it's all changed – I do this:

First of all, I say, can you explain to me what you have to do? Can you explain to me which bit of it you don't understand?

Then I say, were you shown how to do this by the teacher? Were you given a piece of paper or a book or a website where it's explained?

Can you repeat anything of what the teacher said? Or if it was on a worksheet or on a website, can we look at it together?

Then, we try to see if there is a website where they may

explain how this thing works. Tip: quite often, I've found that the best ones are American.

Now here's the key point: you don't have to understand all this stuff yourself. All you have to do is to help your child take it step by step. And – most importantly – ask your child to try to explain it to you as they're trying to get it. This means that they're putting the process – whatever it is – into their own words. Also, without you knowing, you might be raising questions and problems that will help them understand the whole thing more.

I repeat: you don't have to be able to do whatever it is – chemical equations, say – as well as them. You are the bridge over which they will travel to get to being able to do them.

So, chemical equations are something your child may have to do somewhere around the second year of secondary school. If you've not done much arithmetic since school and no chemistry, then they can seem like gobbledegook. They turn out to be not gobbledegook, if you sit with a child who has been told some stuff about it by a teacher and who has, say, a few notes on it. Then, as and when you start looking things up, the gobbledegookness starts to slip away. Things start to make sense.

What's really exciting, is that there often comes a moment when your child gets it before you do, or more than you do. What you're offering is the support of listening to them trying to explain what the difficulty is, and trying to explain how to do it. You're offering them the importance of sticking with it, of going back to what you were told or given by way of explanation. You're offering them what's available 'out there' that enables all of us to find out and learn things. This is offering them some strategies of what to do any time and every time it seems as if they can't get it.

There are also some basic principles that you can return to. Usually, in difficult homework there are stages in the work. That is, you can only do the second part when you've sorted the first part. It's the furniture self-assembly principle. One of the key things you can show your children is that a good deal of the kinds of problems they set in homework involve exactly the same method. Only move on to the next stage when you've sorted the stage that comes before it. If it's science or technology and there are procedures or methods that are rules, then you must stick with these.

So, this needs a good internet connection. It needs loads of scrap paper and pencils. You need to feel free to play with putting in different search words into Google. The key words will probably be in the title of the homework, or in one or some of the technical words of the work.

Not only are there websites that help with these things, there are also people on YouTube explaining them. Some of these are very good.

Now, flip all this over and think what happens when your child comes to you with something that you do know about. The strong, strong, strong temptation is to start lecturing. And in a matter of moments, you can see that your child isn't listening or is getting cross with you. Either way, more often than not, lecturing doesn't work. This is because, as we know, there's a huge difference between knowing something and being able to explain it. In fact, there's not only a difference, it's really hard to figure out what the difference is!

The way to unravel this knot is to go back to how you act when you don't know something. If you do what I suggest, going through stages and questions, then you can do something very similar – even though you do know the answers. This means holding back from jumping in. You wait for your child to come up with words of their own. You wait for your child to come up with questions. Then, instead of immediately answering those questions, you can say, can you answer that question yourself? And you can look for places where there are answers other than from yourself.

What is really useful or interesting to offer may well come later. Let's say your child gets it and it's sorted. At that moment, you can offer an observation or thought that is a slightly different view of it. At first, this might seem like messing everything up, or that it will wreck everything that's just been learned. In fact, if you do this, what you offer is something very important about knowledge and learning as a whole: there is never one fixed way. This means that knowledge and learning is something you can always ask questions about. Nothing gets wrapped up and put away for ever. What's more, if you raise these alternative ways of looking at things, you suggest to your child that they can do exactly the same.

In saying this, I'm reminded that this is what my parents did for me. I had the repeated experience of thinking that I knew something, that it was all settled – no matter what it was, whether in grammar, history, French, or maths – and my father or mother would show me that there was another way of looking at it. I remember having to do an essay called 'Why Chartism Failed'. I had my notes from the lesson, I had the piece in my history text book that said, 'Why Chartism Failed'. All I wanted from my father was some help with my opening paragraph.

'The essay is "Why Chartism Failed",' I said.

'Failed?' he said. 'Chartism didn't fail.'

And then he went through all the things that the Chartists called for and which we now all live by and take for granted. In that one moment, he showed me that history is not a matter of learning stuff, it's being able to debate stuff and in the debating you learn the stuff.

WHERE GOOD IDEAS COME FROM

THE
HOME

The places we live in are stuffed full of scientific and techno-logical biz. All the heating, lighting, freezing, water and building are science in action. At the same time, our homes are full of art and design: all the colours, shapes, pictures are art in action. And homes are among the most emotional places we will ever know as we fill them up with all our loves, losses, desires, fears, hopes, dangers, memories and feelings. Combine these three aspects of home – science, art and emotions – and we have a potent mix. This mix gives us a springboard for learning, the emotions often giving us the motivation for wanting to find out more or to make and do more. Our job as parents then is to tune in to moments when this can happen.

DIY AND BUILDERS

Every moment during the hundreds of jobs done by you or anyone else involves choices, decisions, skills and knowledge. Mending, refurbishing, patching up, brightening up are full of questions. They're also moments full of the stories of disasters, rows and triumphs, going back through decades of family life and into the history of the building itself.

During my childhood, my dad was a DIY freak. I don't know whether he was keen to pass on his DIY skills, or whether he just liked company, but he got me to stand next to him for hours and hours on end while he prodded, poked, toshed, drilled, glued, planed and painted.

What was nice about this was that he was never afraid to tell me how he was not good enough at it, that he had messed up, that other people were really amazingly much better than him. It was then that he was reminded of the rooms he had lived in during that mysterious time in his life before I existed. I heard about a tiny house in the East End of London where there was no electricity and he shared a room with an uncle he refused to talk to. For twelve years! he said.

There were tools he loved, like a very old wooden plane. And others, like an old screwdriver, that he cursed because they weren't good enough. Or he would moan about how it was all too complicated, too messy, too time-consuming, as if the makers of tools and materials were in a great conspiracy to make DIY hard for him. It was personal.

The toolbox was a place full of words: bow-saw, pincers, claw-hammer, rawlplug, Polyfilla, Philips screwdriver, wrench . . . and each had a job to do which he could explain even as he could tell me why his particular one was not up to it and that was why 'No job ever takes two minutes'. This was his DIY slogan, a mantra that he repeated often enough for it to become a family motto. So if, say, my mother mentioned that a door was sticking, or that the lino had cracked, we would sing, 'No job ever takes two minutes' before my father had time to say whether he was up to doing it or not.

And each job had a lingo too: unscrew anti-clockwise; 'runs' and 'curtains' when you paint; 'water looks for a way out'; the plaster's 'shot'; shelves are 'plumb' or 'pissed' and so on.

But this was also arithmetic in action – weighing, testing, counting, calculating. Measuring up walls, floors, alcoves and chimneys, and heading off to shops and builders' yards with calculations about screws, paint, wood or sheet metal. Then, finishing it all off with decisions about sofas, wallpaper, curtains, lampshades. Did this 'go with' that? Were these two colours 'clashing'?

It's easy and convenient to cut children out of this stuff. We are often doing these things in a rush. Some of us feel so uneasy or reluctant or 'grown-up' about it that we don't want to share our fed-upness or superiority with our children. It makes us look less than brilliant. Alternatively, people who are really good at it sometimes feel worried about letting children in on it, in case they mess up. If you've taken on a builder, it can easily feel as if this is all very grown-up stuff to do with money and very technical matters, and you go off into a corner and mutter about 'architraves' and 'acros'.

And when you discover that a builder you got in ten years ago made an enormous screw-up, do you really want to admit that to your children?

A builder once took a fireplace and chimney-breast out of a house I lived in. Some years later, I was lying in bed in the room and found myself wondering what the builder had done – if anything – to support the ceiling where the fireplace used to be. I shared the problem with my teenage son. 'You see,' I said, 'when you take a fireplace out, there's a whole chunk missing . . . I mean, up above, there's another fireplace, so what's that resting on?'

We both looked at the ceiling and we talked about how he must have put something in . . . a bar that goes across . . . a lintel . . . some kind of concrete beam, and it must be sitting there in the gap between the ceiling in this room and the floor of the room above, like the filling to a sandwich . . . yes, we agreed. And I said, 'But if there is a lintel in there, what's it resting on?' Well, er . . . we thought . . . er . . . probably on . . . er . . . something in the gap . . . joists perhaps? We drew pictures of what that might look like and we got stuck trying to work out which way the joists ran. Then we looked at the fireplace and chimney-breast in the room above. We looked up and up to the ceiling in that room. There were cracks running from the chimney-breast out into the room . . . as if the chimney-breast were trying to crack away from the wall.

And come to think of it, I didn't remember the builder ever bringing a concrete beam into the house. I don't ever remember him saying, 'I'll put in a lintel . . .'

I rushed out to get the bloke next door to come and look at it. He was someone who knew all about buildings. He came downstairs and looked at the room that had had the fireplace and chimney-breast removed. No, there was nothing to worry about, he said. No one would take out a fireplace and a chimney-breast without supporting the fireplace and the chimney-breast above, he said. So my son said, 'So where is the lintel, then? And what's it resting on?' The bloke next door said that it would be in there and it would be OK.

I wasn't happy. I rang a builder and asked him to come over. He looked at the cracks upstairs. He stood in the room below and looked at the ceiling. 'There's only one way to find out,' he said, 'cut a hole in the ceiling and feel in. If there's a lintel in there, we'll feel it.'

So he climbed up a ladder and cut a hole in the ceiling. Just big enough for him to put his hand in. He stuck his hand and arm through the hole and waved it about in there.

We waited.

'Nope,' he said, 'nothing there, Mike. Nothing at all.'

I went up the ladder. I groped around. There was nothing there.

My son went up the ladder. He groped around. He agreed. Nothing there.

So we looked at the builder and I said, 'So what's holding up the fireplace and the chimney-breast upstairs?'

He went up the ladder again. He felt in deeper.

'Nails,' he said. 'The builder has hammered nine-inch nails into the joists underneath the fireplace upstairs. It's all resting on nine-inch nails.'

This story has gone round and round in my mind, I've shared it with my children and with many others. It seems to tell me all sorts of things: there's me, the gullible one, who believed the first builder, when he told me it was all OK. There's him, the con-merchant, who risked all our lives – and possibly the neighbours' lives too. And there's the science of it all: weight, structure, support, the right (and wrong) materials . . . stuff that's been worked out over thousands of years of making buildings, putting one storey on top of another. In fact, whenever I hear these awful stories of factories and blocks of flats falling down, I think of my nine-inch nails.

Now I could keep all that quiet. But I don't. I tell people. And like a lot of stories, it's also partly about warning others, warning my children: you don't want to be as gullible as your dad. One day, you might want to alter a building; there are right and wrong ways – there are ways that work and ways that don't work – and that's because of the science of the thing.

So, investigation, interpretation, storytelling and sharing all mingle here. In fact, when it came to working out what to do, it also brought in some invention too. Should we put back the fireplace and chimney-breast? Or would two pillars do? And if we put in pillars, what would they rest on down below? There wouldn't be much point in putting in pillars if all they ended up doing was resting on the earth under the house . . .

Whatever our misgivings about sharing building, decorating, shopping for materials, mending, patching up and the rest, there is also a way of thinking of it all as a time to learn, talk and share. And you'll never know what will spark off that moment of curiosity, that wish to know more, to understand more.

At any given moment, you may get asked by your children or indeed you may want to ask them questions like these:

Why and how do plaster, cement, concrete and mortar set?
How does damp rise?
What is the grain in wood?
How do you decide when to use a nail and when to use a screw?
Why are there three wires in a plug?

THE HOME

What is plastic made of?

What's the difference between volts, amps and watts?

How does the roller hold the paint?

Why does the shower-rose get furred up?

These questions and the hundreds of others in this book won't necessarily be answered. Most of them won't be. I mean them to be 'triggers' for you to share with your child. Alternatively, you can use them to spark off other questions that you or they might want to ask. Once you're in the asking-questions frame of mind, it spawns yet more queries.

Trying to find the answers to questions is as important as knowing the answers. It's as important finding out how to learn as it is to do the learning itself.

As I've said, books, libraries, the internet, tablets are vital. Just as important is talking to an expert like a plumber, a roofer, a builder, a pest-control person and the like who will give you answers . . . and more questions. And more questions.

BEASTIES

Depending on where you live, homes are full of creatures and life that you may or may not want to live with: mould, mildew, fruit-flies, mites, lice, crabs, house-flies, fleas, tics, ants, wasps, woodworm, bedbugs, moths, mosquitoes, daddy-long-legs, beetles, cockroaches, spiders, mice, rats . . . and there are occasional visitors who burst in on us: bumblebees, birds, foxes, frogs, ladybirds . . .

Again, it's very easy to deal with the whole lot as if they're the enemy and the only thing to do is to squash or poison them. Even if that's what you decide is necessary or desirable in the long run, the moment is full of possibilities.

How do these organisms and creatures live?
What is their life-cycle?
How do they reproduce?
What do they feed off?
Where do they go in winter?
How come they survive winter?
How do they make their nests?
How do biologists classify them?
Are they 'insects' or 'crustaceans'? Or what?
And what's the difference?

Against what might be our most powerful feelings, I will now make one of many requests in this book: buy a version of the 'Creature Peeper'. These are very cheap, plastic viewing chambers. You put the small beastie, alive or dead, in the chamber and you can view it through an in-built magnifying glass on top or from below. I've yet to meet a child who isn't made curious by this. You can see the hairs on a flea, the sting on a bee.

It's at moments like these that you get a sense that your home is not just *your* home, it's a 'niche' – or many niches – for other creatures to make their home in too. Depending on how warm or cold, how damp or dry, how many pets, how many crumbs, hairs, bits of dead skin you leave lying about, the different parts of your home make up an ecosystem. That's to say, there are many links between how your family live in the home and the beasties that live with you.

If you are a poisoner – and most of us are:

How do you choose your poison?
How does the poison work?
Is the poison killing us too?
Is some poison not so bad for us humans as others? Why? How?

In my life I've often been to France, and, as all Brits know, the moment we leave the UK we find ourselves in daily contact with beasts we haven't met before or, if we have, they're much rarer. Enter the hornet. Of course, there are hornets in England, but they're not massively common. In France, there are millions.

So, I'm sitting in a kitchen at around ten o'clock at night, with my back to the door, which is open to the garden. Suddenly, I hear a low droning sound, getting nearer, and before I have time to react, something chunky has hit the back of my head and instantly starts to crawl through my hair. In a flash, I know it's a hornet. So instead of doing what I should do, which is get up slowly, walk out of the door and gently put my head down to encourage it to fly off or crawl off, I leap up in a panic and start to shake my head around. I hopped out of the door, making the growling noise that I seem to make when I panic.

The hornet flew up, back into the house and landed on one of the beams in the room. Then it started to crawl very slowly over the beam until it got to a crack. It stood still, and then I heard a crackling, crunching sound: *pchrrrch, pchrrrch* . . . It seemed to be trying to eat the beam.

I'll spare you the details of how I got rid of it, other than that it found its rightful place in the Creature Peeper so that my children could investigate it the next day. I also put it there to demonstrate how massively brave and fearless their father is, how ready and able he is to risk all to defend them.

But then we got interested in hornets. What did it think it was doing? Why did it fly in a straight direction right into the kitchen? Why did it stop flying and start crawling about – in my hair and then on the beam? And why did it start crunching and crackling on the beam?

Believe me, hornets are fascinating and incredible. Almost certainly, this was a young queen, on the hunt to start a new nest. She was flying headlong at walls, trees and bushes to land on something that had a hole or crack where she could perhaps start to build a nest and lay eggs. That's why she was on her own. That's why she started using her strong scissor-like jaws to cut away at the wood of the beam – *pchrrrch, pchrrrch* . . .

Hornets usually hang about with hundreds of other hornets. We found out that one of the amazing and scary things about this is that if you come across a hornet near its nest and you alarm it, it is likely to release a chemical that the other hornets can smell. This alerts them to fly very fast towards the hornet that released the chemical and the moment they land on something warm and moving – like a human arm – they will start to sting it. Unlike bees, hornets can go on stinging someone for several minutes at no risk to themselves. Then they can pull their stings back in, and stock them up with poison for another day.

The effect on a human of being stung several times or indeed many times by hornets is usually lethal.

In its own scary way, the hornet is a thing to be marvelled at, I think. Loud, fast, deadly and very good at protecting its own.

We got to know about hornets.

I have one strong reason to remember this with a shake of the head. Many years before my experience with the hornet in my hair, I was staying in France with my stepdaughter and my son, who were young teenagers. We were staying on the first floor of an old farmhouse that acted as a kind of porch over a barn. On the wall of the barn under our first-floor accommodation was a hornets' nest. Don't worry about that, said the farmer. You don't bother the hornets, the hornets won't bother you. And I believed him.

Whenever we were indoors, we could hear the low, insistent drone of the nest. They sound like the Lancaster bombers of the Second World War: grumbling in an uncomfortable, irritated sort of way.

One day, the children and I went out and when we came back it was dark. The windows were closed, but the shutters were still open. The rule in France is that the moment it starts to get dark, you shut the shutters. But we were too late for dusk. My stepdaughter said, 'Shall I shut the shutters?'

Now there's every chance that a French person would, at this point, say, no. After all, to shut shutters, you have to open a window. If you open a window at night, anything outside, particularly something attracted by the light, will fly in. That could be a moth, a fly, a mosquito, a bat or indeed a hornet.

So I said, yes. And as she went to do it, I said, 'Yeah, but watch out for hornets.'

I'm not sure why I said that. I'm not sure how you 'watch out for hornets'. After all, they move very quickly and the moment you're watching out for them, they've decided to do what they want to do, and they've done it.

She opened the window and in flew a hornet.

'Shut the window!' I shouted, as if I had meant that all along.

My children ran out of the room, down the corridor, into the bathroom, closed the door. And locked it. Hornets, they thought, can easily force a door open, unless you lock it.

And I was on my own in the room with the hornet. This one, I now know with our expertise on hornets, was not a lone queen. It was an irritated drone who wanted to get out.

You know what to do with an irritated drone who wants to get out? Obvious: open the window. But hang on, if you open the window, the others will want to come in. Either because the bright light looks like fun. Or because they smell irritated loner hornet, who is pumping out his alarm-gas.

So, now that my stepdaughter has shut the window, surely the best thing to do is face up to the hornet. Man and beast. Face to face.

I put on my coat and hat and gloves. I covered my face with a scarf. I took a towel and menaced the hornet. Yes, I menaced it. I whirled the towel. I showed the hornet that being near me was a dangerous matter. The hornet cruised about, droning. I whirled. I tried a flick. And a stab. And a lunge. In the end, I clipped it. I got it mid-flight. It reeled to the floor where it rotated like a Catherine wheel and it fizzed. But I wasn't intimidated by this fizzing.

As I told my children, I was brave and strong. And resolute in my job of defending them against nature.

I trod on it.

And this is how the phrase, 'Yeah, but watch out for hornets!' became a 'standard' in our house. Shall I go by bus? Yeah, but watch out for hornets! Shall I do my homework now? Yeah, but watch out for hornets!

Family stories attach themselves to our encounters with beasties. Gruesome, farcical, absurd, these episodes show us up as vulnerable and ignorant.

If we are in a mind to let them, they can also be the gruesome, farcical and absurd triggers to arouse curiosity about these beasties' habits.

I mean, is it true that hornets spend a lot of their time killing and eating other insects?

And if a bat or a house-martin ate a hornet, would the hornet sting them? And would the bat or the house-martin be affected by it? If not, why not?

We can make these moments matter.

THE KITCHEN

Your kitchen, whatever it's like, is the best classroom ever invented. The easiest thing to do is treat it as the place where we 'service' our children. We do the cooking, we call for them to come in, we dish up the food, they eat it, they leave. Of course, for very, very young children, it's hard to do much else. Just as hard, is to change from this way of treating them to another way as they get older. Or to keep changing. After all, kitchens are very personal places and to let our 'baby' start cooking is, for some of us, a big leap to make.

But it has to be done.

There is too much talking, thinking, sorting, investigating, figuring out, remembering and passing on of 'culture' that can go on in a kitchen to risk missing out.

And there are subtle messages to do with who does the work to keep a household going that we teach children in our kitchens.

And kitchens are our laboratories. Cooking uses physics (heat, light, microwaves, refrigeration), chemistry (mixing things together to make other things – what helps, what hinders our getting a good result), biology (that's the ingredients: seeds, veg, fruit, meat, herbs, spices), and maths (weighing, measuring, timing, buying, calculating, estimating).

Kitchens are about culture and tradition: mundane chores we do like laying tables, putting away plates, knives and forks, hanging tea-towels, storing detergents and cleaners, how to wash up are all things we probably learned from our parents and friends. We can tell our children anecdotes and chat about, say, how our mothers used to lay the table, or what the 'glory-hole' cupboard or drawer looked like, how our fathers or grandparents behaved in kitchens.

I tell my children that we didn't get a fridge till I was in my teens because we had a larder, a cupboard with a hole in the wall to the outside, covered over with gauze to keep the flies out. I tell them how my brother and I used to 'raid the larder' and 'make mixtures'.

Food, taste and cooking are 'cultural', no matter how ordinary and plain it is. A slice of bread and butter is as cultural as coq au vin or rogan josh. When my children are making their sandwiches for school, I might tell them about Pan-Yan Pickle and mixing peanut butter with chocolate spread . . . and how chocolate spread 'in my day' was of course much better than Nutella. I tell them about how they're not the only ones who love caramel wafers. Once my brother used his pocket money to buy a whole box of them and he hid them in his room. And I snitched on him. But, outrageously, my mum didn't tell him off! She just said that perhaps he could share them.

And I tell them about my grandparents ('bubbe' and 'zeyde' in Yiddish) and how Bubbe used to keep chickens in the back yard. Or I might go back even further and tell them that my mother used to tell us that the most embarrassing thing for her as a girl was to go with her mother to the market and hear her haggling in Yiddish with the stall-holders on Hessel Street about the price of a chicken. That's me passing on a family memory from the 1920s and the place such stories are most likely to arise is in the kitchen.

*

One of my strongest memories of this Bubbe was her trying to tell my mother how to make pickled cucumbers. My mother asked her how much salt she should use.

'To taste,' Bubbe said.

'What do you mean, "to taste"?' my mother said.

'To taste. Add the salt to taste.'

'But how much salt is that?' my mother said, getting irritated with her.

'I'm saying, I'm saying,' said Bubbe, surprised and cross that my mother didn't understand, 'to taste, to taste.'

This became one of our family sayings. Whenever someone asked a question about 'how much' of something, we would shout out, 'To taste, to taste.' How much coal do we need to get in? 'To taste, to taste.'

Meanwhile, my father would lapse into nostalgic dreaming of glorious dishes he had had decades ago, dishes that we had never seen or heard about from anyone else but him. 'Oh,' he would sigh, 'chulunt. The way my Bubbe made chulunt. You know, boys, you can't just make chulunt like you fry an egg. It takes twenty-four hours to make chulunt.'

'What is it?' we'd say.

'Ah,' he says, 'aha. Yes, what is it? Exactly. It's like, it's like . . . there's . . . y'know, I don't exactly know what there is in it; there's lamb – well, there should be lamb – and there's barley . . . but, when you have chulunt, you don't really know what's in it. I mean, when my Bubbe made it . . .'

And so on. We found it funny. We would tell him that he had told us this a hundred times before. We would tell him not to tell us again. And I've remembered it. Somehow in the great scheme of things, it matters.

Sometimes he would get finicky with what my mother had made. Maybe she would make a potato salad and he would go

91

off on one about the incredible, wonderful, extraordinary potato salads that Bubbe made. 'The onions were sweet. You could get really sweet onions in those days. I loved onions.' Or it was the prunes. 'Boys, you've never seen prunes like the way my Bubbe made prunes. You see these prunes? They're tiny. And shrivelled. I don't know where my Bubbe got her prunes but hers were huge. And soft. And sweet. They were giant prunes . . .'

And we would marvel at the idea of giant prunes. We wanted to have soft, sweet giant prunes like his Bubbe made.

But my mother wouldn't be drawn in. She wouldn't let him yack on and on about how his Bubbe made this and his Bubbe made that. She would blurt out, 'Well, if you don't like this caff, find another one! And I'll tell you something else: I'm not your Bubbe! She spoiled you. You know that.'

And this was a whole other tale. This was a big deal. Behind those words about food, and us laughing, there was the story of how my father was born in America, his parents split when he was only two, how his mother brought him and his sister and baby brother back to England to live with her mother and father, aunts and cousins in a tiny little rented house near the London Hospital. And in that house is a little boy (my father) that the Bubbe thinks she has to protect from the angry aunts and cousins who are cross that this family has turned up from America and is squeezing them all up in what was already a tiny space. This is a little boy without his father. A little boy whose mother doesn't cook or work because she has one arm that was weakened by polio or because she's gone to a meeting, where they will either save the world or hear what their dead ancestors are saying – socialism or spiritualism. Socialism on Tuesdays. Spiritualism on Thursdays.

And all that comes out over cooking and eating.

That's why, if we let them, kitchens are so special.

*

But what of the cooking itself?

There are many excellent books and websites on cooking with children. They are a must. The recipe book is a great example of a bit of 'literacy' that children will want to read and use because of the end result: fried rice, biscuits, meringue or whatever, is something that they want. And recipes take some interpreting. They're written in special recipe-language. If you do exactly as they say, buy every bit of the stuff they say you should, weigh it out exactly as they say you should and follow the instructions exactly, you will usually get a good result.

But more often than not, we don't follow the recipe exactly. Or for some reason we can't and we try improvising: hah, we couldn't find any vanilla essence, so let's use cinnamon. It says 'put in a hot oven and cook for twenty minutes' but this oven's getting old so let's leave it in for twenty-five.

This is chemistry. We are finding out what goes with what to make something else. We find out how ingredients change under heat. We find out what happens if we heat too much or too little: the difference between the dark brown crust or the squidgy middle. The secret of all good science is getting to understand why and how mistakes happen. Every time we don't get something right in the kitchen, we use a bit of science to try to figure out why not. It's vitally important to share this bit of thinking with our children: was it too hot, not hot enough, did we cook it too long, or was there too much flour in it?

But how does cooking work anyway?

How come if you mix flour, egg, sugar and milk and then heat it, you get something dry and fluffy and crumbly? In some cookery books they try to explain this little miracle. They tell you that the reason why you have to mix and stir and whisk and beat is because you are bringing each grain of flour into contact with a tiny bit of milk, a tiny bit of egg and a tiny bit of sugar. Then, when you heat that little grain of flour covered in all that stuff, the grain of flour makes a little puff of gas. That little puff of gas is what makes your cake light and crumbly rather than dense and heavy.

And there are health warnings about not cooking a chicken enough.

Why? Why would an uncooked chicken be poisonous?
How come whatever it is that's poisonous goes away if you cook it long enough?
Where does it go?
Or does the poison change, because we cook it?
And where does the blood go, when you cook a bit of meat for long enough?
What is blood pudding?

And talking of chickens, as you carve a chicken we have names for parts of it that are chicken names that are different from zoology names: wish-bone, parson's nose, breast meat, 'eyes'. My father called the leg the 'pulka', the wing: 'fliegel', the fat: 'shmalts' and off he'd go on one about 'lokshn soup' (chicken soup with noodles): 'my Bubbe's lokshn soup . . .'!

Our names for food are full of personal and linguistic history. To take one basic oddity: people don't eat 'cow' or 'bullock' or 'bull' or 'cattle'. It's 'beef'. The meat is not called 'pig' or 'hog', it's 'pork'. In the mixing up of English and French that happened after the Normans invaded Britain in 1066, people started using the French words for cattle-meat and pig-meat: 'beef' and 'pork'. Go to France today and the 'beefs' and the 'porks' ('les boeufs' and 'les porcs') are running around in the field.

Then again, there are the ingredients written on the packaging. There have been times we've been in the kitchen, pouring something out of a packet or bag at the very moment experts on the radio and television have been talking about 'too much salt' or 'too much sugar' in processed foods. We've been able to pick up on exactly that point, at that very moment, by looking at the side of the packet. Moments like this have to be grabbed. They are precious coincidences that spark off questions and problems.

And why would 'too much salt' or 'too much sugar' be a problem? And if the government health officer is saying it's a problem, why can't the government just say to the food companies, 'Stop putting it in the food'?
Why do the food companies go on putting 'too much' in, when the medics say they shouldn't?
And what is 'healthy food'? How can a food be 'healthy'?
And what is a 'vitamin'?

One of my children got the baking bug. It seems to have come from watching cooking competitions on TV but then plenty of us watch those without dashing off to the kitchen to bake cupcakes. That's where she started: cupcakes. I can see why. A cupcake is very unthreatening. It doesn't seem like a great complicated business to bake a cupcake. Then, when you've made twelve cupcakes, people grab them and eat them and tell you how good they are.

I could see that she loved the precision of it, and experimented with timings so that they came out exactly the right colour. Just as important as the ingredients and mixing is all the stuff to do with the apparatus: having or getting the right trays, learning how to grease the pan, or how to get the right paper cups to put the batter mix in.

From there, it went to getting a cupcake book, another book about other kinds of baking and then to being given a very flashy purple electric mixer by her parents. Rather bizarrely, at any time of day on a weekend or in the holidays, she would get up out of her chair and say in a kind of pleading sort of a voice, 'I want to bake something . . .' As if we would say no!

One of her special turns was at a family party where she decided to make Victoria sponge (not my favourite, I confess) and she spent hours decorating the tops of them with ornate patterns of raspberries. They were like town hall flowerbeds. I think she made three or four of them and they got eaten in about an hour of the party starting. Mind you, I'm still waiting for the return of the apple, cinnamon and raisin cupcake. I think she is getting as much satisfaction from withholding making me something I beg for as she gets from pleasing a house full of people at a party.

THE BATHROOM

The bathroom is another lab. The passage of water down tubes – pressure, flow and heating – and mirrors are all physics. Alongside that, the soaps, shampoos, cleaning fluids, deodorants, moisturizers, anti-perspirants, toothpaste and make-up are chemistry. If you keep your first aid in the bathroom along with pills and medication, that's the biology, along with all the stuff – whatever it is – we do with our bodies behind closed doors in bathrooms: hair, teeth, nails, beards, armpits, genitals, dry skin, rashes, athlete's foot, verrucas, nits . . .

Boring and annoying though it is, we should share the problems of hot-water tanks and boilers with our children.

How does the water get into the house?
Why are they copper pipes?
How would you heat water if you didn't have a boiler?
How does the water stay hot in the tank?
What's a jacket round the tank made of?
What's insulation?
What's a thermostat and how does it work?
What's water pressure?
If you made bigger taps, would the water flow into the bath faster?

I never forget to remind my children of the 'geyser' that stood over our bath, wheezing and coughing hot water into the bath, with its gas flames roaring. Whenever the racing is on and I hear that word 'Ascot' I think of our 'Ascot' geyser filling our bath. Comparing how we heat water in different places and different times is physics.

The bath itself demonstrates the 'displacement' theory every time you get into it. Isn't there a story of Archimedes working that out when he got into a bath?

And the bath is a great scientific playground. I am very proud of having invented the flannel game. You lay the flannel out flat on the surface of the water. You make your hand into a cone shape, with your fingers pointing upwards. You take that cone-shaped flannel with your hand still inside, down below the surface of the water, still pointing upwards. The flannel with your hand inside it is now like a wet tower poking up out of the water. Make sure that all the four edges of the flannel stay below the surface of the water. Note how the flannel appears to suck round your hand. (Vacuum effect!) Now take your other hand and make a ring shape with your fingers around the wrist of the cone-hand. As you do this you have to include in your ring-shape the edges of the flannel. Now gently withdraw your cone-hand through your ring-shape fingers. Now close up the flannel by drawing your ring-shape fingers together into a fist shape. You should have a kind of flannel-balloon now, held at the bottom by your fist.

Pull this flannel-balloon down below the surface of the water. Then, using your other hand, squeeze it. Hundreds of bubbles come floating to the surface, often with a ripply, farty sort of a sound.

Thank you.

This game is really an experiment that investigates the properties of gas and liquid (in this case, air and water). It also looks at 'leaking'. Our whole lives and bodies revolve around leaking. Every part of our body, inside and out, leaks. All machines, tubes and buildings leak. We spend our whole lives dealing with leaks. When the flannel fills up with air, that's because the pressure of the air causes it to 'leak' into the flannel through its holes. When I squeeze it underwater, that's to give it enough pressure to force it to 'leak' out. The flannel is not impermeable. It's holey.

Then we wash and shampoo.

How does that work?
How does rubbing soap on yourself help you get clean?
What does getting clean mean?
Is what we think of as dirt all the same stuff – or very different stuff?
Is shampoo the same as soap?
What are these things made of?

In fact, what we call 'dirt' is usually made up of three main ingredients: the greasy, fatty stuff, oily stuff got from cooking, eating, handling machines along with our own natural body oils; and organic particles of food, wood, paper, our own body (skin, blood, dried mucus) and the like; and particles of soil which itself is a mix of organic material (rotted-down plants) and tiny particles of rock. Analysing this tells the story of our lives – as any forensic detective knows.

Soap on its own can only deal with one part of this concoction – the greasy, fatty, oily stuff. When we mix soap with water, and we wash water over it all, the soap breaks down the grease, fats and oils and helps mix them into the water. The muck that's attached to grease then flows into the water and we wash the whole lot down the plug-hole. The scummy stuff that floats on the surface of the bath- and sink-water is usually the broken-down oil with some of the muck still attached. The rest of it has 'gone into the solution' of the rest of the bath-water.

Why does the scum float on the surface?
And where does it all go then?
Why does the plug-hole get jammed?
What does it get blocked with?
What clears it?
How does that work?

Then, there's your body. Clearly our bodies are different. Similar but different.

This is usually immensely interesting and puzzling to our children. They wonder if they will grow to look like us. In a broad sense, they will. They will have adult bodies. This is odd. For some it's a matter of anxiety or even fear.

Will I have bits like that?!

There's every chance that the grown-up carries a bit more 'sub-cutaneous' (under the skin) fat than the child.

How did that get there?
Why's it there?
Will I end up looking like that?

Conversations about hair, teeth and nails are often what are called 'displaced' conversations about other things. If you talk about them, you are often also talking about such matters as old age, death and puberty as well as the more obvious subjects like what I look like in public, my body-image, what I think of as beautiful and not beautiful.

The bathroom is a great place to do important affirming, reassuring our children that they're OK, they mustn't worry, and if someone at school said something horrible, they only did it because they themselves are full of worries about what they look like.

This is a conversation that has to be repeated many times.

Grown-ups have stopped growing in height but their hair, nails and skin keep growing.

Are hair and nails alive?
If they're not, why do we say they're 'growing'?
Are teeth white all the way through?
What are fillings made of?
Why do some people need fillings and other people don't?

The bathroom is ideal for weighing and measuring of course.
Do you do imperial or metric or both?
It's interesting to do this regularly and to mark the points on a graph, set against time. So on the vertical line on the graph you put the height measurement. Along the bottom you put the months. You measure the child once a month on the same number of the month. At key moments, you get to see that your child grows faster and slower. Then, when someone says, 'My, you've grown', the child can say, 'Yes, one centimetre in January and February but two centimetres in July and August.'

This reveals that nice thing about your own personal science: on the one hand we have our 'autobiography' – the stuff that we call 'memory' and 'what happened to me' – and on the other there's a load of other stuff that's invisible or not known until such time as we use modern systems of measurement. There's something both very personal and very scientific about knowing our own rate of growth. Quite often it's that bringing together of the personal and the scientific that sparks off in children a wish to find out more, learn more and know more. It's what makes science come alive and mean something in the real world.

The bathroom is also where swellings, bumps, cuts, rashes, bruises and scabs make themselves known. Each of them has its own natural history, full of biochemical activity: cells rushing towards the hole in our skin, special proteins that harden when they hit the air to make a scab, old dead cells sitting under the skin making wonderful colours.

What is blood?
What's it made of?
Do plants have blood?
How does blood get round your body?

And the skin is the 'marker' that humans have used in order to play a massive part in 'ranking' ourselves. To our great shame, it's been the means by which we have discriminated, segregated and persecuted. Whatever our or our children's skin colour(s), in the present day skin colour is often a question from children. They hear about the history of, say, Nelson Mandela; they hear about, say, 'racism in football'; there is a secret underground conversation about race that goes on in schools in nods, glances, slang and rhymes. The bathroom may well be where questions like this surface. After all, there's often a lot of skin around in bathrooms.

THE BATHROOM

So, why does skin come in different colours?
Why are different parts of a person's skin slightly different shades?
What makes it into different shades?
Why does the sun make skin darker?
What are freckles?

Why did this 'chemistry' of the skin come to mean so much?
Why couldn't it be that it wouldn't matter any more than the difference between the colour of our eyes?

And, talking of eyes, why are they different colours?
What is an eye made of?
Is it true that some people eat sheep's eyes?
Have you ever eaten a sheep's eye?
Have you ever eaten a sheep's testicle?
Go on, say! Have you?
Dad, tell the truth: have you?

Medication is another area that raises questions. I have no thyroid gland. This means that I have to take pills to replace what the thyroid gland produces. Every morning I go to the bathroom cabinet, take down the boxes of pills, pull out a silver sheet with pimples on it, and pop out the pills, put them in my mouth and flush them down with a few mouthfuls of water.

Why do you take them?
What's a thyroid gland?
Why haven't you got one?
Have I got a thyroid gland?
Will I get what you got?
How did you find out that you didn't have a thyroid gland?

And I tell them the story of how bit by bit over ten years I got slower and slower and colder and colder, and my fingers and toes swelled up, my voice went gruff and my hair went frizzy . . . and the doctors told me that it was my kidneys. Until this clever consultant at the hospital figured out that I had eaten my own thyroid gland. My antibodies had attacked it and consumed it. And I tell them that he was a kind of detective, piecing together what he could see that was odd about me, how my speech was slurred and even my lips and eyelids were swollen.

Then there's the scene where he gets the students in and tells them to diagnose what's wrong with me. He goes out of the room.

'Tell us,' says one.

I don't.

The consultant comes back into the room.

'Well?' he says.

'Kidneys,' they say.

He explodes.

'Just because I'm a kidney specialist and the patient has been referred to me doesn't mean that it's kidneys. You haven't even felt his skin, or taken his pulse, or tested his reflexes! Look at this,' he said.

He picked up small rubber hammer and whacked my knee.

'See that! Nothing! No response at all! Ask yourselves, why? What illness results in a lack of reflex, swollen eyelids and lips, cold skin and a slow heart-rate? Mmm?'

I love this story, and I love sharing it with people – especially children – mostly because it's about me (!). I like the fact that in the story I'm reduced to a set of symptoms and an illness. I'm like a slab of meat. But I also like the way it shows a detective or a doctor or a scientist at work, observing, comparing, contrasting, listening and coming up with possible reasons and solutions. It's at the heart of much that's important about learning: finding out things, observing, investigating, using what you know (interpreting), making informed guesses (a form of inventing), talking (co-operating) and so on. He could have been wrong. He wasn't. He was 100 per cent right. And that's why I'm not dead. Though part of why I'm not dead is that people like him did a lot of experimenting and figuring in the early 1900s and worked out how you could treat people like me. And that's why every morning I pop pills out of a silver strip.

Medication is a great starting point for talk and finding out things.

If you have different kinds of mirrors in your bathroom – the ordinary one on the cabinet, say, and a hand-held magnifying mirror, there's the question of how a mirror can magnify things. Ultimately, the answer to that question goes back to the lens in our own eyes, which we have the power to make thicker or thinner. Optics – another branch of physics!

THE SITTING ROOM

We are at another one of those moments in history when the positions and activities that happen in the rooms of our houses are changing.

When I was a boy, for the first ten years of my life we had no TV. For the second ten we had a TV that was the focal point of one room in the house – the 'front' room, as my parents called it – and that TV was controlled by my father. In the time that I've had children, I've gone from being a one-TV house, to a two-TV house to a three-TV house with at least one of the teenage children having a TV in their room.

Now the change is that for much of the time my children aren't watching TV as it is transmitted, they are watching 'box-sets' of series they like, or the same thing taken from the iPlayer and the like. And they're supplementing that with various kinds of entertainment for themselves on the internet made up of YouTube clips, social networking, games, or sites that have put up material they want to see.

This means that for much of the time, they are not on a lead attached to the TV set, in the way that I was when I was a child – or indeed I still am, if I feel like watching something. In fact, I still say Stone Age things like, 'I would really like to watch a drama or a film, I wonder what's on?'

'You wonder what's on?!' my children shriek. 'You don't have to wait for them to tell you what to watch. You can go and find something for yourself.'

'Where?' I say.

They groan.

When TVs and radios were focal points for households, they were also focal points for debate, argument and discussion. I remember that my parents didn't seem to think of the TV and radio as having very much authority at all. Much of the time they watched the news, current affairs, or discussion programmes, and kept up a running commentary of disagreement. I remember once coming into a room, and my father was sitting there, on his own, shouting at the radio.

In a way, I quite like that. Though it gives radio and TV status, it doesn't give it reverence. My parents seemed to be saying, these are people like you and me. They have their skills and opinions, so do we. They happen to be on air, but we have our lives and experience and words, and this counts, this matters.

I guess I've taken that on board. I confess I do the same, though of course there's an irony in that I am often on the radio and sometimes on TV myself. Mind you, I am quite happy knowing that there are people out there who are shouting at me as my voice is going out.

One of my present delights comes in the morning. My daughter gets up very early and usually I'm the next up. While she gets her breakfast and makes her packed lunch, the radio is on. Our conversation drifts in and out of things to do with her news, my news, good vs bad food, homework, hairstyles, the life of our cats, what we are each going to do today and what's on the radio. Quite often all this is about ideas. What I like is that this conversation makes ideas seem debatable and fluid. No matter what is being said on the radio, or by me, she has a big say in debating them and a big say in controlling the flow. I like the way we sometimes end up drifting into family memories and talk about films and TV programmes. My view is that when we make memories overlap with the fiction we read and watch, this is where the real 'work' goes on to figure out the meaning of things, and why they matter to us. All we need is the space and time to do it.

Front rooms and sitting rooms are also good places for games. I've noticed that my own children are much keener on these when we're on holiday, particularly on wet English ones. I'm a fan of wordy games – Scrabble, Boggle and Lexicon – but I can't always wing it with everyone else. I sometimes try the 'but it's very educational' line, but my youngest fobs me off with, 'Play it with yourself, then.'

Much more popular with our youngest are charades and Who Am I?

Picture the scene: adults, including grandparents, flopped out on sofas and armchairs, one or two dozing gently, children bouncing around . . .

'I'm bored.'

'I'm sooooooooo bored.'

'Let's play charades.'

'Let's play Who Am I?'

'Pleeeeeze.'

What do you do?

Do you demand dozing rights?

Do you say, 'Later'? Or, 'Tomorrow'?

Or do you stir your mind with a big spoon and agree to play?

The old TV *Charades* show gave us a good structure of gestures that I don't remember from my childhood. If by chance you don't know it, it's well worth learning it. This complicated sign language lets you cover titles from movies, books, TV shows, songs or anything else you want. And you get into talking about words and syllables and rhymes. There are moments of surrealism when you think up rhymes for syllables and these will probably have absolutely nothing to do with the original title. So while you're trying to get your audience to think of the 'gone' from *Gone with the Wind* you're miming 'con'.

Who Am I? is good to play with bits of paper stuck on your face, but you can play a version of it the other way round. In Who Am I? with paper, the person with it stuck on their face doesn't know who that person is, so they have to ask the others questions to find out who they are. The other version, you simply have a moment before the game gets going where one person decides who they are. Then everyone else does the quizzing until they get the answer. Both ways work and it's vital to keep the youngest on board with help and advice.

Perhaps I don't need to say, but these games are of course very verbal, they invite discussion and argument. There are disputes that sometimes need verifying with consultations with Wikipedia. The subjects range (as they used to say on serious radio programmes in the 1950s) over centuries and the whole earth. They can range from the serious to the crazy and for young ones, fill in all sorts of info to do with how lives are lived, who becomes famous, who doesn't and why.

In my life, the sitting room is where the deadly serious matter of debate about sport takes place. This is one of the times TV-watching reverts to the old pattern of clustering round the one set. What's quite funny about sport is that the event itself is usually mostly non-verbal. The effect on those watching it, though, is to smother it in talk. We are all experts, know-alls and commentators. We argue with players, crowds and commentators. We become soothsayers and fortune-tellers. We arm ourselves with stats and facts and biographies. It is a talk-dense, knowledge-dense area of our lives. And full of passion.

I've become very interested in how children move from being interested in a sport in a rather non-verbal and physical way – no harm in that, of course – to this verbal, fact-obsessive way. It can seem as if there were some god telling them to mug up on thousands of bits of knowledge: sport homework. And they stay in doing hours of what would in other circumstances be 'boring' and 'too long'. They will do complicated calculations about points won, points dropped and what-ifs. They see the stats come up on screen and compare these with previous games and matches. They become prosecution, defence, judge and jury on moments, players and teams. And in different places, their talk changes. If you eavesdrop, you can hear them engaging in furious debate with their peers in the playground. It's then that you realize that the sport homework is in part a way of getting yourself briefed for the chat tomorrow with your mates.

Equivalent sudden build-ups of knowledge go on with music, clothes, gigs, shows, films, actors and the rest.

Of course much of it goes on and has always gone on without parents getting involved. Sometimes, it's actually a matter of 'parents keep out' – though that's not usually the case with sport.

One way some of this gets a bit more depth, however, is precisely through the kinds of comparisons that we as older people can give. It's not that we bring more wisdom, just the fact that what seems entirely new and of the moment also has a history. What's funny or odd for our children is that the feelings they're having are very similar to the feelings we had about people who to them look or sound old or crap.

And this is where 'connection' happens. I mean, when we remind ourselves of our own lyrical, passionate moments of yearning and fantasy that were wrapped up with singers, actors, music, film and the rest, it gives us a window on why it's mattering so much to our children.

That's valuable in itself.

THE LOO

From children's first words (or earlier), wee and poo and the places they come out of are fascinating. Some of this is about the taboos and bans we put round talking about it. Some of it is, I think, down to the fact that this is stuff we make several times a day. In its own way, it's an achievement.

How we talk about it with children, how we create the spaces and places where it goes on is 'cultural'. We only have to travel to see that. It's not all that long ago when the public loos in France were 'squatters': two foot-shaped ledges to put your feet on and a hole below. In homes in Germany, plenty of the toilet bowls are, in effect, inspection zones. You poo on to a platform so that you can inspect what's going on in your guts. All this makes for great conversations about what are or are not the best arrangements. It's loo technology.

Same goes for the deep mysteries for the cistern. Some of my finest moments have been in solving such things as the perpetual dribble (I don't mean me!), the non-flush, the perpetual overflow and the flood. Next time one of these happens – if not before – just go with one of your children, lift the lid of the cistern and admire home technology at its best. It's usually a beautiful system of a lever, tap, float and pump. When the lever is down, it opens the tap and water flows into the tank. When the lever is up, it blocks the opening and no water flows into the tank. When you flush, a 'plug' rises and then falls, pumping the water into the loo itself.

These days, the whole thing is usually made of white and orange plastic but just sometimes you'll come across old ones where the float or 'ballcock' (always worth a laugh) is made of copper and there is plenty of furred-up brass in the machinery. You'll find online or in books some delightful stories about someone called Thomas Crapper who played a crucial role in the invention of all this.

Your children will probably know some rude rhymes about farting, weeing, burping and the rest. I know many. When I was a child, they were banned everywhere except in my own home, where my father seemed to know hundreds and was always happy to share them. I don't think I'm exaggerating when I say that part of my love of poetry comes from collecting his and my friends' rhymes.

I offer you (learned in the 1950s):
(to the tune of 'The Yellow Rose of Texas')

There is a winding passage
that goes up to my heart.
And what comes down this passage
is commonly called a fart.
The fart is very useful:
it sets the mind at ease.
It warms the bed on wintry nights
and disinfects the fleas.

Along with this are the various scenes we see each of us playing out in relation to our digestive system at work. Adults – often without knowing it – do endless commentaries and re-runs on what this or that food or drink will or won't do to our systems. Whenever the regularity of our routine is disrupted – too often, not often enough, too loose, too whiffy – the commentaries start up. Once children twig just how repetitive and boring we are, they love to comment back about this.

My mum, sad to say, was a loo-smoker. She always smoked a cigarette in the loo and then tried, but failed, to flush it down afterwards. So the ciggy paper and bits of tobacco were often floating on the top of the water. If you mentioned this to her, she just denied it. 'No, not me,' she'd say.

Meanwhile, my dad would tell us that he couldn't eat stewed fruit: 'Gives me the squitters,' he'd say. He couldn't drink cheap red wine: 'Gives me the squitters.' He made a big deal out of making sure that we all washed up 'properly', otherwise – 'We'd get the squitters.' It seemed as if 'the squitters' was a near-death experience. Or at the very least, something lethal.

In my parents' case, it was where their own home language surfaced, so they 'grepsed' (burped), 'fotzed' (farted), a worthless person was a 'pischer' (pisser), an old man was an 'alte cacker' (literally, an old shitter), nonsense was 'dreck' or 'bupkes' (both words for poo) and so on. Somehow, this enriched the world of the loo. Most people have a variety of slangs to cover it all and one of the delights of reading English literature pre-1700 is to find that Shakespeare, Chaucer and the rest were much freer with all this than writers from about 1700 up until the 1960s, happy to let 'flee a fert as loud as a thunder-dent'.

As this topic is surrounded with 'don't say that' and 'not in front of Granny' and the rest, it's interesting – and important, I'd say – to get into why we should have become so edgy and touchy about it. We not only flush away our wees and poos. We try to flush away talking about it too.

Why's that?

And talking of flushing, what is bleach? Where does it come from? And how does it work?

And talking of bleach, why do loos stain with something other than the poos and wees? What is that stain? What's in the water that stains a loo? What's it made of? And if it's in the water, does it go into our bodies when we drink it?

And talking of bodies, how does digestion work anyway?

It really does seem odd that our whole lives revolve round a tube that runs from the top to about halfway down our bodies. At each stage along the tube, another kind of job is done: wetting, cutting, mashing and breaking down chemically at the top; more mashing and squirting with acid (among other things) in the bag at the bottom of the first bit of the tube; more squirting, squeezing and drenching with yet more chemicals for many, many centimetres of tubing; cunningly absorbing all the stuff we need through the walls of the tube; making a sausage in the last bit of the tube and squeezing it out.

And if that seems amazing, then consider the wolf, the pelican and the cow. If you go to a wolf sanctuary you can see wolves eating meat. They swallow chunks of meat on the bone and their digestive systems can deal with that. Pelicans can put a whole pigeon in the pouches under the beaks and then swallow the whole pigeon. And cows can sit in a field making chewing movements with their mouths while they pass food from one stomach to another to another to another to get what they need from grass.

Comparing our bodies to animals, talking about the taboos, having fun with each other about how we keep repeating ourselves when we talk about digestion are all great ways to encourage children to be curious about how their bodies work.

CHILDREN'S ROOMS

I can remember the exact shape of the flowers moulded into the cast-iron fireplace that was in my bedroom when I was a child. And when I say 'remember', it's not only in my mind as a picture, but it's also a fingertips memory, because I used to run my fingers along the stems of the flowers.

Most adults carry memories like these from twenty, thirty – in my case from fifty – years ago. This should tell us that there is something very deep and lasting about what our childhood rooms mean to us. In what may well turn out to be quite a short time in a person's whole lifetime – let's say zero to eighteen – the words, thoughts and actions that go on in that small space are among the most powerful we will ever know.

Before all else, they should be places where a child feels safe and loved – whether we adults are there or not. So, whatever I might say about it being a place where curiosity can be encouraged, this curiosity rests on those feelings of safety and love.

I found out what beds are made of because I kicked up a fuss about how my bed wasn't as comfortable as my brother's. My bed, I claimed, had lumps in it. It was, I said, 'a potato bed'. My brother's, I said, was low and soft and – if I had known the word then – kind of 'classy'. Mine, I found out, was an old squeaky metal-frame bed. My brother's was a 'divan'. 'Why can't I have a divan?' I asked.

My parents explained how beds have springs. There are springs on the bed bit of the bed. And springs in the mattress. We went to a bed shop that had pictures of cross-sections of beds. I love cross-sections. They're like secret views into the worlds behind the world we live in. Posh beds, they said, have horse-hair in them. 'Is that real horse-hair?' I asked. 'Yes,' said the man. It seemed so strange that you would want to sleep on bits of horse. 'There's even horse-hair in some old walls,' my dad said. 'And in violin bows,' said the man.

Horse-hair was important stuff.

And I got a new bed.

The bed was where my mother read to me. She used to sit next to me reading *Squirrel Nutkin*, *The Little Red Engine*, *Miskito Boy*, *Raff the Jungle Bird*, *The Amazing Pranks of Til Eulenspiegel*, *Raggylugs* by Ernest Thompson Seton – whose name sounded as interesting as his books. I still have these books, the same ones that my mother read to me.

These moments and these books are the building blocks that took me into reading and studying. They laid the basis for almost everything I got out of school and enabled me to do what I have wanted to do in life.

That easy. Reading to me every night . . . and leaving space and time to talk about what she read to me. And it couldn't have been all that easy for her. From the time I was three, she was a teacher. She had children's work to mark and lessons to prepare.

It was also a time when any worries came to the surface. I'm an '11-plus' child and in 1956–7 when we were doing tests and homework leading up to the exam day, I got more and more worried. I was desperately worried that I was going to let them down. I was worried that I wasn't as clever as my older brother. I was worried that if I went to secondary modern school, I would be beaten up.

So I couldn't sleep.

And I would call out to my mum to come and sit with me. She would come with hot milk with dark brown sugar in it, so that it tasted a bit treacly. And she told me over and over again not to worry. Then, when it got near to the exam, she let me into a secret. She said that there was this thing called 'Headteacher's recommendation'. She said that even if a person failed the exam, if that person had the headteacher's recommendation, that person would 'pass'. 'I asked Mr Scotney [our head teacher],' she said, 'if you had his "recommendation", and he said yes.'

I wasn't absolutely sure that I believed her, but it helped that she said it. And the hot milk with the dark brown sugar helped too.

These kinds of conversations – hundreds, maybe thousands of them – that take place in those moments between the day and sleep, are key moments in our lives. It's as if they happen when we are at our most raw, when the armour that keeps us clammed up and removed from the world is off and we can ask the questions that really matter to us, and get answers that stay with us for the rest of our lives.

When I'm in schools, I often ask children if they've got TVs in their rooms. In many schools, most children tell me that they have. They say that they go to their rooms at about seven o'clock, put the TV on and doze off with it still on at any time from ten till twelve.

Is this OK? Do we really want to hand over our children to the TV and miss these moments I'm calling 'raw'?

Just to be clear, I am not against TV. I know that plenty of people who write this kind of book advocate anything from rationing it to banning it. My own view is that TV is something we talk about rather than ban. We get into conversations with our children about the programmes they like and don't like. We offer views other than the ones they have in their heads or with their friends. We give them 'comparison and contrast' – key in the business of building up curiosity and thought.

Bedrooms are also places full of choices: What's the decor? What goes on the walls? Where should things go? Who tidies up? Who cleans? What kinds of curtains or blinds? How should things be stored? What kind of shelves? Who throws things out?

I think we should make as much of this as we can a conversation. These are vital moments when children can explore and find out about stuff that matters to them. This is where they create their taste.

I can remember going with my parents to the paint and wallpaper shop to choose what was going to go on my bedroom wall. In the rolls, I spotted a wallpaper that was made up of small, repeated scenes from Paris: a café, a bus, the Eiffel Tower (of course). The background was a light mauve and the scenes seemed to have quite a lot of yellow in them. I loved the way it would bring what I thought of as busy city life into my room. My parents bought it and I would lie in bed, daydreaming, looking into the scenes trying to make them come alive. It also covered up the hole in the wall that I had made with a metal ruler, trying to drill through to my brother who had moved out of what had been 'our' room, into what was now 'his' room.

Bedrooms are also mostly where illness happens. Again, these are profound moments in our lives. They are full of mystery, pain and worry. And full of words: temperature, antibiotics, virus, bacteria, dose and the names of the medications: Nurofen, paracetamol and the rest.

As it happens, we don't necessarily have to go to the internet to find out more, though the sites on children's illnesses are now really good. Inside the medication boxes are leaflets that people have spent hours putting into language that we are supposed to find helpful and easy to understand.

Children ask questions about their illnesses – and about ours too, of course. If we are not medics, this can often lead us to shortcut the questions with words or phrases that indicate that we don't really want the children to know about the illness because we think it might make them more worried.

I suggest that of course we need to tell children that we don't know everything and we don't, say, really know the difference between bacteria and viruses, or that we don't really know how 'Nurofen brings your temperature down'. But we can also say, 'Let's see if we can find out . . .'

What is coughing?
What's it for?
Why does sniffing make you cough?

Yes indeed, the mysteries of mucus. There is no reason why a child would know or could know that the tube inside our noses links to the tube at the back of our throats and when we sniff, we shunt mucus up the nose tube and round into the back of our throats.

Our bodies want to keep the airway to our lungs free of mucus – otherwise we won't be able to breathe – so we cough to blow away the mucus. If we sniff, there's more mucus flowing around the top of our windpipe. Even when we blow our noses – as we think 'down' our noses – we also blow some of it back up into the tubes ('sinuses') above our noses so that some of that will dribble down the back of our throats.

The best way to cough less when it's mucus from up inside our nose that's flowing, is to let the mucus dribble out of our noses.

I am only delivering this sermon because it's a lovely example of something as everyday as sniffing and coughing, but which is, for many people, mysterious or unknown.

And why or how do we make mucus anyway?

How does it turn into bogies?

What are bogies for?

And, Dad, you've got hairs growing out of your nose . . .

Why does it happen that sometimes after a long run of coughing, we're sick?

What is sick?

Why are we sick?

Why does sick smell?

Why is it that when you smell sick, it makes you feel sick?

Some of this links to another mystery in our bodies: the 'autonomic nervous system'.

One way or another we get to know about the nerves that we can feel do things for us: we feel whether things are hot or cold, sharp or blunt, rough or smooth. We can taste whether things are sweet or sour, hot or cold, rough or smooth, dry or wet. And we can sense the way some parts of our body are better than others at feeling things.

Then we can give instructions to parts of our body to do things: pick up, let go, kick, blink, smile, frown, sit, stand up. These are all instructions to muscles to do things. Muscles 'contract' and we do it.

Some of these are emergency reactions, ducking, putting our hands up in front of our faces, blinking.

But all through our lives there is a nervous system running the hundreds of bodily processes we need in order to live: heart pumping, the squeezing and pulling of our guts, taking sound from our ear into our brain, light and colour into our brains from our eyes and so on.

This autonomic (self-managed) nervous system is extraordinary. It's all connected to the brain. We can affect it by the way we think and by, say, what we eat or what we do (like running makes our heart beat faster) and hormones (chemicals that come from glands) can affect this autonomic system too.

It's all vital to our staying alive and being able to do what we do.

Now just a glimpse or mention of this with children can conjure up for them images of secret tunnels, tubes and wires. How can there be what is like a secret world of message giving and taking, actions being taken on account of messages received, going on inside us, without our knowing? It's both magical and scientific at the same time.

Whenever I hear ministers talking about all the things they say that children should know by the time they're eleven – or some such – it nearly always seems to involve stuff 'out there': Shakespeare, the area of a circle or who is the prime minister of Portugal and the like. They very rarely seem to talk about the basic parts of our bodies: what they are and how they work.

And there we are, lying in bed, our ears on the pillow and we can feel our pulse in our ear. But what tells the heart to beat to make that pulse? And talking of pulses, why can't you feel the pulse in the veins in your arms or legs?

OUTDOORS

If there is a 'great outdoors', perhaps there ought to be a 'little outdoors'. That's not to diminish walking out of the door and into the ordinary outdoors of our modern lives. Just the opposite. Our 'little outdoors' is a highly diverse environment that we humans have created and yet it's very easy to use it without noticing it. There's a reason for that: we created much of it in order for it to be easier to use than the wilderness that was there before. And some of it – like some features of the climate, say – is more of a by-product of what we've done. A lot of the work that humans have done to make the world around us, then, is invisible. We live in and among the results and consequences of our actions. The challenge is to investigate and discover what the 'little outdoors' around us can do for us, what we can do for the 'little outdoors' and how it all came to be the way it is.

GARDEN OR WINDOW-SILL

I was brought up in a flat over a shop but we had a back yard that we shared with the shop-owners. It was a triangle of beat-up concrete with a cherry tree in one corner and an elder tree in the other. Along one side there was a coal bunker, big enough to climb in – good for flying to the moon – and in the bit next to a downstairs scullery was a concrete drainage ditch – good for hide-and-seek, crouching in the waste water from the sinks.

Beyond the yard was an alleyway where the delivery vans could get access both to the shops in our road – some twenty or so shops – and a builders' yard where they 'prepped' the stuff they were putting into buildings.

This alleyway was covered in pebbles and on all sides the different kinds of refuse chucked out by the shops – wine bottles, broken-up antique chairs, chemists' jars, butcher's bones – spilled out into their yards and bins.

When people ask me about my education, I think of course about my schools and universities but part of me always wants to say, 'And the back yard, window-sills and the alleyway where I lived.'

One day, we were out and my parents decided to bring back some caterpillars and put them – and the plants they were on – in an aquarium on the window-sill. The plants were nettles.

Every day or so, we went out and got more nettles for the

caterpillars to feed on. Eventually, the caterpillars made themselves into chrysalids and we waited for what seemed like several years. I'm not sure if my parents knew what species of butterfly was growing and waiting inside those little waxy pods, but eventually the chrysalids' bottoms started to wiggle and bit by bit butterflies climbed out of their shells – while we watched.

It was a delicate, seemingly painful procedure, full of what looked like caution and hesitation. We spotted some red fluid next to where they hatched. But, thrillingly for us, sitting in our aquarium were several tortoiseshell butterflies which flew away from the window-sill to eat, lay eggs and start the whole cycle over again.

It was a captivating thing to do. Whenever people talk of life-cycles and metamorphoses the images of this time come to me. How can it be that something as slow and plump as a caterpillar can turn into something as dry and flittery and multi-coloured as a butterfly? It doesn't seem possible.

My parents triggered off a feeling of wonder. Their own enthusiasm was infectious. I was curious and fascinated.

Another thing: tortoiseshell butterflies are very attractive and it's quite possible to be drawn to them and become interested in their wings and colours. In my mind, in addition to that beauty, for me, thanks to my parents and that old aquarium, there is a solid, basic, down-to-earth side to that beauty: knowing that it's all based on caterpillars eating nettles.

Nettles! Those plants you skirt round because their hairs drop something that stings you.

What is that stinging stuff anyway?
Is it true that the hairs on the stems don't sting but the hairs on the ends of the 'teeth' on the leaves do?
Why would that be?
Does rubbing a dock leaf into the sting help?

And come to think of it, we never, ever called them nettles. They were always 'stingers'. That's their name. Not nettles!

It's also an interesting idea that a given species depends on one specific plant. Children won't know that unless they get a chance to see something like this. That old elderberry tree in the yard used to be thick with black-fly. And when I say 'thick', I mean thousands and thousands of soft, furry flies all over the stems and leaves. At the time, we didn't do much more than wonder at them, or sometimes shake, poke or brush them off with sticks. Yet it's these connections and links we know as adults to be the key to understanding how the world of living creatures works: everything is in an ecosystem. We are all co-dependent. The moment one part of the dependency changes or is changed then another part is changed too.

I loved the look of the elderberries on this lone tree in the corner of the yard and was convinced that they could be used to make something. My mother sometimes experimented with making jams and pickles but she always said that there was nothing we could do with the elderberries.

Was she right?

I know we could have made elderflower wine, but is there really nothing you can do with those luscious-looking berries?

The lone cherry tree in the other corner produced thousands of tiny bitter cherries and I pleaded with her to make something with these. She said she would stew them and we could see if we liked them. So we picked a pile and she stewed them up with a heap of sugar. She was right, though. Even with sugar in the cherries and some added on afterwards, they were unbearably bitter. We didn't try again.

So what was the difference between our cherry and the cherries we bought at the greengrocer? I remember my mother trying to explain plant-breeding. I didn't understand. Looking back on it, I suspect that she didn't either. I'm still fascinated by the production of strains of fruit trees, though.

My father suddenly caught the urge to garden. As he often said on a Sunday morning, 'C'mon, Mick, let's go up the dump.'

The dump was at the end of the alleyway, where the builders dumped any of the stuff they had taken out of the houses they were working on, or any of the waste from the pieces they were making in their workshops. These workshops sat round a little square yard, and there was a plumber, a carpenter, a glazier and the like, each one making what he would install in the house.

The dump was full of treasures and my father started to raid it for old sinks, which he brought back down the alley to put in the yard and plant with flowers. For me, it was the dump that was endlessly fascinating, not the flowers. Looking back on this dump from now, I wonder how it is that I'm not scarred, missing a limb or dead. It was full of broken glass, lead-piping, broken asbestos, 'red lead', lead-based paint, jagged edges of bathroom enamel-ware, saw-blades, broken drills and so on. I am often puzzled at the pleasure and fascination I got from rifling through this stuff, finding treasures of copper and brass, but I am appalled now by the danger I was in. I wonder how it is that we can give our children experiences of rifling through junk, looking for treasures, wondering where this or that comes from, who made it and what for without it being such a massive risk.

I haven't solved that one.

I also know that I loved to watch the plumbers, carpenters and glaziers at work. They would let me stand in the doorways of their workshops and see them bending pipes, making window-frames and cutting glass. Looking back on it, that was a privilege. I was watching artisans using years of training and experience making the kinds of things that went into houses in the 1950s: the very things that my father lamented he didn't know how to make, while he was roping me into helping him with his DIY.

Again, I wonder how we can give our children the experience of watching artisans making and mending, without it being a risk. If we are people who take on builders, we sometimes get to see it in our own homes. I once wanted to repair a stretch of a Victorian cornice and a craftsman came to the house. He cut a piece of the cornice and showed us all how the cornice is made up of repeated stretches no longer than a foot each. He said he would take this piece away to make a mould, and he would make some twenty or so new pieces from the mould, bring them back and put them into the broken part of the cornice. He told us that in London alone there are thousands and thousands of different patterns. Sure enough, he came back with a pile of the sections of the cornice, and fixed them into place with plaster, while the whole family – along with other builders who were in the house – watched him at work. For a moment he had star-status.

He told us that he was crazy about Dickens. He loved Dickens more than anything else. He had read all his novels, and had found out about all the places he had lived. He said he always watched the films and TV adaptations of the novels and liked spotting the differences between the books and the films.

I like these links between people, buildings, artisan skills and writing and, in this case, with the stuff we throw out. I picked that up from my parents, and perhaps some of my children have picked that up too. It's part of making the world we find ourselves in, peopled with the makers and doers who change it. It means we don't take it all for granted.

*

Nearly all my life I've had cats. Never a dog. That back yard was where we trained the first kittens I ever saw. My mother showed us how to get them to wee on a tray full of ash from the stove from our front room. It seemed so strange that you could tell these little unruly roly-poly fur-balls where to pee. Why would they know next time or the next time or the next time that that was what you do and that was where you did it?

'Let them scratch it,' she said. 'Just make sure they don't wander off.'

The mother cat was called Simpkin, who is the cat in *The Tailor of Gloucester*, one of my favourite stories, a story that I would ask my mother to read again and again. One problem: Simpkin is a male cat. I can remember how we named some of her kittens: Sherpa because he liked to climb our blanket mountains when we put our knees up under the covers; Share because we spotted a division sign in her fur. My parents called one of them Archy, because they said that Archy appears in a very funny set of stories called *Archy and Mehitabel*. My mother used to like saying in a wistful, nostalgic sort of a way, 'Toujours gai, Archy, toujours gai.'

'What does that mean?' we asked.

'She's telling Mehitabel that she'll always be happy,' she said.

Many years later I found out that it's Mehitabel who is the cat, not Archy. Mehitabel is the one who is 'toujours gai'. Archy is a cockroach who types poems on a writer's typewriter by jumping up and landing on one key at a time.

One day, when Simpkin was sitting on my bed, I noticed that she had a soft bump on her back. We took her to the vets and they told us that it was cancer and she was 'put down'. That was the first time I knew about animals being put down.

This was a first encounter with death and one that links to and through all the deaths I've known. How we as parents handle death with our children will affect them for the rest of their lives. I once interviewed a boy on the radio for a programme I was doing called *On Saying Goodbye* and the boy said that when his cat died, that was when he came to realize that death means 'not being there'. My parents were quite matter-of-fact about the death of Simpkin, though I suspect something much more troubling was going on under the surface.

My mother had lost a child before I was born. She never mentioned this. Never. I only ever found out about it because once, when we were going through old photos, I had spotted a picture of my mother with a baby on her knee and had asked my father who it was. He then, for the first time, told us of this boy, Alan, who had died. As I say, my mother never mentioned him, though my father did once or twice. Many years later, an old family friend told me that my mother and father had once had a row when their cat died. My mother had said angrily to him, 'You care more about the cat dying than you did when the baby died.'

Because I was part of the moment when Simpkin died – it was me who had spotted the soft lump – and because my parents handled the matter rationally, answering any questions I asked them; and also because, I guess, we had kittens to replace Simpkin, I got some of my first insights into death without fear.

We gave away the others and Archy stayed.

Since then, I've had a stream of cats who've lived alongside children and they've taken part in their naming and dying, their accidents and times at the vet. One of them was named after the great Arsenal striker, Alan 'Smudger' Smith. I was lucky to meet him once. We were standing together on the back line of a photo-call at the wedding of the director of Community Sports at Arsenal Football Club.

'My children named our cat after you,' I muttered, just as we were supposed to be saying, 'Cheese,' for the cameraman.

'Is he nippy?' he said.

'Not really,' I said, 'and it's a "she", actually. She's grey and has a white Hitler moustache.'

'I once heard that someone had named a goldfish after me,' he said in his slightly lugubrious Midlands accent, 'but never a cat.'

This story has gone into family folklore, and whenever we hear Alan Smith on TV, one or other of us will say at some point or another, trying to do the Midlands accent, 'Is he nippy?'

At the moment, our cats are two ginger brothers who eat together, go out together, hunt together and sleep together. We've never seen two cats so intimate. They loll over each other, taking it in turns to lick each other's faces. Of course the great advances in social attitudes to same-sex relationships enable us to take all this in our stride.

I say to the children, 'I think . . . I think – don't hold me to this – that ginger cats are always male.' This stirs up a bit of a Wikipedia flurry.

'Nope, you're wrong, Dad. It's about 75 per cent to 25 per cent.'

'Yep, that's what I said.'

'No you didn't.'

'So why is it 75 per cent to 25 per cent?'

'Yeah, why is that, Dad?'

Then in a flash we're into X and Y chromosomes and recessive and dominant genes and we play at lining up Xs and Ys . . .

We make close observations of the cats as they jostle for power to see which one is top dog. If a cat can be a top dog. We found out that cats use height to dominate each other.

Whichever cat can find a position higher than the other is the top one. Sure enough, the one who is nearly always higher than the other is the one who jostles the other out of the way if there's only one bowl of food. There's the pattern of animal behaviour played out in front of us.

All we need to do is talk about it, read about it, or watch TV programmes about it, and apply it back to our own animals. The science is played out in front of us.

The underdog cat is also the twitchier of the two, we've noticed. But that's ever since he lost half his neck to a bite and the vet's knife. He seems to have remembered it, and doesn't let us get near him any more. We have conversations about how he could remember such a thing.

Do cats remember?

The garden is full of birds. There are various bird-tables and bird-boxes left over by the previous owners. We stand at the window and watch the birds hopping about in and out of the holes. A starling has a bath in an old bowl that got left out there. It dives in and sploshes about in short bursts. Into the bowl, splosh, pokes its head out to have a look, back down, in, splosh, up, look, back down, in, splosh . . . and so on.

Why would it do that?

Sometimes the holes in one of the bird-boxes are like an underground station, with blue tits bobbing in and out. We wonder if they've got a nest in there. And it's good news that it's too high and inaccessible for those ginger brothers to get them.

And there's a robin. One step into the garden, front or back and he's there, bobbing about within arm's reach.

What does he want? I ask the children.

Is he trying to tell us something?

Does he want company and thinks that we're cool people to hang out with?

Is he hoping that I'll write a children's book about him?

Or does he think that we'll dish up some spag bol for him or something?

Or will we turn over the ground and bring to the surface grubs for him to eat?

We talk about how unafraid he is.

And the foxes.

At night we hear them wailing. Once, we went to the window and saw two or three of them chasing each other's tails in the middle of the street. They were like young men on the way home from a club, who stop to give each other a bit of a kicking. We did that thing that comedians have been doing for years: giving the foxes different voices and names, as they ran about under the streetlamps. The big media story of the fox that got into the back of a house and bit a baby, feeds into what we see foxes doing. One time, we watched while our cat and a fox had a face-off on the top of the garden wall. We were ready to dive in and protect Tiggs. We didn't need to. Tiggs did some hissing and teeth-flashing and foxy turned tail. We often talk about what a fox would or wouldn't, could or couldn't do. I think of my own childhood when foxes were rare, shy creatures who were only familiar through stories, songs and poems.

'Is a fox a kind of dog?' says one of my children.

'No,' I say.

We look it up.

'It is,' they say. 'Wrong again, Dad.'

I'm not quite sure why proving me wrong is quite so pleasing to them, but I'm glad that it is.

THE PARK

Parks are great places to become curious. What's more, most of them belong to us. They are part of what we are entitled to.

In fact, that's an interesting conversation to have.

Who does this park belong to?

Us.

How can it belong to us?

It's public.

Who's the public?

All of us. We're all the public.

Who runs it?

They're people who've been put in charge of our park by the people we vote for.

You voted for this park?

Kind of.

I think there should be more swings.

Well, you could tell them. Or you could join the Friends of the Park.

There is a science devoted to playground apparatus. Mostly, it's developed as an out-of-sight technology, until a moment occurs when a council or school says that the old play-park has to change. It's then that you discover firms that have been experimenting with this stuff for years, trying to find ways of making parks safe but challenging.

With our youngest children, the trick is patience. It means standing for hours as they explore a metal tunnel four feet long. It means working out routines for climbing 'spiders', jumping on to 'flying foxes', climbing the stairs of slides and helter-skelters. These are sequences of tiny achievement which, if encouraged, build and build body-awareness and confidence through fun. It always saddens me when I hear parents or grand-parents saying things that can make a child feel that they're not good enough: 'You're six and you can't climb that?!'

One funny rule I've worked to, which some people think is crazy, is that I'll never lift children higher than they can climb themselves. My thinking is that no matter how frustrating I'm being in the short term, in the long term the children learn how to climb up, get just as high as they want and – even more importantly – how to climb down. Well, if nothing else, it gives us something to argue about!

Another good thing about parks is that they invite compari-son. Going to new places, staying with friends, means comparing swings, pitches, slides and facilities. The children remember idyllic moments at the park they've only been to twice, where, say, there was a flat concrete surface where you could ride round and round on bikes, or an especially high slide, now built with health and safety thoughts in mind into a mound. Joining in these chats is in its own way how we talk about how 'author-ities' behave towards the very people who put them in power. It's not often that children can get a full sense of how govern-ment works in relation to something that they want and care about, but with parks and playgrounds it's stripped bare.

And it's in parks where I've spent what must by now be years playing football and cricket both as a child and with my children. I've even taken my children to see the tree that stood as a wicket for me and my friends sixty years ago! I suppose when I do this, and when I witter on about, say, 'this is where my mother lived', I'm saying something about history. There is the history in books. There is the history we come across in country houses or castles. And there is this very ordinary, unrecorded history of 'where I kicked a ball around' and the like.

Playing ball games in the family groupings of two, three, four or five, sometimes expanding with friends and relations, sometimes shrinking back to twos and threes, comes to have important meaning to us all. We express powerful things through how we win and lose, how we are 'fair' or 'unfair', how we argue about points and goals and runs, won or lost. I'm always shaken at hearing the way some parents shout at their children when they're playing ball games with them in the park. I try to listen in to hear what they're shouting about. More often than not, I can hear disappointment. They are demanding that their children run faster, catch better, kick harder or whatever and this means to me that they're disappointed that their children aren't showing that they're going to be world-beating sportspeople. I think it's possible to argue that deep down they are saying to themselves, not to their children, that they are disappointed in themselves that they were never world-beaters! I guess I am.

I would have liked to have been Arsenal's goalkeeper, played rugby for England, swum breast-stroke or done the 50K walk in the Olympics. But I didn't ever work hard enough at any of it. I was never going to. I knew I was OK at some of these sports but never more than a bit OK . . . sometimes. This doesn't give me any right to do a number on my own children about it. I think we have to think of park sport as a time to show our children that we love seeing them run and jump and catch; control a ball, hit it with a bat or racquet or whatever. We have to find ways to show them how to do things without making the child feel that they're no good. And though falling over, missing the ball, not winning are frustrating, they're not a disaster. Part of any sport at any level is learning how to get over being disappointed so that you can enjoy whatever it is next time – and perhaps get better at it.

Another way to get a kick out of park sport is to over-dramatize it, fill it with fantasies about who you are. At various times in our lives, most park players have said things like, 'I'm Ronaldo!' It's like putting a costume over what we're doing, so that we become our heroes. This is also part of growing up, where, in stages, first we play out a fantasy of being wonderful and all-powerful. Next, we learn that we're not really that good and then we get a glimpse of just how incredible the super-sportspeople's skills are.

As adults playing the games, I've learned that the prize is really not in winning. I just have to suppress the child in me. The prize is in making sure that the whole thing is fun from the time we get ready to go till the time we get back. Sometimes that means cooking the books so that it looks as if I'm winning but my child gets to win in the end. That might mean winning a game but losing the match. It might involve building in handicaps like only being allowed to shoot at a goal from further away.

Then, later, when we're watching the same sport on TV, seeing close-ups of sportspeople showing their skills, we can compare the goalkeeper's dive, the off-break, the smash with what I and our child did over in the park last weekend. Next time we go we try to do what that sportsperson did. I can't think how many hours either my various children and I have spent trying to kick a ball so that first it bends one way and then another. In fact, one of my now adult sons points out a park in London whose main point of interest is that it's 'where we tried to bend the ball'.

THE PARK

All these moments are ways in which we get to matter to each other. We discover whether people care about us. Building on that, they can also be ways in which we explore and find out stuff to do with the sports, the players, the stats, the skills and even the science of it all. It may well seem casual, trivial and small-time, but on the basis of it being pleasurable, it can give a kick-start to all sorts of lines of enquiry and ways of thinking. It may turn out to be the one focal point for reading.

Many sports involve ways of thinking that are a bit like a kind of constantly moving 3D chess with you guessing what the opposition is doing even as the opposition is guessing what you are doing. Talking, reading and writing about this involves logic, geometry and psychology. You might be taking it in turns to take penalties on a bit of rough ground, thinking that you're Lionel Messi, but you're also in an abstract world of angles, speeds and curves.

If that's all it was, for many of us it wouldn't matter very much. The truth is that we can't do anything without using our minds and our personalities. This means that when we mess about with a ball in the park with our children, it can easily be a moment that we as adults use for our own benefit. On the other hand, if we can lay to one side our own frustrations and what we might imagine are our thwarted ambitions, we can help our children to want to do more and know more.

Just as important, in these moments of argy-bargy, what-ifs, near-misses and the rest that every sport creates, we lay down a kind of blueprint for how to behave with other people. There really isn't much point in spending hours at the park if all it does is turn out bad losers, spiteful winners or players who can't share and can't co-operate.

THE SKY

Most of us experience the weather on the ground. We're not pilots or astronauts. Weather feels like it's about puddles, putting on scarves, slapping on sun-cream. Even when we watch the weather forecast, we instantly translate it from the diagrams on the TV screen to what it'll mean to stand at the bus stop tomorrow, or what clothes to wear.

Meanwhile, it's up there, up above our heads where most of the weather is being made. Obvious, of course. We know that. But because it's obvious, it's easy to pass on a lack of interest in it. So, though children hear us talking endlessly about how it's a bit chillier today, or that it feels like spring or that the wind has turned, they much more rarely see us – well, most of us – looking up at the sky wondering, asking questions or figuring. Above us is an ever-changing wonder available to us to think about either like scientists, measuring and predicting, or as artists, imagining, drawing, writing, dancing. Or both.

Why do some clouds rain and some don't?

What is a rainbow?

What is wind?

Why are some clouds darker than others?

What is hail?

Do the weather rhymes work?

THE SKY

Red sky at night, shepherds' delight.
Red sky in the morning, shepherds' warning.

What makes a sky red anyway?

Playing the cloud-shapes game is fun, studying the clouds to see if you can find animals, plants, giants, demons, people and faces in the shapes of the clouds. One spin-off from this is that if we ever find ourselves looking at paintings by people like Turner or Constable, there's a shared way of thinking and talking about them.

Scientists play with cloud-shapes too. For them, it's about naming the types: 'cumulus' and 'nimbus' and the like. But it's also about looking at a particular shape and predicting what it will do later. I remember my brother had a little book about the weather and once he had figured out what some of the clouds would do later, it felt as if he had some kind of crystal ball. He could look up at the sky and say things like, 'You see those feathery bits all over the sky? They're going to turn into great puffy clouds later and it'll probably rain.'

All this makes the weather and the sky ideal for keeping a log. The easiest thing to measure is of course the temperature and the moment you do this, you get into the way the weather people measure temperature 'in the shade'. If you put a thermometer clearly not 'in the shade' you get a different reading from the one we hear on the weather forecasts. Measuring windspeeds, air-pressure and rainfall can involve buying bits of gear – some of it expensive – but in the books for children about weather they show ways of improvising this very cheaply. An ideal thing to set up with grandparents who are keen weather-watchers and who live in a different climate is to get them swapping weather info with the children.

OUTDOORS

There's a rough and ready way of working out whether a storm is getting nearer or further away. You count the time-lapses between the flashes of lightning and the thunderclaps. So, when the lightning flashes, you start counting (or measuring on a watch). When you hear the thunder, stop. Wait for the next lightning flash, count again and stop when the thunder comes. Compare your scores. If the second one is shorter, the centre of the storm is getting nearer; if it's longer, it's moving away.

This is also a great way of having a conversation about what is lightning, what is thunder? Which may well lead on to the big one: what is electricity?

We can grab weather on camera and put it on our computer screens or send it to each other as texts: 'Sky frm bus wndow'.

I like the way birds handle weather. The mysterious thing about the wind for children is that we can feel it but not see it. Same goes for air and an idea like 'warm air rising'. Watching birds is a way of 'seeing' wind and air. Some birds glide more than others. Some flap more than others. Gulls are good gliders. Pigeons are good flappers.

What are they gliding on?
How come they can glide up as well as down?
Why does spreading their wings slow them down as they land?

Making paper planes and darts imitates birds and the history of kites, gliders, planes and the new generation of solo flying machines is bound up with hundreds of years of people watching birds and wanting to be like them. A way into the art, history, technology or science of any of this might come from no more than watching gulls, having paper plane competitions or flying kites.

TV is a wonderful informer but, cruel though this might sound, a TV news item about a weather disaster is also put there for entertainment. The talk about 'climate change' and the reports of tornadoes, hurricanes, droughts, floods and storms is made much more real when we look more closely at what's going on above our own heads.

The sky at night takes us to a world of art and science mostly downplayed or even ignored in school. How people have described the destiny of humankind has been wrapped up with thinking about the sun, moon, earth and stars. Sitting in the dark, looking at the sky for ten minutes is as big a starting point for questions as any I know. It may start from nothing more than, 'What's that one called?' or 'Which one is Mars?' There is now a phone app that helps you name and plot the constellations. Even with my very limited knowledge, there is always something stirring – shocking even – looking at a star or constellation that I recognize and thinking about how far away it is, how long it's been there, how millions of other humans can see it too, how trillions of humans have been looking at it over tens of thousands of years.

In my experience, I've found that these moments always, always, always spark off amazing questions about the whole history of humanity, the movements of the earth and the other planets, the nature of the universe. I really like it that these conversations may well be full of information – or lead to digging out books or websites – but they are also full of don't-knows, what-ifs, and I-wonders. In a matter of moments, we move from hard facts about, say, the distance of the earth to the moon to the very edge of what any of us knows.

In these night-sky wonderings, we soon end up with whatever is our core belief-system: what's it all for? My own is that it's not 'for' anything! I don't impose this on my children. I don't tell them that this is what they should believe. I always say that this is what I and some other people think, and there are plenty of other people who think differently. I try not to close off talk and thought about such matters, no matter how firmly I believe what I believe. I guess it's a tough message that I come up with. Standing in the dark looking up at the stars, saying that you don't think that there is any purpose to it all, would, on its own, be a comfortless thing to say. That's why I don't leave it at that. I say that instead of looking out to the stars for a meaning, I look to us, I look to ourselves, I look to how we live together and get on together, I look to how we make and share the things we need. So I don't duck saying what I believe. I just don't lay it down in such a way as to be saying that they have to follow me.

These few minutes underneath the night sky link up to many other things: visiting ancient monuments like Stonehenge, reading Greek myths like Daedalus and Icarus, going to a planetarium or on a long-haul flight, watching space exploration stuff on TV, talking about gravity, coming across Einstein or Galileo, talking about February in leap years. I can't think of the number of times I've 'done' the solar system, the twenty-four hours of the day, how day and night or winter and summer happen or what makes it 365 and a bit days of the year, with oranges and apples from the fruit bowl on the kitchen table. A tilted apple for the spinning earth and a little bit of paper stuck to the apple for the UK is useful too.

(By the way – and it really is a 'by the way' – the commentary on the planetarium show in New York is done by Robert Redford. One word of warning though: taking a very young child in there may not be ideal. Our youngest hid under the seat. Even so, every time Robert Redford turns up in a film on

TV, we all turn to each other and say, 'He did the commentary on the planetarium show in New York, you know.' And then we turn to our youngest and say, 'And you hid under the seat.' Some day, he'll get his revenge.)

THE BEACH

The sea and the beach are gigantic living museums. The sea collects the exhibits and spreads them out for us along the shore. All we have to do is slow down and look. Any beach displays hundreds of specimens and offers them to us to pick up, and find out more about them in books and online. Even things that look like scraggly bits of weed might turn out to be egg cases for creatures we've never seen. Seaweed that blurs into heaps of greeny-brown veg will turn out to be different plants. A dark red stone might be a bit of brick or tile worn smooth into a pebble by the sea and sand. A beautiful blue stone that glows when you hold it up to the light might be a bit of a bottle worn into a pebble too. If there are rock pools, and you're prepared to spend an hour or so, you get rewarded with seeing anemones, starfish and sea-urchins.

At the same time, the soft sand of a beach is a great surface to fall on to and roll about in. This way, it offers children new things they can do with their bodies. This is all about extending ourselves, discovering new ways of expressing ourselves. I think this is partly why we find such times so uplifting. These are strong and real reasons why we can get a sense that we are refreshed. Doing new things helps us to think new things. Doing new things helps us to say new things.

*

I find that no matter how often I go to a beach and no matter how often I look things up, there are always other creatures, plants and shells that I don't know about. My trick is to sidle up to people who seem to know what they're doing and then, with my children, ask them what they're digging up out of the sand or what they're trying to catch. Apart from this revealing things we didn't know, it does the job of reminding us that knowledge and expertise are not only kept in books and scholarly websites.

I've found in the past that sometimes the best experts have been local children. On one occasion in France they had found some kind of sea-slug that they had in a bucket. We crowded round to have a look. Every so often, it squitted a deep purple ink. It wasn't long before someone explained how delicious they taste cooked in butter with garlic and parsley. In a moment, the beach had changed. It turned into a free deli, with people putting in views on the tastes of shrimps, scallops, oysters, crabs, lobsters and the best way to cook them, along with strong divisions of opinion on which kind of seaweed was edible. It's fascinating to be in on a moment when the animals and plants around you are moved from being the things you 'spot' to things you can eat. I asked a man who had a basket full of oysters how often he came here to collect them. 'Nearly every day,' he said. 'I don't go home till I've got enough for my evening meal.' In just this one meeting, there was a history of how people all over the world have survived by knowing where to look, how to catch and how to cook. Of course, we can read about that sort of thing in a book. You're reading it now. It may or may not hook a child's interest. A hundred times more infectious and vivid is seeing and talking with someone doing exactly that.

Perhaps a day or a year or a decade later, there'll be a conversation or a TV programme about fishing the seas till they're empty, the cost of oysters or the diet of the Romans and the man with his basket or the children with the sea-slug will pop into our minds – adults' and children's.

Beaches make geology naked. I find pebbles and sea-washed junk irresistible and try to pass my enthusiasm for it on to my children. Each pebble or pseudo-pebble is a bunch of questions:

What are you?
Where do you come from?
How old are you?
Why are you the shape you are?

One holiday we decided that the stones looked so much better wet than dry, so we brought back a box of pebbles, varnished them at home and they looked as if they had just been picked off the beach. Some people put them into jars, fill the jars with water and a little vinegar to stop them going green. It's a way of making holidays survive on the window-sill. Children talk of them as 'treasures'.

My father once went to tremendous efforts to find a home stone-polishing machine. It was a present for one of my children. The polisher turned out to be a little barrel that you filled with polishing powder, mounted on an electric motor and then left to turn and churn for about a week. The results weren't sensational but good enough.

Occasionally any of us can come across crystals, fossils and semi-precious stones like cornelian. A band of bluish rock runs across England from Robin Hood's Bay in Yorkshire to Lyme Regis in Dorset and in some of the pebbles there are perfect fossils. When we were on holiday near Robin Hood's

Bay, my friend looked it up in a book and said that the pebbles were 'nodules'. We loved that word: 'nodules', we said, and giggled. He conjured up a picture of dead creatures sitting in blue mud at the bottom of pits. We went to the fossil museum in Whitby and stared with amazement at the giant snail-like creatures on show, the chambers of some of which had crystallized.

A close look at the stones on one or two of the bridges across the River Thames or in the stonework in Victorian museums and churches will reveal yet more fossils – sometimes hundreds of them in one slab. These show us a view of what the seabed looked like millions of years ago. Most museums, but especially the Natural History Museum in London where my brother has been a palaeontologist (fossil expert) for most of his adult life, display and explain the worlds that these fossils come from. There are links between the living creatures and plants we find on beaches and the fossilized life we might also find on that beach or on a bridge, on an old window-sill, or in an exposed bit of rock somewhere. As always, these links can seem very abstract in a book or on TV until, say, you find a fossilized sea-urchin in a cliff in Norfolk as we did once, or indeed while looking at a stone table-top in a junk shop. Words like 'ammonite' and 'belemnite' are sometimes not much more than difficult words attached to a far-off, non-human world until you find the spark between us now and those times from millions of years ago.

My own children have got a buzz out of going to those shlocky stone and crystal shops just by the beach. Whenever we go in, I fear that my brother is there in spirit, making the point to us that these are places full of loot with a trail of blood and treachery behind the treasures. I can hear him warning us that it's rubbish science. The pieces have been plucked out of their 'context', nothing links with anything else. You get no sense from them how old they are, how the rocks were formed, how the now fossilized creatures once lived. They're just for gawping at. Even worse, he might say, as the children are highly unlikely to find anything as stunning as the stones on sale, they may look at the stones on the beach and think of them as not good enough.

True, true, I say to myself, but I don't want to spoil the children's awe. At times, they've spent their pocket money on polished agate 'eggs' and amethyst crystals. They sit alongside the pebble of white rock from a strange, isolated windswept hill, made entirely of this rock. Sitting several inches from me as I write this is an anonymous, dull-looking pebble. It was once yellow, now grey. I picked it up from the side of a sleeping volcano on the Italian island of Vulcano. Just as it sounds, the island is a volcano, the volcano is the island. Apart from the volcano, there's not much more than a couple of grey beaches and a hot-plopping mud-pool where people sit slapping the mud on their faces. In the water, you can see bits of lava floating. Everywhere you walk there is the strong smell of sulphur, that boiled egg smell, once purified for the making of stink-bombs.

I picked up a pebble and put it in the little breast-pocket of my shirt. When I took my shirt off that night, the stone had made holes in the fabric. I show my children the dull, inert thing. 'It made a hole in my shirt,' I say. The sulphur in the stone mixed with the water of my sweat in the heat of the day turned into hydrosulphuric acid, and that acid was strong enough to 'eat' the cotton of my shirt . . .

A walk, a stone, some heat, some sweat and I did a chemistry experiment without knowing.

THE SEA

The sea that's washing all these stones and creatures is full of power, mystery and beauty. A few moments on a beach shows us to be creatures who are captivated by it in so many different ways.

I'm always interested to see how people from the very youngest to the oldest love to get involved with the sea as a force. We build sandcastles and trenches at the sea-edge in order to watch its power wash away what we make. Sand gives us a material that is more messy, more malleable, more changeable than almost anything else we'll ever handle anywhere else. We cover our hands and face with it, we get up to our knees in it, we dig it, we throw it, we heap it, we pat it, we scoop it, we make lines and shapes in it. This is not trivial.

As I say, for many of us this will be almost the only time that we feel this free to make and model with a material. We do it without fear of failure. When it falls apart with the tide, it's a wreck but not a disaster. We can mix the sand with shells, stones and flags. We can write messages on it. We can experiment with dry, damp, soggy sand. We can dribble watery sand on it. If we make things near to where a stream runs into the sea, we can make dams and see how the flow of water builds up the pressure of a pool and sweeps away what we build.

If you eavesdrop on children doing all this building and

151

designing, you can hear them making plans, discussing possible outcomes, comparing designs, making up jokes, describing to each other what they look like with sand and water all over them. Activity like this is one of the most powerful motors for talk. Many children who find it difficult to put their thoughts into words, or who find it difficult to finish what they want to say, can become fluent in the company of one or two other children making and doing, changing and watching sand and water on a beach.

There's usually room for them to move away from each other if they start arguing or fighting. There is space for children to learn that important ability of knowing when to 'leave it'. One of the stories of the overcrowded world of small classrooms, small playgrounds, small rooms in flats and houses and high-emotion online chatrooms is that we all find it very difficult to 'walk away'. All of us, children and adults, often find that we go on much longer than we need to, nagging, snarling, getting the last word, backbiting, digging. Whether we're 'giving it' or 'getting it', one of the sad features of it all is that people on the receiving end of stuff that they don't like to hear often find it hard to know how to disengage. A beach is a space that offers that glorious possibility of moving off – of making another sandcastle a few yards away. It can be very hard to learn how to do this in the overcrowded places; easier to learn it on a beach.

And there is the endless variety of the waves.

The sea is beautiful to look at. Staring at waves has always seemed to me to be a wonderful thing to do. Same goes for listening to them, feeling them and smelling them. We usually think of the word 'rhythm' as something to do with sound: drums, beats and pulse in music and poetry. We can hear the rhythm of the waves but we can also see it. Looking out to sea or along a beach we see one row of waves lying in front of another and another and another. As our eye hops from the top of one row of waves to the next, it makes a visual rhythm. Artists, film-makers and photographers know this. They make rhythms in their paintings, films and photos with people, lamp-posts, trees, cars and the like. For the rest of us, going about our business, we don't often stop and think of the rhythms we can see. The one time perhaps when we do stop and see them is when we look at the sea. And the great thing is that when we come to the next day, the rhythms are different. This is visual music. Talking about this gives us a way of talking about the work of painters, photographers and film-makers too.

Again, just like the sand and water experience, these moments face to face with visual rhythms may feel new and different. Just knowing about waves from books, TV and film is not the same as standing and looking at them for a few minutes.

There is also the matter of respect and terror. There are thousands of stories, poems and real events that tell us about the power of the sea. As a teenager and young adult, I loved swimming in the sea. I have loved the space and depth of it. I have loved the sense that under the water was another place. My favourite book was Jacques Cousteau's *The Silent World*. Though I've never really ridden the waves in boats or on surf-boards, I've loved being shunted towards the shore by waves. I've loved feeling that moment when the push of your own legs is made insignificant by the push of the waves. Of course, you can hire a machine to throw you about, you can run on tread-mills, ride switchbacks at the fair, or be tugged along by people. The waves are special because you are immersed in the very stuff that is doing the pushing. A cup of it does nothing. A sea full of it shoves you. Like a lot of the other moments I've been describing, this can be new and rare for our children. It makes your body do new things which in turn makes your mind do new things.

It goes without saying, perhaps, that doing any of this can be lethal. One of the scariest moments I've ever had was on a little beach in Spain. The waves were knee-high. A group of us, adults and young teenagers, were swimming about within our depth when we noticed that we had drifted along the shore to where the waves were a bit more powerful, there was a 'hole' below us so that we couldn't put our feet down and because the tide was going out, we couldn't get back to the beach. In moments, we were struggling against the waves but not making headway. Twenty feet away, there were people standing and playing in the same waves on the shoreline. Twenty feet in front of us, there were dozens of people sitting about on the beach in the sun. With calm and forethought, we could have just let ourselves float. We were all good swimmers but something makes you try to force it and we struggled against the waves, trying to get to the shore. We tried much harder than we should have.

In a matter of seconds, we were all feeling heavy, arms and legs seizing up. We were gasping and crying out. But no one could hear us. Or if they did, they would have thought we were mucking about, calling to each other for the sheer pleasure of being in the sea. I could see that the young people were panicking and even though I was panicking myself, I pushed them as hard as I could towards the beach. Once, twice. It worked. I remember that as I got tired I struggled less against the waves. Not because I thought it through carefully but because I had to. And that was the best thing to have done. The moment I stopped fighting, I stopped seizing up. I could glide on the surface. I knew how not to sink. The sea wasn't that rough after all and in a very short while the waves took me sideways to where I could put my feet down and I walked on to land. I sat down in the sand, exhausted. My mind and body were shaken and bewildered. The young people huddled together and looked at the place where they had just been. Incredibly, there were families with young children further out than where we had just been. They were just frolicking about in the waves. Laughing and shouting. And others on either side of the 'hole' where we had been were rolling over in the waves calling out to each other, having fun. How come there had been that moment of terror?

Each of us who was there that day has put those feelings and thoughts, those mind and body experiences into what we hear and see about news of sea-storms, tempests, hurricanes, tsunamis, tornadoes, whirlpools, currents, accidents, disasters and much more. Part of being human is being vulnerable. Part of being human is living in and being part of the powers that are in nature: wind, rain, snow, sea, mudslides, rockfalls. Ideally, we should get a sense of these forces without being unsafe, without taking risks. I'm certainly not someone who wants to take risks – either for myself, or for my children. I'm no dare-devil. I don't get a buzz out of feeling that I'm Mr Big, Mr Brave, defying these forces. Every day, we make decisions for our children about this sort of thing. We say: don't climb any higher, come away from that low wall at the top of the castle, don't get any nearer to the fire, don't go into the sea today.

As some experts lament, we have become 'risk-averse'. The argument goes that we have got to a point where we have made our children less safe precisely because we have kept them away from risk. I learned to canoe without a life-jacket – unthinkable today. My parents let me play on a beach and go swimming without them being anywhere near me – unthinkable today. What this tells me is that 'risk' is not something objective that can be measured like a quantity of flour. Risk is something 'cultural'. We have the means to share the news of children being 'grabbed' by a wave and washed out to sea, we know of the terrible accident when a school canoeing trip in the sea turned into a disaster.

So nowadays, we create situations where such accidents and disasters are much less likely to happen – even if it means narrowing down the life-experiences available. In the great sum of things, I have much less of a problem with that than many people in the 'risk' lobby. The reason why I am not so worried about a lack of risk in our ways of being with children is that I believe that we can be cunning and inventive enough to cook up non-risky ways of putting ourselves and our children into situations that are new, exciting and challenging. I think we *should* find situations that are challenging. But it's not as if 'challenging' has to come along with 'life-threatening' as its inseparable buddy. I'm in favour of life-jackets in canoes. I think we need 'challenge', because it's in the challenge that our minds and bodies move in new ways, we ask ourselves questions, we try out new things, we learn to adapt and change.

THE WOODS

When I was a child, I spent a lot of my free time in woods. These weren't great forests. Far from it, they were the little spinneys and coppices at the edge of parks, or next to the bypass.

How many different leaves can you find?
Which trees make leaves that stay green all the year round and which ones lose them?
What's under the bark of a dead tree?
What's the oldest tree in this wood?
Which trees are 'native', which trees were brought in from another country?

Woods are constantly changing, changing colour and shape with the seasons, making and shedding different things, and being cropped and trimmed by rangers and foresters. Many of the woods we can go in are hundreds of years old. Some of the trees we see are the descendants of trees that were there when the Tudors, Normans, Saxons and Romans were there.

As you walk through them, you can hear birds reacting to your presence, calling out to each other that something potentially dangerous is coming. If you live anywhere near them, you can hear owls calling to each other. If you go online, you can now check the sounds with the birds you've heard.

Woods are great for what we used to call 'Wide Games', like Smugglers and Customs where the smugglers hide paper money on themselves and try to get through and beyond a line of customs officials. Hiding in a bush brings you up close with the layers of leaves on the woodland floor, slowly sifting down into black humus, berries and seeds on the leaves like haws on hawthorn, ideal for splitting open and using as itching powder. A handful of autumn leaves spread out on a white sheet is an instant collage.

How do trees shed their leaves?
Why are sycamore seeds, ash keys and lime seeds like helicopters?
Why are blackberries juicy and their stems so thorny?

Many of the woods in towns and cities have had to be claimed, fought for and protected. Sometimes there are signs up that tell the story of how this or that landowner bequeathed it to the people. Other times, it was councils who protected them against developers and house-builders. These are the footprints of battles from long ago fought by people on our behalf. The sign may well tell us who runs the wood today and how you can become a 'friend' of the wood. Near us there's a walk that runs along the path of the old railway. Sometimes it runs like a deep trough between and below the backs of houses. Sometimes it emerges and looks out over London. Here and there, children have hung an old tyre so that they can swing from a tree and there are dens halfway up the old cuttings. Years ago, I sat on a garden wall looking down on one of the trains that used to run there. My youngest doesn't really believe me. There are no railway lines, he says. We talk about how they took up the tracks, and how over my lifetime trees and bushes have 'claimed' the land. Perhaps they've claimed it back, we say. Maybe when they cleared the land to make the railway, there were trees and bushes that they cut down and burned. For eighty years or so there was a railway, and then they took up the tracks and the trees and bushes came back. Now it's a long thin forest. Even the bridges are part of the woods.

In one of the woods near us, the ranger has a house right in the middle. How strange, to live in the middle of a city in the middle of a wood. At night, when we're on the bus, and the woods are utterly dark, we can look through the trees to see a light on in the house. It's like a Grimm fairy tale. We wonder who lives in the middle of the wood.

Then, one day I find that I'm playing with a band and the guy playing 'pans' (steel drums) tells me that his daughter is a forest ranger and she lives in that house in the middle of the woods. He's from Venezuela and she's brought up three children there. I tell my children. We wonder what it would be like growing up in the middle of the wood. We talk about getting up in the morning and walking out of the house, through the wood to get to school. It seems so medieval, so Hansel and Gretel. Or what would it be like, waking up in the middle of the night in there?

Other histories sit in woods: holes where bombs were dropped off by planes running low on fuel heading back to Germany; hunting grounds for kings and queens who loved the taste of venison; common ground for owners of pigs wanting to fatten their pigs on acorns; hidey-holes for runaways; dark ponds where someone slipped in and never got out. In some woods, there are the furrows and humps made by prehistoric settlers. In one part of Epping Forest there is a ridge marking the edges of a camp, supposedly made by Boudicca on her way to burn out the Romans. Now, beeches and oaks grow out of the slopes and bumps. In other woods that flank the road it's said that highwaymen, like Dick Turpin himself, used to hide ready to jump out at carriages full of moneyed folk.

In summer, there is the magic of beams of light angling down to the woodland floor. Looking up to the canopy is like looking through a kaleidoscope. A walk through the wood shows off something hugely variegated and diverse; there are details in close-up, middle distance, high up and far away. Engaging our children in the world can sometimes mean just putting them in places that are full of diverse sights, complicated and unfamiliar patterns. In autumn, fungi emerge. Fascinating because we can scare ourselves with how poisonous they might be. How one tiny taste of one and we'd be rolling on the ground crippled with pain. Some tree trunks and fallen logs seem to sprout stacks of shelves, fungi in layers. In France, people head off into the woods and come back with basketfuls of lumpy green and brown fungus. They share them around, pleading with us to fry them in butter and garlic. How can they be so sure that they haven't picked a poisonous one by mistake?

The children watch while we eat them, wondering why anyone would ever eat such a thing. The idea of unlabelled food, food that didn't come in a wrapper, seems outlandish. I point out the dried version in a packet with a bar code in the supermarket. They look like misshapen wood-chips. I can see that the children are wondering why adults inflict such horrors on themselves. Soon we are talking about foods, taste, customs and culture. Amazingly, some people in the world don't like Marmite, I say.

CAMPING

I am an ex-camper. My parents were fanatical campers and so for ten years or so, every summer and Whit week, they took us camping in many places in England, Wales and France. By the time I was sixteen, I had my own tent and went off with friends with our tents on our backs. My enthusiasm hasn't lasted into adulthood and part of me thinks that I have deprived my own children from that face-to-face with the elements and beasts that camping gave me.

If you camp, you can't escape weather, flies, wasps, grass, cold water and uncomfortable chairs. You become expert in stings, bites, scratches, bruises, sunburn and mouldy feet. You discover that your body's edge – your skin – is merely a surface for hundreds of creatures to use as a landing-strip. You discover that this landing-strip is nothing more than a temporary obstacle for hundreds of small beasties intent on getting through your skin to something beautiful on the other side: your blood. Any ideas you might have of your skin as being protective have to be junked. If you think of your skin as being there for the purpose of presenting yourself to the outer world, this too must be forgotten.

You and your children become expert in who or what can puncture your skin, and inflict pain on it because of these beasties' suspicions of us as death-bringing giants. Conversations turn to antihistamine, venom, malaria and anaphylactic shock. Lists of stingers and biters are drawn up: horse-flies, mosquitoes, wasps, bees, hornets, some spiders, some ants, scorpions, nettles, daddy-long-legs. No, I say, daddy-long-legs don't bite, and nettles are plants. We wonder what midges are. One time, on the Isle of Arran, we discovered that daytimes are midge-free. Then, you could be playing cricket in a field and the second the sun went down behind the houses, millions of midges appear out of nowhere and start eating your face. The trick is to stop playing cricket and get home before the sun goes down behind the houses. We've been known to hit a ball, start to run the run and to keep on running to get home in time.

One of my children trod on a scorpion. 'I've trodden on a scorpion,' he said.

It was in Australia. I carefully and patiently explained to him that they don't have scorpions in Australia.

'It's a scorpion,' he said.

'I don't know what it is,' I said, 'but whatever it is, it's not a scorpion. They don't have scorpions in Australia. I'll come over and have a look.' I did just that. I went over and looked. 'That is a scorpion,' I said. 'No one go anywhere near it. It's very, very dangerous.'

'I know,' he said, 'that's what I was trying to tell you . . .'

I remembered a French summer camp when I was a teenager. It had rained so much, the farmer let us sleep in his barn. In the middle of the night, Alain woke up and started shouting and swearing. 'Some bastard has stung me,' he shouted. We put on our torches. He pointed to a red hole on his ribs. We flicked our torches round the barn floor. A scorpion skidded under a stone. 'I was stung by a scorpion,' he announced. He was in pain but oh so proud.

I looked at my son's foot. He seemed to have squashed the

scorpion before it stung him. We looked closely at the wondrous-
ness of the scorpion, with its long flexi-tail, the hook on the
end, the bulb of poison just below the hook. Another creature
who knows how to puncture the human skin.

On that holiday, we met and ran away from giant grey spiders,
stick insects and brave, fierce little lizards called blue-tongues
that hang about in outside showers and drains. What I didn't
know was that when I went running through the boggy area
next to the lake in my trainers, I must have been within millimetres of being stung by tiger-snakes, and when the children
swung from a tree on a tyre that hadn't been swept out for
months, they must have been millimetres from deadly red-back
spiders. Brits are people who go to Australia and make an enormous fuss about relatively harmless beasts while taking huge
risks bashing about unprotected near the really deadly ones.

Every summer, the newspapers explain to us how ultraviolet
rays affect our skin. They tell us about melanin cells, radiation,
sunblock, skin cancers, factor 50. We see cricketers and athletes
covered in creams.

Now at this point, I might have to concede that the whole
argument of this book collapses. Even as the sun beats down
and every child is directly and immediately affected, it seems
as if any child I have known shows no interest whatsoever in
any of this information. All those newspaper articles and ultraviolet ray warnings are not much more than an annoying background burble. This ought to disprove everything I say in this
book where my point is that when the immediate environment
presses itself on the child, there is a perfect opportunity to set
the mind racing, to ask questions, find out things, express what's
going on in words, drawings, photos, collections, dance . . .
But with the sun, I am shown to be a fantasist. In children's

eyes, sunblock is just irritating stuff that tastes like soap that grown-ups make you smear on yourself: grown-ups, they think, probably do it out of spite. The sun doesn't 'do' anything. It just 'is'. It just 'is' hot, so go away and don't bother us with stuff to do with how it goes through your skin. Of course it doesn't go through your skin. How can light go through your skin? Your skin is like a castle wall. Covered in thick plastic. And even if it did go through your skin, how can smearing yourself with a bit of grease stop it? Der.

OK, I concede, sometimes all this practical knowledge stuff is a struggle. I shouldn't have suggested it's always easy.

THE
STREET

I see streets as a place of many meetings:

- between buildings and people
- between vehicles and people
- between those who designed and built it and those who live and work in it
- between those who sell and those who buy
- between those who travel through and those who stand still
- between those who produce signs and symbols and those who read and interpret them
- between those who dig, build and work below the street and those who move over them
- between those who demolish and those who conserve
- between those who thrive and those who go bust
- between those who say nothing and those who say a lot
- between those who left marks but are anonymous and those who put their names all over the place . . .

. . . and many more.

This makes them great places to feed our curiosities, awaken interest, get us wanting to find out more.

THE GROUND

The ground level of streets and the ground itself is punctured by hundreds of covers, gratings and lids often made with robust but beautiful designs, labelled with odd words that you hardly ever see anywhere else: 'hydrant', 'ductile', 'slideout', 'rapide', 'telegraph' and the like. Makers' names and the places where the cover was made often appear too: Adams Ltd., York; Brickhouse, Dudley. I like 'spotting' these and with some of my children we've 'collected' them. It brings you into contact with what must have been a flourishing cast iron business, turning out covers for the whole country. You can look these up online and on Google images. Some of them have a date on too. Just looking at a date reminds you that the everyday matter of walking down a street has history too. 'Someone put that drain in a hundred years ago; people walked past and saw that a hundred years ago. Who were they?' It's good to think aloud like that when we're with our children.

In many parts of the country the small round coal-hole covers are still in place and their lovely designs vary a lot. You can get a piece of thick tissue paper and a soft black pencil or black wax ball from an art shop and make rubbings of coal-hole covers. If you're worried about the hygiene of it, then take some baby-wipes and give it a good old wipe first. If you don't fancy anything as hands-on as that, then you can stand over them and take a photo on your phone. Then you can cross-check them with the ones on Google images. Or better still, print off a sequence of them as a display or frieze. They are nearly as varied as snowflakes. Perhaps that's what they are: giant cast-iron snowflakes!

In the wake of collecting these, you find yourself getting into conversations about coal, coal deliveries, fireplaces and heating. After all, if you look down a street with coal-holes in front of each of the houses, you get a picture of how thousands of people used to live. An everyday sight in some streets was of coal-men turning up outside your house to tip coal down the hole. But where did it go?

Usually, you can see the place where it went, a basement or small room beneath the pavement. Sometimes there are steps down to an 'area' below the ground level. On one side is the basement of the house itself, while on the side below the pavement there are doors to what was the coal-shed. These days, the basement is often lived in and the shed is for bikes. There's a whole conversation to be had there about how streets are places that we re-use and adapt. Coal turns into bikes. A kitchen used by servants becomes a flat.

Occasionally, as we walk along a road, the covers and lids are in use. A workman is peering in, going down, coming up, mending or cleaning. If it's the telephones, there is a stunning show of coloured wires, which you see the engineer trying to 'read'. There is a magical moment when you can imagine out loud with your children the phone conversations of the street whizzing along under your feet.

Sometimes, I play it a bit nutty and whatever the sign on the cover says, I say, 'But where is it?' So, there are the cable TV covers which sometimes have the initials CATV written on them.

I say, 'Where's the TV? It says here that there's a TV here but all there is is a bit of metal.'

'Yeah, yeah. OK, Dad, no need to get excited about it.'

'No, we've been tricked. We could stand here for days and we wouldn't get a TV picture out of that.'

'Come on, Dad, we're late.'

'I'm going to write to the newspapers to complain.'

'Yeah, you do that, Dad.'

We walk on.

A few minutes later one of them says, 'What does the 'C' in the 'CATV' stand for?'

'I don't know,' I say, 'maybe it's something to do with cats . . . some kind of TV for cats. That's why it's on the ground. The cats come along and peer through the little hole and watch Cat TV down there.'

'But that would be CAT TV.'

'Cats aren't very good at reading so they just give them "CATV". They don't know any better . . .'

Looking at all these different covers, lids and caps reminds us of all the different services that come in and out of the places where we live and work: mains water, waste water, sewage, gas, phones, cable TV . . . and the teams of workers over decades who've dug and lined the holes and tunnels, laid the pipes and wires and nowadays come along mending and replacing. We can wonder aloud about these too: 'Look, that must be where the gas for the gas stove comes in . . .'

Sometimes this connects with TV programmes about someone like Bazalgette who planned the great sewer system of London to deal with 'the Great Stink' and cholera. Or it might be news items in winter about burst water-mains, sewage overflowing into rivers. If we mention or notice such ordinary things as drain covers and we have a conversation about them or even just a few jokes, these make a link with the more difficult or more abstract news items or 'topics' at school. We help children 'fix' what they hear from TV or history lessons to real objects that they see.

Also at ground level is the constant redesigning of pavements and roads. There's a road near where I live which I'm sure has had parts of it in a state of re-build non-stop for over ten years: pavement widening, speed bumps, pavement narrowing, putting in 'islands', taking out 'islands', altering the 'right turn', creating a one-way, getting rid of the one-way. It's a joke. We cheer the latest 'Road-up' sign. A conversation about it leads into who decides how wide or narrow a road should be? Who are the planners and where are they?

We talk about council meetings and the signs that go up in the street, that you sometimes see attached to lamp-posts telling us that the matter is 'under consultation'. We do have a say, I say. And in a matter of moments we might be talking about councils, votes, local elections and the council tax.

As for the holes in the road, my rule of thumb is: where there's a hole, look in it. You never know what you might see, you never know who you might get a chance to have a chat with, you never know what you might find out about. This connects with the great finds that we hear about when builders are digging holes in city centres and come across skeletons and treasure. The ground beneath us becomes much more than just the stuff we walk over.

Looking in holes shows up the kinds of soils we live on too. Most of my life, I've lived on clay, and when you look into the holes that builders make, you can see the slice through the raw clay, looking like a slice of fudge cake. Then you can talk about how clay shrinks when it's dry and expands when it's wet, and

THE GROUND

I tell the story of my brother's house. The front of the house nearly fell off because one hot summer the clay beneath it shrank so much.

The paving and road surfaces vary too. In a good few towns, the old Victorian – even Georgian – stones and cobbles are still around. Sometimes there are just twenty feet of cobbles in an alleyway, or the kerb at the edge of the pavement is obviously really old. I remember the graffiti from Paris in 1968: 'Sous le pavé – la plage': 'Under the paving stones – the beach'. We talk about what that might mean . . .

What kind of stone are these stones made of?
Where do they come from?
Who cut them?
Why do Americans write 'curb' and we write 'kerb'?
Why do Americans say 'sidewalk' and we say 'pavement'?
What are tar and tarmac?
What's the 'mac' bit for?
Where does tarmac come from?
Is there really a tar lake in Trinidad?

I find that it's sometimes the children who ask the questions, sometimes me. Mostly Google and Wikipedia have at least the first stage of an answer.

EYE LEVEL

The next 'layer' up of a street is the level we usually look at most often: shop windows, cars and car names, registration plates, vans and lorries with their signs on the side, street furniture, bus maps and timetables.

Some of the old stuff is nearly invisible – horse troughs, pumps, fountains, benches and bollards – and it's only the new or temporary things we notice: grit bins, traffic cones, temporary fences and barriers. Once you're on to all this, some streets seem to be full of it. Quite a lot of it is covered in inscriptions too: horse troughs put in place by the 'Metropolitan Drinking Fountain Association'. Who were they? Why did they build the troughs? What have the council done with them? Are they just beds for weeds where people chuck their beer cans? What else could they be used for? Benches in memory of people who once lived there; the difficult code of the bus maps and timetables. I told one of my children that 'bollard' is a swear word. When you're really angry, you can shout, 'BOLLARDS!'

The world of cars, car names and registration plates used to be scope for endless collecting when I was young and we had various car-spotting books to help us. If you have any of these still hanging around, or any old annuals with pictures of great cars of the past, it's worth digging them out, to compare the older models that you were familiar with, with the ones that the children will see today.

There are various kinds of car-name games you can invent. At the first level, there's the job of identifying the make and the model. So, one of you can 'spot' the make and the other has to reply by naming the model. You can upgrade this sort of game by making the naming require a link. So, one person names a model or make and the next person has to pick up the last letter of the model or make and use that as the first letter of a model or make – like a chain. Meanwhile, registration plates have become a flourishing industry for people who want to celebrate their names, initials, jobs and hopes. Because a registration must include numbers as well as letters, there is an inventiveness being used to manage this in order to make words: SA33D is SAEED, for example. For many years, the people who issue the registration plates have banned rude words and double entendres but they can't keep up with new ones or rude words in non-English languages. A 'BUT' is worth a cheap laugh, at the very least. Two of the languages I know, French and Yiddish, have one or two insulting three-letter words that occasionally turn up on registration plates. Again, worth pointing out, if only to explore the way we live in a multilingual community but we can't expect the car registration people to keep up with every single possibility.

Also at this eye level are the shop windows. They do their own inviting, begging us to look at their displays and signs. One of the shops where I live has a miniature village in the window which the owners update with seasonal changes. We stop to look at these, of course, and talk about what else they could put in the display. Apart from these very inviting windows, it's sometimes good to stop and look in the windows of the ones that our children might think of as less interesting:

How many different kinds of bread are there in this window?

I wonder why there are five guitars for sale in this charity shop. Are people suddenly getting rid of their guitars?

Sometimes there's a cake shop that says that you can order up your own design and in the window there are some examples: a rocket-cake with 'Happy 3rd birthday, Spaceman!' written on it in icing. You can go far with imagining cakes for different people.

When the pound shops, food shops, bag shops and the like spill out of the shop on to the pavement, the street becomes more like a market. I'll come to markets in a moment but looking at these open shops that occupy the pavement, I've found myself wondering out loud:

How can there be so many different kinds of loo brush?

Do those carpet-cleaners really work?

You see those shopping trolleys? Well, I say, when I was a kid we had one that was like a basket, made of basket-straw and the handle was a walking stick, nailed into the basketwork. It was my job to go to the Co-op at the end of the road to pick up the order that my mother had dropped off a few days earlier. I was the only child I knew of my age who did this. And I used to walk through the street with this shopping trolley desperately hoping I wouldn't bump into one of my friends. I drop that story in as part of my permanent propaganda to get my children to do the occasional 'chore'!

On that theme, I've always thought that in an ideal world I should be able to convince my children to come and do the dullest shopping as well as the exciting stuff that they want to do. I should have enough brain-power and enough cunning to be able to wheedle and bribe them to do it. But – I have to admit it – I have by no means been as successful at this as I should be. I don't like the idea that they might think that they have the right to sit about at home ordering up their delicacies for us, their adult carers, to go off and fetch. It feels odd to see an able-bodied thirteen-year-old stretched out on the sofa, watching TV, eating an apple and giving me a list of what they would like from the food shop round the corner. I try various tacks – not all of them successful: if you want me to get the stuff that you want, I say, then you'd better come too. Or, I need a hand. I can't carry it all. Or bribery: if you come, you can have a . . . etc.

I want them to know how much effort it is, how boring some shopping is, how much things cost. I want them to see how other people are shopping with different budgets, different tastes, different styles of shopping. I want them to guess quantities, look ahead to what they might be eating later, tomorrow, or when their friends come over.

And there are shopping moments that are treasures. For years my brother would weep with laughter at the memory of asking for a packet of hankies and the shopkeeper saying to him, 'Sorry, sir, but we don't sell hankies in the summer.' It's also great to talk about the different ways in which you get treated in different shops. There's a particular kind of second-hand shop where the people behave as if you're an intruder. We often talk about one that's become a family joke. The shop was open so we pushed open the door and the man in the shop said, 'What do you want?'

A bit taken aback, we gestured in the direction of all the second-hand gear around the shop and said, 'We just wanted to take a look.'

He said, slightly rattily, 'But is there anything you want?'

One of us said, 'Well . . . er . . . we don't really know yet because . . . er . . . we haven't looked.'

'Then I'm closed,' he said.

You so want your children to see and hear moments like this. I have a friend in the States who has a way of talking to people when things like that happen. He simply says to the owner of the shop when he hits a brick wall like that, 'Are you *in* business?' This has become a catch-phrase for us, so whenever we see a chi-chi, boutiquey sort of place, we say to each other, before even going in, 'Are you *in* business?' Catch-phrases like that intrigue and puzzle children because they are obviously not real conversations. We are not really asking each other that question, we're quoting my American friend. This invites them to ask us why we are saying that, and who said it first. Who is he? Where does he live? Why did he say that? And then I've got the story of waiting in the freezing cold outside an apartment block in New York (a 'building') waiting for a car that never arrived and my friend yelling down the phone, 'Are you *in* business?!'

Another encounter with the chi-chi boutiquey thing was a little shop that was selling second-hand clocks. These weren't complex antique timepieces, created in the workshops of clock-makers from hundreds of years ago. They were mostly 1950s plastic shop-clocks that had been run off production lines, with garish shop signs and product labels stuck on to them: a bit of sentimental fun just looking at them, actually. We looked around. It was a bit of a journey round the kind of clock I used to see in shop windows when I was a child and the children could spot how some of these had changed their logos. In the middle of our looking, we heard the owner talk quite loudly to someone and say, 'I wasn't prepared to sell him the clock – he didn't understand it.'

Again this has become a catch-phrase, very good for saying when you see the most ordinary of objects, whether in a junk shop, supermarket or department store – a packet of cornflakes, a plate, a pair of shoes – 'I'm not prepared to sell you that, you don't understand it.'

Charity shops, junk shops, second-hand bookshops, antique furniture places, auction rooms, car boot sales, jumble sales and the rest are museums. Something or other will arouse curiosity in children. I have a memory of being on holiday in Pickering in Yorkshire and we went into a big second-hand furniture place. My dad was on the lookout for a desk and he spotted one – or what he thought was one. It was the kind you sit at with your knees in the gap between two sets of drawers. What was slightly different about this one, they said, was that it was 'bow-fronted'. The drawers were curved. The man running the place was very old and – I can see now in my mind's eye – he was pickled. My parents asked him how much for the desk, and I'm pretty sure he said £25. For my parents, who were classroom teachers and who spent all their spare cash on holidays, this was quite a hefty outlay. I could see that they were torn: should they or shouldn't they? They were thinking that it was a bit of an extravagance. But then, it seemed so inviting, the bow-fronted sets of drawers, the leather mat, neatly fitted into the wooden top. 'Mahogany,' my father kept saying. 'Antique.'

'Yes, antique.'

So they bought it. It would be delivered after we got home.

For a few days, they panicked that they had parted with their money without having any kind of surety that they would get the desk. How did they know that it would be delivered? But it came. And my parents were very pleased with it.

But then over the next few months I picked up something odd in the air. Neither of them actually sat at it. They put stuff in the drawers. They put stuff on the top. But neither of them worked at it. They explained that it was a bit low. A bit low? Couldn't they sit on a lower chair? No, that wasn't the problem. What was the problem? Well, they said, slightly sheepishly, it's not really a desk. What? Not a desk? Of course it's a desk. No, it's a dressing table. But you said it was a desk. Yes, we thought it was a desk, but in actual fact, it's the bottom part of a dressing table. On the top, there would have been a mirror. How do you know? Have a look at this, said my father, and he pulled the 'desk' away from the wall. On the back, there were two downward stripes about three feet apart. In the stripes there were screw-holes.

'That,' said my father, 'is how the mirror was fixed – with two battens screwed into the back.'

'Were you diddled, then?' I asked.

'Well, not really. It's just that . . . he must have heard us calling it a desk. Put it this way, he didn't bother to say that it wasn't a desk.'

This story comes back to me on all sorts of occasions like, say, whenever I'm watching auction shows and the *Antique Roadshow* on TV and people look at objects and try to figure out what they are, how they're made, whether they've been damaged. I always give myself a little nod when we see the experts looking behind, under and in, in order to find out whether the object has always been like that or whether it's been changed. If I'm in a junk shop or watching the TV, I tell the children that story and it links to that business of looking under and behind objects to find out more about them.

It also tells me about my parents who were usually rather cautious buyers – their parents had been very poor – suddenly giving in to impulse. And the follow-up scenario of having been tricked or diddled or nearly so.

Moments like these stretch across generations, wrapped up in the objects we own, the things we put up on our walls, or the ones we sit in the corner. They are part of what those objects mean. Intertwined with all the technical stuff about hallmarks, glazes, veneers and the like, there are personal stories to do with who gave what to whom, what the owner of the junk shop said or didn't say, who bashed the corner off, and so on. Sharing these stories invites more conversation, more wondering and gives depth to the objects we live with.

It may seem an obvious thing to say, but everything, ourselves included, exists in relation to other things and people. The clearest way is in the present: we sit on a chair in order to sit at a table in order to eat some breakfast that was in the fridge. These are the relations of the present and it's very easy for children to live in this 'present', particularly if most of their lives is laid on for them. There is no immediate need to question anything or find out about stuff, because it just sits there and, mostly, they just fit their lives into it. But everything – ourselves included – also exists in relation to other things (and people) backwards in time, in history. The chair I'm sitting on was bought or acquired from someone in the past. So was the table, the fridge and the food. Each of these things has a personal history and also a 'cultural' history. These histories are explanations for why it's a chair you're sitting on and not a stool or the floor, or the shape of the table and what wood it's made of, or the food you're eating.

Now, all this is usually much too complicated and abstract to talk about with children out of the blue. Talking like that is what I'm calling 'unattached' or 'unfixed' knowledge. Talking about such things separated off from real things that the children know and live with is likely to end up forgotten even as you're saying it. If you go through an episode (like the one about my parents and the 'desk' dressing table), though, you find yourself face to face with precisely this interesting fact about how we exist: as part of the present and as part of the past simultaneously. The point about junk shops, car boot sales and the like is that they offer up loads of odd, intriguing things that take us to the very point where past and present meet: we stand in the shop in the present trying to fit an object from the past into it.

Loads of feelings to do with our memories of parents and grandparents are often wrapped up with why we might like that jug, or dislike that table. By talking about all this, having fun with it, investigating it, we fill out our children's lives, make them more multi-dimensional than the one dimension of the present. The one-dimensional present is how ads and shopping are usually presented to us: you want this car, don't you? If you buy it now, you will feel wonderful, now. So, you buy the car, now, and you drive it, now. With children, it's quite hard to break through the ordinariness and unquestioning, that's-the-way-it-is nature of this 'now'. As I say, junk shops and old stuff of any kind may, if nothing else, take us into this other dimension of the past, where lives were different, people made things differently, behaved differently towards each other. Not necessarily better or worse, just different. And my view is that the business of 'comparing and contrasting' is a great tool that we humans have invented to enable us to think up new possibilities of how to live, how to change things. Long live junk shops and car boot sales.

Back in the present, I hate it when people are rude to the men and women on the tills in supermarkets. Another reason for trying to conscript children to do the shopping run is to show them that treating people with contempt is horrible, or vice versa – that thanking people and wishing them well is right and a good thing to do. People behind tills are no better or worse than anyone else and it upsets me to hear shoppers behaving as if someone on a checkout deserves being shouted at simply because they are on a till. Why should the act of buying a heap of groceries give us the right to boss around someone doing your bill? Again, thinking of my parents, they made a point – perhaps once too often! – of explaining and showing us that. We can talk about these things in finger-wagging, sermonizing ways as much as we like, but it won't really make much sense to children unless they see us in action, behaving in that way as part of everyday life.

Shopping at its most basic level is also arithmetic. If we can bear to slow down, if we get our children to do the calculations we're doing in our heads about quantities, costs and change, we show them that these are practical sums. I suspect that one of the reasons I wasn't much good at arithmetic is that my parents were both very quick at it. Though they got me to pay the milkman, do the weekly shop, take clothes to the launderette or 'nip across the road to the newsagent' to buy the paper, more often than not the sums were done for me. Though I loved to watch the gasman tot up the shillings and pence he took out of the gas meter, pile them up on the table, he did that, not me. There's something odd, isn't there, spending time with our children helping them with their arithmetic homework, but not spending time with them doing the arithmetic of shopping? I'm as guilty of this as anyone! Sometimes the sums involve exactly the same things they're supposed to be learning – addition, subtraction, multiplication and division. I remember when I was a child, a fair used to come to where we lived. The show-people's children were quite often put in the kiosks to collect our money. I was always amazed at how quick they were with the change and working out how many goes we had left. Now, I find it quite ironic to think that these children were almost certainly regarded as being hopeless cases when it came to traditional schooling and yet here they were, mastering one of those traditional skills: the arithmetic of money. Perhaps, given the right encouragement and the regular chance to use them in similarly practical ways, they could have mastered some other traditional skills.

Before we actually get ourselves to the shop there is the list. I've often thought that working with a child on lists is one of the best things we can ever do to help them get the hang of sorting out what a person needs to do in life, what order to do them in and how the very business of turning thoughts into words on a page (or on the memo app on a phone) is among the most useful things we'll ever learn. It shows us that putting all that thinking into slow motion – that's making the list – has its rewards at the end: we come home with everything we thought we needed. It helps us in working out budgets, choosing between what we want and what we really need. That's surely something worth helping children to get the hang of too.

I've found that even the youngest children love doing this, especially if they can't write! I mean, they love having a piece of paper and doing what we might think of as 'pretend writing'. People in education prefer to call it 'emergent writing' – an important stage in getting what writing is for and what you have to do to achieve it. After all, there is nothing 'natural' about making squiggles on a page that then enable you to make sounds, which lead to you having thoughts, which in turn allow you to get things done. What's more, you can't expect children to leap from the point at which they don't know this to the point at which they do know it, simply because we tell them that this is what writing is. How much easier it all is for a child, if they see it and feel it in action. So, while we as adults make our list, our very young children can make their 'list' of squiggles and bring it with them. When they're a bit older and can write the kinds of squiggles we call words, I've often given up on making a list myself altogether and asked them to be my guide:

'What else do we need? Is there anything on there we haven't got yet?'

This way of shopping also puts children closer to the food and other purchases in the home. These haven't arrived by magic, or care of the domestic fairies who look after them. They've arrived care of the effort that people have put into it.

When it comes to the 'what' of shopping, there are of course many, many directions we can go in, if we talk openly about why we buy this rather than that. The whole debate about 'healthy' food is played out in concrete detail each time we shop for it. Anything that children hear in school, see, hear or read in the media is directly related to the shopping lists we make with them, or the face-to-face meetings we have when we get to the shops. This is a brilliant lesson in 'theory and practice'. What we might know and say is right (that's the 'theory') may not be what we actually do (that's the 'practice'). This is fascinating to children. We know that one of the most common accusations they make against us is: 'But you said . . .'

So, face to face with food on a supermarket shelf, we are forced to think, Will this harm me? or Will it harm me if I only eat a little of it? And so to food labelling. This is a hot topic. By sharing the issue of food labelling with our children, we and they are right in the middle of a debate that we and they can hear regularly on TV and radio. The moment this becomes all joined up and we are looking at the labels with children, we are discussing big concepts like truth and lies, information versus lack of information, language to inform or language to deceive. We can talk about the exact meaning of words like 'healthy', 'reduced fat', 'scientifically proven', 'no additives' and the mystery of 'E' numbers. We have hundreds of examples of this language and science – or non-science – sitting in our fridges and cupboards.

And it applies to off-the-shelf medicines too. I often wonder how many of us have fully got the hang of the fact that a) we can take ibuprofen *and* paracetamol, b) some off-the-shelf medicines for colds and flu contain ibuprofen *or* paracetamol, c) if we take those medicines it's dangerous to take ibuprofen or paracetamol if the medicine contains it, d) but we can take the one that is *not* in that medicine. So if we want the kind of relief that medicine gives you, it's good to know. (Incidentally, this is a little lesson in logical thinking!)

However, the information we need in order to know all this is usually written in very small print on the sides of the medicines or on the sheets inside. Getting young children to understand the point of reading labels gives them a great foundation for treating them seriously later.

Same goes for looking at the labels that tell us about the country of origin and what anything else apart from food and medicines is made of, or any other claims made by such labels as 'Fair trade'. This might be no more than the extraordinary fact that a shelf full of goods of any kind may well be showing us the output from a score of countries across the world. Or, it might trigger off more political concerns about the conditions of work that produced that shirt, that picked those bananas or made that chair. Our children see programmes about this. Again, the label is the link. Then again, if one shirt says it's '100% cotton' and the other says it's '50% polyester', why should that matter? And why did I – a highly educated twenty-one-year-old – put my absolute favourite, very posh, all-wool sweater in a hot dryer at the launderette? Because being 'educated' isn't the same as having the 'nous' to read a flipping label! That's been a good egg-on-face story to tell children.

And it's at the shop level that the economy of high streets is being worked out. When I was a child, a high street hardly changed. The shops that were there when I was four were mostly still there when I was seventeen. In most places in Britain today, it's very different. Shops are opening and closing, many lie empty, some are demolished to make way for supermarkets, and there is a shift away from what are clearly single-owner businesses to chains and franchises.

This is a great thing to talk about with our older children. Right under our noses, at eye level, discussions about prices, convenience, variety, cost of living, standard of living, quality of life, minimum wage, small businesses, online versus face to face and the rest are going on in and around the shops we see and use. There's a chain of questions and possible answers, running from the cost of a pound of tomatoes to how the whole economy is run. Ultimately, this is about whether we think everything is just about as good as it's possible to get or whether we think anything should change – and if so, how. These kinds of discussions can be very airy-fairy and not very connected to how we live. Walking past an empty shop might mean nothing more than a slight moment of regret that no one mentions very much. Or it could be part of talk and debate that comes and goes again and again about why a shop might close. This then turns into the way we understand, agree or disagree with what politicians and commentators are saying to us on TV.

Alongside shops, there are plenty of other buildings in streets that can make us scratch our heads and start conversations: the post office, places of worship, the converted chapel or church, the library, fire station, garage, the pop-up, the squat. If we think of a street as if it's a book, we can help our children 'read' it. We can do a lot of this simply by wondering out loud. This not only starts something up but it encourages the children to wonder out loud too.

What is that illuminated board in the window of the post office with little flags and numbers on it? It tells you about 'exchange rates'? What's an exchange rate? It's when you want to go to a country that doesn't use pounds. You have to buy some of the money in that country? You can buy money? Yes. Why don't we all have the same money?

Talking of post offices, the red postboxes in the street tell a little story. On each of them there is a monogram of the king or queen who was on the throne at the time it was made and put there. The monograms themselves are mostly interesting shapes – and difficult to draw – but they tell us how old the postbox is. It always seems incredible to me when I see one with Queen Victoria's monogram on it. It means that it must have been put there before 1903, which means that people have been putting letters in it for over a hundred years. How many letters is that? And what wonderful or terrible or amazing things have been told in those letters?

Then, there are places of worship. If it's one we don't usually go into, we can of course ask if we're allowed to go in and look. If not, what is the religion? What do people do in there? Schools do a lot to tell some of this but, again, it's good to make the link between what the children might learn about the religion and the buildings and people coming in and out of them. Christianity poses interesting questions the moment we realize that there are many kinds of buildings for the different branches of the religion. What does 'Unitarian' mean? What's the difference between a chapel and a church? What is a 'Friends' Meeting House'? Some churches put witty and pithy slogans up outside: 'We are the soul agents in this area!', 'There are some questions that can't be answered by Google', 'Down in the mouth? Come in for a faith lift.' I'm not a follower of any religion but these posters and signs are always worth a conversation or two. What do they mean? Who are they for? And of course children are interested in what we believe and why.

I'm Jewish in origin so I know a bit – not very much – about synagogues and so we might have conversations about the different branches of Judaism, or my children have sometimes asked me how is it possible for me to call myself a Jew if I don't go to any synagogue. Good question! Some synagogues are now completely anonymous, with no sign outside. This has led to conversations about who has attacked synagogues in the past and why. Other times, they've asked about why some Jews wear hats and some have curly side-locks. We can talk about our beliefs or our origins or what other people believe in open or closed ways. A closed way is to suggest that what we are saying is the only right way. An open way is to say clearly, 'This is what I believe', while making plain that other people believe other things. I've always thought that being open and honest about my origins, my non-belief and my belief in religious toleration was probably the best way to do this. Sometimes these conversations have led into such topics as how do I decide what to believe if it doesn't come from a church or synagogue? Big stuff!

Old traditional churches in Britain are usually open for visiting and they are of course not only places of worship but also museums and offer an incredible show of architecture, sculpture, wood-carving, tiles, stained glass and much more. Quite often there is a little booklet on sale that explains the history of the building and why it's named after a particular saint. Whether you are a believer or not, this is part of the history of where we live, and much of what we read and hear is represented by the shape and look of these buildings. A civil war and the execution of a king resulted from these matters, and there are traces of these battles in many of the speeches that politicians make and in most English literature written before 1900. Just being curious about why one church looks different from another can be a trigger to take us and our children down a route thinking about that.

There are naturally hundreds of inscriptions in and around

churches and graveyards. These are keyholes into how people lived and died and how people wanted to commemorate each other. In some churches, there are less obvious carvings such as gargoyles outside, carved heads high up at the top of pillars or on the ceilings or sometimes under the wooden seats at the front of the church in the part called the choir. These carvings are often funny, sometimes rude, sometimes in a strange code showing, say, something like a monkey carrying a purse. Sometimes they tell a story from the Bible. There may be a booklet on sale that explains these. Sometimes, if they are too rude, they don't!

And of course in some high streets, we still have a library. What can I say about libraries?! I would say (wouldn't I?) that these can be among the most important places we can take our children to. If we can't afford to buy books then we should never forget we have actually already bought the books in our library. They're ours. Another fact to remember is that it's not only the books on show or even the books being borrowed from that library that are available. We can order up books from right across the library service. And again, if we are a member of a library, we can get ebooks for free too. We don't have to go online and pay for them.

As far as children are concerned, the most important gift we give them by taking them to a library is the skill of browsing. I have written about this elsewhere in this book, but let me say it once more. Taking a young child again and again to one of the big book-boxes that are on the floor in children's libraries, or going to a shelf with them and looking across a range of books on a given subject or theme is a massive education in how we store and order knowledge. This isn't just an exercise in 'book knowledge' but in the way we store all knowledge –

online as well. If a very young child knows about looking, scanning, rejecting, choosing – moving on to somewhere else – and then doing it again, then unpicking and unpacking the huge jungle of the internet is that much easier.

Another tip: we should always try our hardest *not* to choose our children's books for them. Or if we do, let it be one or two, and the child choose more than we select for them. When we don't choose for them, we give them a chance to see if the reasons why they pick one book over another are good. Have they brought home a book that is interesting or not? If not, why not? What else could they do to find one that *is* interesting? What would happen if they talk to the librarian? How does a library show you where all the books are – even the ones you can't see on the shelves?

The other great thing about libraries is that they're full of books we think we're not interested in. If we let ourselves wander away from our comfort zone and stroll around the shelves, look at the recommendations' trolleys and posters, we come across ideas and worlds that we probably would not come across anywhere else. Libraries are mind-changing, outlook-changing, life-changing places.

Most libraries let children borrow at least ten books at a time. This is like a curriculum all of its own. This can be the curriculum that our children make for themselves and with us. They can follow their noses, follow their lines of interest, grab whatever takes their fancy, or follow up series and favourites. This curriculum is like a parallel to the curriculum laid down at school. What's vitally important is that it's one that our children choose, make and re-make.

One of my great delights in life is to talk to parents who have come into a library with their children because they can't afford to buy books, and perhaps because they (the parents) can't read

English very well. I look at the expressions on their faces as they watch their children drinking up the books. It reminds me of the stories my father told me about his grandparents – who couldn't read English very well – taking him to the local library in Whitechapel in London. This is where he learned that quality he passed on to me: entitlement. We are entitled to find out about and learn anything we want. Books in libraries tell us exactly that. And it's one of the most powerful ideas we will ever get. Just by going regularly to a library we learn that. It doesn't cost any more than the council tax we've already paid. In that sense it's free. By the way, every single thing I talk about in this book has a book about it in a library somewhere!

Finally, in this chapter, we can think about markets.

Many markets are raw, in-your-face places. They have a very different feel from shops and supermarkets. For a start, you can usually smell them and hear them much more strongly than shops and supermarkets. And then, markets show us the changes that happen in how we live much more quickly. In the part of London where I lived, the markets used to reflect that its population was largely Jewish. The stalls and shops next to the stalls sold food and goods that had links to the countries where the Jewish population came from: Poland and Russia mainly. The language that the stall-holders and the shoppers spoke in the market was the one they spoke in Poland and Russia – Yiddish. As that population moved out and new communities came in, the stalls and shops changed, the foods and goods changed, the languages changed. The market became Greek, Caribbean, Chinese, Ghanaian, Indian, Bangladeshi, Nigerian and so on. Sometimes the cultures overlapped and mixed: you could buy bagels filled with halal meat, cassava started turning up on stalls that had only ever sold 'English' root veg like carrots and parsnips. The street cries changed as people of, say, Indian or Turkish origin started calling out their wares. The sounds on the CD stalls changed from reggae to West African . . .

Not all markets are so international, but to a greater or lesser degree they all show change and experiment. Stall-holders are usually people who will test the buying public the moment their sales go down, or the moment they see that another guy is doing well with his gear.

All this gives us plenty to spot, plenty to listen to, plenty to figure out. A shifting, changing scene is more likely to start a conversation than a static one. If a new food turns up on a market-stall, we can ask people what it tastes like, where it comes from and how to cook it. If we hear music coming out of the speakers on a stall, we can ask to buy it. If we go regularly to a market, it doesn't take long for stall-holders to know who we are and conversations start.

And there is stall-holders' public lingo: 'strawbs', 'two pound banana', 'cukes', 'bowl of apples' and the more private lingo that you might sometimes hear: 'cabbage' (meaning clothes rejected by the factory), sums of money like a 'monkey' and a 'pony' and all sorts of words and expressions of Romani and Yiddish origin like 'shmatte' meaning rubbishy clothes.

Many markets have a very long history, particularly those in town squares or village high streets. In a local library there'll be pictures of these going back many years. Sometimes these are related to the 'fairs', the seasonal events, which often needed a charter from the local aristocrat or even the king. This may be on display in a local museum. On its own, sitting on a wall, or in a book, it won't mean very much. Linked to the living market, that we can and do go shopping in, is a way for history to mean something. What did the charter say that the stall-holders could or could not do? What did it say about people getting drunk and fighting? Does the market today ignore some of these clauses – e.g. if they are to do with music?!

Farmers' markets have brought a bit of change, though in some ways they hark back to what markets always were – and still are in places like France. Local – or nearly local (!) – people bring to where we live, stuff that they've grown and made. I, for one, find the food on offer at these usually absolutely delicious, if expensive. I'm a total sucker for the olive stalls, Middle Eastern cooked food stalls, and anyone selling burgers, cider, honey or crêpes. It may not be the cheapest way to spend a couple of hours, and perhaps I've been 'done' more than once – a subject for a chat in itself – but the sheer pleasure of drinking a warm, mulled cider with a crêpe in the cold, open air somewhere, along with my family, each of us eating and drinking stuff we've chosen, talking about where the food comes from and why we like it, has been wonderful. I like the way the farms and stalls sometimes have leaflets with explanations of how they produce this and that, where they're from, why they are organic, or where the recipe comes from. When we come home with leaflets like that, we can leave them around for a day or two, so that we read them and make the connection between words on a page and the flavours, smells and sounds of the day we were there.

This may lead to all kinds of conversations about factory-farming, herbs and spices, the meaning of words like 'mulled' and the supposed or real health-giving properties of a certain kind of soap or oil. These are conversations that may never take place anywhere else. It's the effort of going, sampling, talking and reading that opens up these new topics. And it just happens. There doesn't have to be a lesson or a talk or an event. All we need to do is go, have a nice time and stay friendly with each other while we're doing it!

UP ABOVE

Looking up gets us thinking about whole buildings. It's very easy to walk down streets and residential roads without ever really taking in what's going on above eye level and how whole buildings are made.

The word 'architecture' always sounds like something highly technical and expert. In a way, we are all experts on architecture because we live in and around buildings. Not a day goes by without us using buildings. They are all 'architecture'. We may not have many words to describe them, we may not have the right technical words to describe them, but we all use buildings. What is quite rare, though, is for us to have many conversations about all these different buildings. And yet, the buildings are not only part of how we live, they also make the shapes that outline where and how we live. A small space will pretty well guarantee that we move in one kind of a way. A very large high space may well result in us moving in another kind of a way. Standing in a Manhattan street is a very different experience from standing on a road that has two-storey residential houses all along it, in the type of road that was called 'ribbon development'.

One way to start thinking about houses, flats, factories, churches and the like is to wonder how old they are. The older buildings have plaques with dates, and occasionally churches and town halls have 'foundation stones' with the names of dignitaries who laid the stone. Sometimes these older buildings are under threat of demolition and there are campaigns to keep them. If this matters to us, it will raise all sorts of questions about who decides which buildings get demolished, which ones stay – and why? Is a building worth preserving just because it's old? Quite often these conversations take us to the matter of what old buildings are made of and who lived there, or what was made there.

It's not obvious to children – or to us – what buildings are made of, and when you look up, above shops, or to second storeys, there are a whole lot of 'features' that may well go by unnoticed: bits of plasterwork with faces or shell shapes, coloured bricks, zigzag markings, bits of wood, cast iron, terracotta twirly bits on the edges or tops of roofs. We don't have to know about these things to be curious about them. That's what I mean about us all being architects – of a kind. We may not be able to design houses but we can look at their appearance.

When I was growing up, we lived in the suburbs, and suburban houses are a fascinating hodge-podge of styles. Sometimes they vary from street to street, sometimes from house to house. Even if the houses in a street were all built to the same design, by now, after eighty or ninety years, the people who lived in them have changed the doors and windows, altered the front gardens, built different fences and walls. On TV, there are of course hundreds of programmes about this sort of thing, but as we're out and about we can see how people have made these alterations themselves, sometimes as a total bodge, sometimes with a touch of fantasy and originality. What could have been a very boring walk to the doctors can turn into a bit of porch-spotting. How many different kinds of porch can we spot? I am an unashamed sentimentalist when it comes to curved windows.

When I was a child, I thought that curved windows on houses, shops and tube stations were slick and streamlined. They reminded me of swish cars and transatlantic ships. Whenever I see one, I point it out: 'Curved window!' It's very irritating for anyone near me – even more so now that I've started spotting where people have removed the curved windows and put in flat windows that go round the curve in the architecture like the edges of a hexagon, say. Irritating though it might be, it means that the children sometimes do window-spotting themselves.

Then there's the shape of arches: round or pointy? The Romans built some churches and castles out of stone, and some of these have survived. Their arches to doorways and windows were round. Then a few hundred years later people decided to make pointy windows. At various times, people have been very keen on rectangles – rectangular windows with rectangular panes – as were the Georgians, for instance. All this makes the landscape of houses, factories, schools, blocks of flats and the like an extraordinary hodge-podge of originals and 'revivals' of these different styles. When the modernists turned up in the twentieth century, they tried to think up functional ways of making windows plain and simple. Their windows and door shapes were made of squares and rectangles – but without loads of panes. Meanwhile, the Arts and Crafts movement liked the look of country cottages with little windows divided up into little panes.

When we look at buildings – from top to toe, as it were – we can see all these different styles, old and new, original and revived, jostling with each other. Occasionally, something from completely outside any of these main types crops up. We live in an area where the windows and shapes come from somewhere else altogether: they are imitations of the kind of houses the British built on hillsides in India during the time of the Raj! This reminds me that for many years people have often built houses as echoes of somewhere else or of another time. What's all that half-timbering about, if it isn't as a memory of the Tudors and the Elizabethans?

Blocks of flats and offices have a history too. When I was a boy I thought that 'mansion flats' – those red-brick blocks built somewhere around the turn of the nineteenth and twentieth centuries, with glass doors at the entrance – looked wonderful. They seemed so swish, and people in children's books from long ago lived in them! Other kinds of flats going back to the same time or earlier were built first by philanthropic bodies such as Peabody and then by councils. Quite often there are plaques on the wall when it's Peabody and the like. We can look at these and find out how they used to run their buildings, locking the gates at night, or demanding teetotalism. Council-built blocks have been vilified for years, but that's mostly been either because councils didn't have the money to keep them in good nick, or because the government of the day has run a propaganda campaign against social housing – or both.

Public building in the post-war era has been a story of prefabrication, right from the prefabs to tower blocks. Children play with Lego and other construction games and it's fun to think what's similar and what's different about building with Lego and building with prefabricated chunks. There's also the strange matter of 'brick-effect' buildings going up all around us. Apparently, we all like the look of brick but having bricks and bricklayers is 'not economic'. So now they build with breeze blocks and put sheets of brick-effect material on to the breeze blocks. Hey presto – buildings that look like the buildings we like. Or not. It's fun to explore all this with children too.

I'm a plaque-spotter. More and more local authorities are putting up plaques and memorials and these are part of the whole world of statues, memorials, cenotaphs and the like. These are all possible starting points for conversations. The older the plaque, the more intriguing the description of the person: 'engraver', 'philanthropist', 'founder of the Salvation Army'. Local councils have taken to marking interesting or important events and institutions. There are flats marked with the date that a rock star recorded his song there, or where something was broadcast from. Wars and battles are commemorated on plaques next to flower-beds. How odd that scores of men went from this village or that town to fight in a place called the Crimea! Where is the Crimea and why did those men have to go there? Or did they choose to go? Sometimes the plaque tells us that there used to be a building on this site. Why do they say that? What was important about that building? My favourite above all is the one that marks the place where Shakespeare first put on his plays, even before he put them on at the Globe. It always seems amazing that this was in Hackney and I found the account (in a library!) of how the men who owned the theatre dismantled it and took it across the River Thames to go towards building the Globe.

Anyone or any event on a plaque will link to something we can find online or in a book. I know it's irrational but I've often found that something local to where we live is that bit more interesting. You might tell me about the fact that there were prisoners of war in Britain during the First World War. Yes, I'm interested. You tell me that there was a prisoner-of-war camp where my son and I play football every Sunday, and suddenly I'm all ears. Tell me more, where exactly? Why here? Were they mistreated? Why isn't there a plaque? Oh there is, I hadn't noticed it! A buzz around the house or – better still – even while you're kicking a ball about, say, can open up a whole line of thought about wars and taking prisoners or something specific about that particular war. What was it for? How many died?

Sometimes there are events and people we know of who we think might be worth a plaque. I remember once just as I was walking down the steps into Bethnal Green Station, a local-sounding father was explaining to his daughter that once, many years earlier, lots of people died here because they were trying to shelter from the bombs. At the time there was no plaque there marking that sad moment – though there is now. My wife and I made a radio programme about the two music-hall song-writers Weston and Lee who wrote, among other things, 'Goodbye-ee' and some of Stanley Holloway's monologues. We dug around a bit and found out that one of them had lived in a road very near us, and later lived in a house a couple of miles away that was still standing. We tried to get a plaque put up for them, but failed. We tell our children about that.

Also up above eye level are the shop names, pub signs, church names and street names (though some of these are mysteriously at waist level just where people can stand in front of them or even lean on them so that you can't read them!).

In a way, the names of shops and the signs that go up in shop windows are like a dialect all of their own. Whether it's the jokey names of hairdressers and cafés, or the signs urging us to buy this or that, there is a whole language of the street (not 'street language'!) that tries to attract us. I think we should play along with this, revel in it, be inventive with it, make up jokes alongside it.

Here are some real shop names:

Wokaholic (Chinese Wok restaurant)
Exchange and Smart (second-hand clothes)
Wooden it be Nice (door salvage)
Abra Kebabra (kebab joint)

Rhythm and Booze (off-licence)
Norman D. Landing (ex-army clothes)

I've had some fun with my children misreading (in other words, pretending to misread) signs. I never call 'CAFFÈ NERO' by its proper name. I always tell my children that it says, 'CAFFÈ NERD'. When we go past 'Chooks' (which only sells chicken meals) I do a mock dialogue that goes something like this:

'What would you like, sir?'
'I'll have some fried chicken, please.'
'Sorry, sir, we don't do chicken. We've only got chicken.'
'OK, then, I'll have some chicken.'
'Thank you, sir, but I should point out that the chicken isn't available today. It's chicken today.'
'Right, I'll have the chicken then.'
'Very good, sir. Would that be without the chicken?'
'No, with the chicken please.'
'Sorry, sir, we're not doing that one with the chicken today. We're doing it with the chicken.'

And so on . . .

Another fun thing to do is look at the lettering of the shop names and try to imitate it in a notebook. A good deal of the last hundred years or so in the history of typefaces is wrapped up in the way shop-front names are written. And people are always inventing new ways to express the feel of their shops.

Some shops have lists of what they do or what they sell outside. If you chant these, they often make a rhythm, even a kind of poem. If you shunt them around, you can turn them into a kind of rap: 'Make-up, nail art, waxing, facials, airbrush, spray tan, manicure, pedicure.'

You can turn that into:

Make-up, nail art, waxing, manicure
facials, spray tan, airbrush, pedicure.

Sometimes it's fun to be plain daft: 'Hey look, it's called Crocodile Antiques, shall we go in and see if they sell crocodiles?'

If the children used to say the names of the shops in a different way when they were toddlers, it's fun to talk about that. One of my children called Marks and Spencer 'Marks an' 'spensive'.

Sometimes, when renovations are being done, you get a glimpse of old shop names and old shop signs underneath the modern ones. They're reminders of the previous history. Books and booklets of local history are nearly always full of photos of what the high street looked like in the past. It's fun to pore over these looking for similarities and differences.

If a shop name coincides with anyone you know, or indeed with your own family name, it's amusing to pretend that there is a link and see what happens. When I was about seven my dad took me to the Geffrye Museum. When we came out, he said, 'Hey, look over there. There's your butcher's shop.' Over the road from the museum there was a butcher called 'M. Rosen'. I think it must have been the first time I had ever seen my name written up big somewhere, and I can remember getting a feeling of excitement. For half a moment, I thought that it was me! Or at the very least, I was confused at why my name was there. Of course, my dad admitted right away that he was just having me on, but it's moments like these that remind us that all these very permanent-looking names and signs are put there by people thinking about lettering, colours, which part of their names to use, or indeed whether to make up entirely new ones.

*

Pub signs offer another kind of conversation, especially as sometimes they are deliberately 'wrong' with a picture of a brick-
layer's arms (limbs!) as opposed to the Guild of Bricklayers'
arms. As a boy, I lived near a pub called the Oddfellows' Arms
and there are plenty of other 'Arms' that are remembered.
Occasionally, local or mythic characters are remembered like
Old Parr, Mother Shipton or Mother Red Cap, Man in the
Moon. The gentry, aristocrats and monarchs abound: Marquis
of Granby, Duke of Cambridge and many Queens and Kings.
You can find all sorts of animals, boars, bulls, eagles, lambs –
most of which have some symbolic importance, often Christian.
It's said of some that they owe their origins to very old events:
the Saracen's Head supposedly dating from the Crusades, and
the Seven Stars to the religious significance of the constellation
of the Plough in medieval times. The Ship may well be a distant
reference to Noah's Ark. In the modern era the naming has been
done for different reasons: sometimes for a jokey, olde worlde
feel, sometimes to make the place sound French, sometimes
because it's a chain. Pubs are closing at a fantastic rate and
sometimes the signs have gone. It can be interesting to spot the
lost pub. Sometimes high up on what is now a house, you can
see in the plasterwork, 'The Swan' or some such.

There are really nice little books on pub names (another
trip to the library) and plenty of the names have entries online.
The descriptions of drinking in pubs in books by people like
Dickens and Thomas Hardy – or even the drinking scenes in
Shakespeare's *Henry IV Part I* – link up with these inn signs,
names and buildings. Sometimes, the buildings themselves are
very special, with Georgian, Jacobean, Elizabethan and occasionally even earlier parts of the building still in use. It's quite
something, I always think, to sit in a pub having a meal with
your children and pointing up at a beam and saying, 'It says

here that that beam has been there for over four hundred years . . . and it's even older than that because once it was part of a ship!'

When it comes to street names, we can say that every street name has a history.

Some are named after people. They may have been famous people, local dignitaries and landowners, or just the local builder. Famous people could be saints like St John, or St Thomas; Priestley Close was named after the Unitarian and chemist who discovered oxygen and who fled Britain. (With saints' names, if you fancy it, you can play the apostrophe game: seeing how many times the name has an apostrophe: St Michael's Road. And how many times not: St Michaels Road.)

Sometimes street names are memories of the trade that went on there: Butcher Row, Pickle Herring Street, Skinner Street.

Often they are memories of important buildings: Old Paradise Street – a name given to streets that passed by graveyards; Orchard Place – from an old pub on the site called the Orchard House.

Sometimes they describe what the road looked like: Green Lanes, Holloway (i.e. Hollow Way or sunken road – often sunk as a result of hundreds of years of cattle being driven down it).

Sometimes they tell us where you'll get to if you carry on down it: London Road, Basildon Road.

In some names you can spot reminders of old rivers and wells: Stamford Brook, Fleet Street.

In others, it's an activity that people have remembered in the name. I was brought up in Love Lane. The story was that it was where lovers went to do their loving.

So we can think of ways to chat about these: 'I wonder why it's called Meeting House Lane . . .'

'Hey, look at that one: Cheapside. I wonder why it's "cheap" and what "side" is it on?'

'Poultry? Not much point in calling it that. Poultry can't read . . .'

YET HIGHER

Finally, right up high in the roads and streets where we live, there are the cranes, tops of towers and tower-blocks.

It's quite something to see, high up in the cabin, the crane-driver operating a crane. Even more exciting is watching the driver climbing up the stairway to get there. Indeed, looking up high often reveals people on harnesses, in slings, or on platforms and the like building, repairing, changing streetlamps, trimming trees. It's simple to stop for a moment and wonder out loud: 'I wonder what it would be like working up there every day?' And this leads to the matter of danger or the view, or the sight of birds, or the things they see that us lot down here didn't know they could see . . . !

Those high places are great for visiting for views over countryside, town or city – or indeed just a better view of the sky. If there are maps and guides at the place, so much the better. If not, you can use an app or map on your phone or one of those antique things – a real map!

Sometimes the walk up the tower or the lift ride is the exciting experience. Open spiral staircases make for strange snail-like photos; trying to go up the Empire State Building in New York has turned into a saga in our house. Rather than it being one ride up, it seems as if the various chunks of the lift (between 20th and 40th, say) have been franchised out, and so as you go up, guys are bidding for you to ride with them. They call out to you that they will take you non-stop to the 33rd floor, or halfway up for $50. And the wonderful but horrific thing about the top of the Empire State is that it's open to the weather. (Well, it was then. I don't know if it still is.) One of my sons has never forgiven me for getting him to climb the ladder into the top of the Statue of Liberty's head. He has remembered it as a piece of extreme Dad cruelty. He's in his twenties (at the time of me writing this) so it's lived on as a key moment.

The views we get from these high-up places are like living maps. Before the days of mapping instruments, high hills and the tops of trees served as alternative ways of knowing a land-scape, so there's no reason why they can't do the same for us.

Looking up at these high buildings and places gets us wondering about how they built them. The modern ones we see with cranes all around them, but how were the old ones built? And why don't they fall down? These are great questions to ask of guides if it's a famous tower with paid visits. Alternatively, we can try to look up how, say, Big Ben was built. And why exactly is the Leaning Tower of Pisa leaning? One of the reasons why those wood-block games, Lego and even sand on the beach are fun is because we can try to build as high as we can before the whole thing comes toppling down. Why does something only three feet high topple but the church tower has been standing there for four hundred years?

Talking of church towers, it's not only amazing that they go on standing for hundreds of years, but also the many different ways they're built. Again, you can start by just spotting that, counting the differences or drawing them. In travelling about, you start to see that one part of the country built its towers one way, and another part of the country in another way. Why would that be? In recognition that we like looking at these towers and wondering about them, more and more churches light up the towers at night, and this helps us to think and talk about them.

And of course, another good thing about church towers is that we can often hear them. I'm hopeless at picking up a tune. I like getting my wife or the children to sing the chimes for me, to see if they can teach it to me. It makes you think about how many bells are needed to make the tune, whether the bells are really being rung by a bell-ringer or they have got a mechanical way of doing it now. In a matter of moments you can get on to ring-tones on mobile phones and the person we know who has got – would you believe it – a ring tone of . . . ! No! Yes!

TRAVELLING
AND
HOLIDAYS

Most of us have bought into the idea that holidays will be a) fun and b) relaxing, yet we may well find that at least one of us is getting bored – or worse. Why not? There might be long journeys cooped up in small spaces, the worry that something might go wrong and endless wet days with nothing to do. And very few families have the experience, except on holidays, of all living together day in day out, for longer than a weekend. And yet we only booked the holiday because we wanted fun. And a rest. And then more fun. For some of us, we remember our holidays as children, teens and twenty-somethings and land with a bump when we realise that being on holiday with children is nothing like that. We have to find other ways of having fun.

TRAVELLING

Travel is hard. We all get anxious and frustrated – it's just that we do it in different ways. Children tend to show it by saying, 'I'm bored', 'Are we nearly there?' and inventing ways to annoy each other. I'm not going to pretend that it's simple to make long journeys easier. All I can say is that journeys do present opportunities for getting children interested in worlds 'out there', beyond what they're used to.

With a decline in audio experiences – or 'children's radio' as we used to call it – car journeys are the last refuge of the audio story. I get letters from people thanking me or cursing me for the hours that their family have listened to the audio of me reading my poems while they were on the way to Cornwall or Spain. I suspect that people like Martin Jarvis get the same – in his case for his many terrific performances of the William books.

Radio producers of children's and 'Schools' programmes back in the day used to talk of the 'world of the ear'. They believed that it was their job to use the human voice, sounds and music to evoke places, feelings, moments in the child listener's mind. It's a kind of storytelling, where the pictures of the people and places you're talking about are not brought to life through pictures. Instead, the listener has to do something in their mind to create visual images, using the words, hints and sounds coming from the audio.

If we consider that this is an important way to extend children's powers to think, then car journeys are a perfect time to introduce audio. Most bookshops sell a variety of CDs for children and you can find plenty more online either as iTunes or as CDs. If you think of solving the problem of a journey in terms of half-hours and not as one single problem, then there will almost certainly be at least a couple of half-hours in these.

Sticking with the audio, my own memory of the car is a time when the whole family listened to radio programmes and this often sparked off debates and arguments. My parents treated the radio as if it were someone sitting in the corner of the room (or car) who couldn't stop lying to them. It was 'outrageous' that this person was trying to dupe them and the rest of the world with these 'lies'. Even cultural programmes seemed to set them off on a running commentary of memories that ran counter to what they were hearing. As a child witness to these, it meant that voices on the media weren't telling us the gospel truth. A politician carefully explaining why he had brought in a policy would be rounded off with an expletive – sometimes in Yiddish or German – like 'Kvatsch!' (meaning 'rubbish', I think). As we got older, my brother and I grew bolder at challenging our parents for their interruptions. Perhaps we agreed with what the person on the radio was saying. Or perhaps we just wanted to hear what they were saying, so we would tell them to pipe down so we could get to the end of the programme without their interruptions, thank you very much. Other times, we were infected – in a nice way – by their enthusiasms for odd, offbeat corners of the radio schedule. That was how I got to hear – on car journeys and on holidays, as it happens – such programmes as *Under Milk Wood*, *Poets Reading Their Own Poems* and Alan Lomax's stunning field recordings of traditional singers. I have a strong and very fond memory of sitting round the car, mid-summer, with the car doors open, in the middle of a field on a campsite in Yorkshire, listening to one of the 'Radio Ballads' by Charles Parker and Ewan MacColl.

In fact, with so much music and so many different kinds of music on the radio, the fiercest debates are often about music. As a car full of people of different ages, there is a limit to the number of times everyone wants to listen to the CD of nursery rhymes that the four-year-old wants to hear over and over again. On the other hand, the jazz greats or Mahler's symphonies that you want to listen to won't necessarily be what flips the egg for the tweens and teens. In the give-and-take of 'I'll listen to yours if you listen to mine' is a cultural leap – opportunities to figure out what these passions for music are about. There's nothing more surprising than discovering that your children like the sound of something from thirty years ago, and that you like something that they like which came out two weeks ago.

On journeys back to London on a Sunday, we sometimes hit a programme made by a colleague of ours and my wife and I talk about how he makes it, what he's saying and what he plays. I find myself wondering if our children in the back are getting an experience similar to mine in our family car fifty years ago. It's as if there's a mini-history repeating itself: radio days on car journeys – fifty years of finding out that we don't agree with our parents!

Something else that crops up on car journeys is the fossil-fuel debate. I've found that the moment children do the environment at school, I've been challenged about why we're in the car, why we're using petrol, why we're pumping carbon into the atmosphere and how many animals and humans we're killing. These are good moments. It's when the science links up with real human activity and human wishes. Do we want to go somewhere warm where there's a beach? Is that something we could or should give up? What are the alternative ways of getting there? What are the alternatives to not going there at all?

I find that conversations about petrol head off into some of the most challenging and difficult questions of all. I listen more and more to people who appear on radio and TV talking about producing energy (or to be more correct, 'harnessing' it) in ways that don't produce carbon. I try to understand the technologies and practicalities of wind, bio, solar, wave and 'heat exchange' and – just as hard – the politics of it all. Put simply and naively, if it's all desirable and necessary, why isn't there an instant worldwide shift to it?

So, filling up the tank and getting back into the car can be one of those moments where we discuss all this. Needless to say, there is wonderful material about this online, and places like the Centre for Alternative Technologies in Machynlleth in Wales pose the problem brilliantly: the technologies have been invented so why aren't we using them more? As this is about the lives of our children after we've gone, these conversations are more than 'good' or 'interesting'. It's more than possible that they are about the destiny of the human race. I wonder out loud in front of my children if politicians' chit-chat today about 'the deficit' or 'interest rates' will in the future look absurd, trivial and irrelevant in the light of the environmental disaster that they knew about but didn't deal with.

At the same time, I don't think that this should be a reason for passing on our guilt and anxiety to children. It's my view that a good deal of the environmental action that reaches children is just this. Information comes in terms of such things as, say, how they should be turning off the electric light. This feels to me as if we adults are saying to children that what's happening to the environment is their fault. 'Turn off the TV at the socket or you children will burn up the atmosphere and we'll all die tomorrow!' When I see homework sheets or TV programmes that talk about turning off running taps, I think out loud about the kind of big political decisions that need to be made to really switch over to sustainable ways of living. I say provocative things like, 'Imagine the UN banning cars . . .' Getting back into the car, with the smell of petrol from the pump still lingering on my jacket seems like a good ironic moment to say that.

QUIZZES, WORD AND NUMBER GAMES

The real attention-grabbers during journeys in my experience have been weird quizzes, word or number games.

I laugh to myself (and at myself) that I, someone who doesn't like the exam and testing regime of schools, find myself on trains and in cars barking out, 'Who was Henry VIII's father?' Of course, I justify this by saying:

- my children said they wanted the quiz – it wasn't my idea (lies, I was the one who first got them hooked on it)
- nothing rests on it – they won't be judged, selected or segregated as a result (that's true)
- they often 'win' (only if I feel like it)
- as often as possible, get them to be the question-masters and quizzers (yes, that's really important)
- the games help us get to the seaside without them killing each other (except that the quizzes can be just another reason for them to start on each other).

Even so, a bit of me wonders whether I should be doing this, and, needless to say, I might even go on a bit about how terribly damaging to their mental health it is. ('Yeah, yeah, Dad, get over it and just ask us another question . . .')

So, here are some quizzes and games you may want to try.

GENERAL KNOWLEDGE

Get the children to pick their favourite subjects. This may well branch out so that they end up quizzing each other on such things as top performers on the TV shows that we adults haven't even heard of. This always sets me thinking about what rates as 'knowledge' in the world. By the time most children are eight or nine, they have vast amounts of 'knowledge' about stuff on TV, film and in music and almost none of it counts as valid or valuable in the world of school knowledge. They know hundreds of names, styles, words, catch-phrases, tunes, cultural origins, and none of it counts when it comes to being judged within education. Why is that? Will that seem strange in years to come? It's as if two streams of 'knowledge' run side by side without the one noticing the other. Is this why some children get to think that what's on offer in the one called school is so difficult or boring? Do such children think, If you ignore the stuff that I know about, why should I take an interest in the stuff that you keep going on about? Or, Why is my stuff so easy to know but the stuff you give me is so much harder?

When the children take over a general knowledge quiz, I wonder out loud about this. When it gets on to who wore what on a TV programme last week, I interrupt: 'Is this general knowledge?' pretending to be some old fart. I've even, at times, got them to imagine sitting in school being tested on this popular entertainment stuff alongside their maths, English and science tests. Why not? I say, pretending to be a not-old fart. (It's important to keep my children hopping about not knowing whether I am or am not an old fart, I always think.) I am, let it be said, someone who in 2014 got sent home after only one round of a famous TV quiz show because I didn't know the names of any of the 'One-hit-wonders'. My vast knowledge of all things deep and important was overthrown in front of millions when I was put face to face with the question: 'Who sang "Who Let the Dogs Out"?'

So the general knowledge quizzes I do with the children start off being quite *Mastermind*-ish sort of things but quickly get democratized by the children inventing subjects for themselves and quizzing each other, or – even worse – quizzing us. With older children, I've found that questions about band names or football line-ups drift alarmingly into exam revision. One moment you're doing, who won the FA Cup in 1971 and the next, which is the only artery in the body *not* to carry oxygenated blood? It's only long journeys that can produce such strange meetings.

CAR REGISTRATION PLATES

Car journeys offer the immense resource of car registration plates – that is, random and endless supplies of numbers and letters. You or your children can devise all sorts of games with these.

So, for example, you can challenge each other to make up words out of the letters you spot on the registration plates. One way of doing this is to give each other a word of the same number of letters and whoever is the first to complete their word is the winner. So one of you might say, 'dancer' and the other one gives back, say, 'hoping' and off you go hunting for the letters of those words off the registration plates.

Another way to use the letters is to have a competition to see who can make up the longest word from the letters you spot. Or, if you want to avoid competition, you do this co-operatively and see if together you can beat the family personal bests for, let's say, words beginning with A, then B, then C – and so on.

You can do this more simply by seeing collectively how quickly you can beat the family best for completing the alphabet in the right order or backwards in the right order . . . A car full of people shouting and pointing, 'THERE'S A "K"!' is a moment to be treasured.

Other versions of word-making on journeys can use the letters you see on road signs too – or only on road signs. So, let's say, you get the child to think of a word and you match it with a word of the same length. Then it's the first to complete the word by finding letters anywhere. To make it harder (in other words last longer), you say that you can only make the word from letters that appear as the *first* letter in words on signs.

Another letters game you might want to play involves picking a letter and a topic. So, you can say something like, 'six animals beginning with "T" '. If you want to give the game a bit of a pattern you can do this working through the alphabet. You can do it co-operatively or competitively. Or, you can use number plates as your cue. So you can take the highest number on the number plate you both see, pick one of the letters (e.g. 'M'), pick a topic (e.g. 'towns') and if that number was five then you would choose, say, five towns in the world that begin with 'M' . . . or as you want. Then it's the other person's turn. You use the apparent randomness of the number plates to make it all hang together.

You can also use the letters or numbers of the registration plates you see to play versions of the TV show *Countdown*. Instead of the source of the random letters and numbers being the tray that the presenter picks from, it's the number plates you spot. If you're doing this in your heads, rather than writing them down, it's easier to limit the number of letters or numbers you choose, otherwise it'll probably be too hard!

The simplest game to play with small children is the one where you call out a letter or a number and say, 'Can we see a nine!' and the like. To make it a bit harder, all you need to do is say, 'Can we see a number plate with the letter "C" *and* the number eight on it' – or any combination you come up with. Then you can up the skill with older children by saying, 'Can we make the word "cat" from the letters we see?' If it's competitive ('First person to see the number eight' and the like), it'll often end in tears, though, as the child psychologists frequently say, not all tears are destructive! Sometimes it's through the tears that children figure out for themselves how to solve problems amicably. Sometimes!

Some people are addicts of number plate cricket. There is the classic way to play this or, if you prefer, you can make up your own versions. At the heart of cricket is that you have six balls to bowl at a batter to try to get them 'out'. The batter has six chances to hit the ball and make runs. A batsman is out when you break his wicket, he is 'caught', 'stumped', 'run out' or got 'lbw'.

The simplest way to play is to ignore 'getting out' and just play who can make the most runs with six number plates that the bowler 'bowls'.

So, the bowler picks six number plates that the batsman has to be able to see. Together you tot up the runs on the six number plates. Then you swap over. Obviously, the aim of the bowler is to keep the scores down. With this version of the game you have to agree how long it takes for the bowler to do his 'run up' to bowl. It's best to do this by counting out loud together. So a game goes like this: you count together, say, 1, 2, 3, 4, 5 and bowl! The bowler has to pick a number plate that bowler and batter can both see. You call it out and add up the numbers. You do this six times and you remember the total. Then swap over.

There are much more complicated and sophisticated ways of playing number plate cricket that you can find online.

PLACE NAMES

Back with signs, there is the matter of place names. This is a wonderful and fascinating subject all of its own. The history of whatever the country, or part of the country you're in is in part told by place names. In England, for example, the dominant language of the place names is Anglo-Saxon, mixed in with bits of Celtic and Roman languages (thanks to the settlers before the Anglo-Saxons), Danish (thanks to the Vikings), French (thanks to the Normans), Latin (thanks to various users of Latin like the old Church) and so on. There are simple and not-so-simple books on this and plenty of information online for each place you go through. It really is worth the effort of digging around in this stuff. You quickly find that there are, say, a lot of names in England that end with '-thorpe', '-ham', '-by' and '-ton', '-bourne', '-cester' or use '-ing'. 'Why's that?' you can ask. Or, 'Let's see if we can find out what they mean.' When it comes to '-by' for example, it tells us that it was a settlement where people spoke Danish. This brings to life the fact that you're going through a place where the Vikings once lived. Though Scandinavia is a long way away and Scandinavians speak Icelandic, Norwegian, Swedish and Danish (and other dialects), here they are in this '-by' village, town or city. It always seems amazing that we've kept this memory alive in the place name. The name is like a tiny museum remembering each time we say it the peoples who came and named or re-named that place.

Go to another part of the British Isles and then other common parts of the names appear: 'Tre-' and 'Pen' in Cornwall, or 'Aber-' in Wales crop up a lot. Why is that? Quite often, there are locally produced books on sale in newsagents that tell the story of these names and they bring to life something of the history of the people who once lived in the place where you're staying.

You can play all sorts of games with place names. One is to imagine what the word of the place name would mean if it wasn't a place name. So, you could say that if Wembley was really a word you could say that if you felt a bit weak and feeble, 'I'm feeling a bit wembley today, so I'll stay in bed.' Sometimes you can cheat and a place name that ends in '-ham', for example, you can turn into '-em' and see if that makes a phrase. So the town of 'Witham' (pronounced 'wittem') you can turn into 'With'em' and tell your children that nearby there's a town called 'Against'em' . . . and they had a terrible fight. That's why people say, 'Are you with'em or against'em?' So, together you can make up mock origins of place names, breaking up the words into the syllables and inventing reasons why they came together in this particular place.

The shorter names are also good for trying to make up limericks. It's good fun to cheat a bit and squeeze words to rhyme with the place, or squeeze the pronunciation of the place so that it rhymes.

Sometimes, the people in a town pronounce the name differently from the way you might read the name. There's Marlborough and 'Morlborough', for example. Places called 'Beauchamp' are often pronounced 'Beecham' and 'Belvoir' as 'Beaver'. Americans find the '-cester' names hard and might pronounce 'Leicester' as 'Lye-sester'. Some people in or near Cirencester call it something like 'Sissester'. It's amusing, then, to come up with posh or American or local ways of pronouncing place names and these can also be squeezed into a limerick to make them work.

RAILWAY STATIONS AND TRAINS

Stations are incredible places, full of the history and use of technology. They also involve complicated systems of passing on information. Human beings have been at their most ingenious at inventing how to get trains through the landscape and into stations. Sometimes they've been at their not-so ingenious in telling us where to go and how to get the train we need – what is nowadays called 'signage'.

One activity to try is to pose these as problems that the children can attempt to solve: imagine how, 150 years ago, you've got to get a train to go under a river.

How do you dig a tunnel without the river falling in on top of you?

Who was the first to do it and how did they do it? (As it happens I often travel through this very first one!)

Children find tunnels interesting or even slightly frightening. And some tunnels are different from others. I was quite surprised that my thirteen-year-old daughter suddenly noticed that the tunnel we were in was bigger and more open than others and that it included two tracks and not just one. Quite by chance we were in the world's first passenger underground railway tunnel. This was a tunnel for steam trains. That coincided with a question she asked not long after about why the big stations in London had such high roofs and I remembered from my childhood how the steam trains used to line up pumping steam hundreds of feet into the air. 'I guess that it was because with a low roof,' I say, 'all the steam would have been pressed down on all the passengers . . .'

How do you get over a river?

What different styles of bridges are there?

Play spot the bridge style – also good for car travelling, especially on motorways.

And how do you get through a low hill without digging a tunnel?

The story of digging cuttings and who did it is an amazing one, so if anyone gets a bit interested in this, it's worth following up. Put it this way, in England alone, it is an extraordinary fact that the built environment of roads, railways and thousands of buildings has come about because of the back-breaking work of millions of Irishmen. Unless we notice such things, they are invisible.

The information that stations put in front of us is, for a child, confusing if not bewildering. There are scores of different typefaces, surfaces, sizes of lettering, strange words and phrases. If we stop for a moment and imagine ourselves back as that child, there really isn't much of a reason for knowing which sign or which word or which phrase is more important than another. There are so many signs saying 'Caution' or 'Warning' or 'Don't' while others direct us here, there and everywhere. The indicator boards are written in a kind of code and in some stations, you know that the station you will be going to won't appear – only the final destination of the train will show up on the board you're looking at.

I think the serious job we have in stations is as translators. We can – if we have time – ask our children to get us, let's say, from the mainline to the underground train; or from the mainline to the suburban line, so that they can get practice at it. Alternatively, we can use it as an excuse to muck about with this stuff.

Whenever I see the sign, 'Help point' or 'Trolley point', I tell my children that they are instructions: 'Help! Point!' or 'Trolley! Point!' as if trolleys need to be told to point.

A sign at one station reads, 'Dead slow pedestrians'. I always say, 'Where? Where are the dead slow pedestrians?'

'Look right!' – 'I'm looking fine, thanks.'

'Dogs must be carried' – 'Quick, find a dog. We're not allowed on here unless we've got a dog.'

'See more by boat' – 'That's handy because my glasses aren't powerful enough . . .'

I sometimes play the full stop game. At school, of course the children are taught how, why and when to use full stops. There's a kind of full stop frenzy as if one of the worst things that could ever befall you is if you leave one out. People on comments threads sneer and jeer at each other for leaving out full stops as this proves that the person who commits this error is sinful or stupid or both. Meanwhile, our stations are covered in full-stop-less sentences and phrases. And we don't mind. If the sign says, 'Meet the General Manager', we don't demand a comma, colon or full stop. If the sign says, 'Hold the handrail Keep clear of the edges', we don't get in a state because there was no full stop between 'handrail' and 'Keep' and we don't mind that 'Keep' has a capital 'K' even though there was no full stop in front of it. And mysteriously, the world doesn't come to an end. So, it's interesting to play the game of counting how many times the posters, signs and warnings have no full stop. Just as mysteriously, some of the signs *do* have full stops.

Who decides why there will be sometimes, and not at other times?

And why?

Who is the full stop judge?

And where does this judge sit?

Even more mysterious is the ad full stop that just appears. 'Mortgages.', says one ad. Another says, 'Planet. Sized. Brain.'

What?!

What's that about?

We know the reason: the people doing the ad decided that we would notice the ad more if they put those full stops in, and it's worked! I've noticed it. So there is another rule about full stops. It's the 'look at me' rule of putting full stops on posters – not one we learn at school. What we do, I guess, is lay our full stop reflex to one side and accept that it's OK 'in this context' – the context of posters and signs.

There is then, a poster-ese or 'sign-ish' language that doesn't obey the 'rules' that are laid down elsewhere. Even the sign 'No smoking' is, when you look at it long enough, a bit strange. How come we take the word 'no' to mean an instruction? If I were to write 'No raining', we wouldn't take it as an instruction. We might think of it as a description perhaps. So, what we have learned is that in some circumstances 'No' attached to an '-ing' word means 'don't'.

All this sort of thing is fun to play with children. It reminds them (and us) that there are many varieties of written English, and that some of the rules they are taught as definite, never-to-be-disobeyed rules don't apply when it comes to writing signs, posters and ads.

Does the sign 'STOP WORKS' mean, 'This bus stop is working'?

Does it mean, 'Stopping is something that works'?

Or does it mean, 'Stop! There are some works going on here'?

I guess, by the time we're about ten we've figured out that it's the last but it's entertaining to think out loud misremembering it and thinking of all the other things it could mean.

We can thus use the language of stations – all the signs and notices – to play with the fact that we write different kinds of language for different situations. As this kind of language use is not often talked about in schools, we are filling in a gap if we talk about it out of school, while gently questioning just how definite these rules really are. Interestingly enough, some of the signs to do with life-and-death questions – safety and danger signs – are those that 'disobey' the rules the most. So, when sticklers for rules say that full stops and the like can be life-and-death issues, I share my chuckles with my children and say, 'Except when it's posters, poster-ese and sign-ish rules instead.'

HOW MUCH LONGER?

Children ask questions about how long will it take to get there, how fast do we need to travel to get there by five o'clock and the like. You probably do this already, but if you don't this is one way to help them:

How many miles will I travel in 1 hour at 60 miles per hour?

Sixty miles.

If I turn that into minutes it's 60 miles in 60 minutes.

Or, 1 minute per mile; 1 mile per minute.

How long is the journey? One hundred miles.

So that will take – if we keep going at 60 miles per hour – 100 minutes. That's 1 hour forty minutes.

Travelling at 30 miles an hour will take us longer to do the same distance.

We only do half a mile in a minute.

So, it takes us 2 minutes for 1 mile.
That means 200 minutes for 100 miles.
That is 3 hours 20 minutes.

If you want to get into it, the equation is:

S = D/T (Speed = Distance over Time)

which can also be 'expressed' as:

Speed = 30 miles per hour (60 minutes) or 30/60 ('30 over 60' as we used to say).

If I keep the units the same:

30/60 is the same as saying 1/2 = half a mile in one minute.

In other words, if I travel at 30 miles an hour, I will travel half a mile in one minute.

Now change the speed and if we want to know the distance we'll do in a minute at this different speed, this distance will equal (let's say, for example) 45 miles per hour (60 minutes).

45/60 is the same as saying 3/4, so that's saying we'll do three-quarters of a mile in one minute.

In other words, if I travel at 45 miles per hour, I will do three-quarters of a mile in one minute.

Once you know how far you will travel in 1 minute, at a given speed, you can work out how far you'll get in 10 minutes or

98 minutes and so on. You multiply the distance you can do in one minute by the number of minutes. And as the children know, phones, tablets and computers have calculators on them to work out the sums you can't do in your head.

HOLIDAYS

Here are some things that you may well have done on holiday, but, if not, I can say that my own children have enjoyed these:

SPORTS DAY

I would never have guessed that this would work so well, but since my daughter was seven, she has organized us all (the family plus my wife's parents plus guest(s)) into an all-day sports day. This was her invention. We each have to choose a nickname for the day – mine is 'Dynamo Nebbish' – and she makes and issues us with admission tickets, which she sells to us on the day. She draws up a set of sports which includes welly-boot throwing, egg and spoon, boules, a bean-bag and bucket-filling time trial, sprints, long distance, paper-dart making and throwing. You can of course invent any 'sport' you like. We have a scorer for each event so that by the end of the day there is an overall winner who receives a cup and a medal which my daughter makes. Careful falling over, sudden outbreaks of bad legs and coughing can guarantee that the youngest wins.

THE EXHIBITION

When you go for a walk, you can say that the point this time will be to make an exhibition when we get back. So throughout the walk we're looking for treasures and interesting things to put in the exhibition. This will involve us in many hours of debate about what is 'interesting' and what is a 'treasure'. You may need to invent criteria, like 'Will it interest Nanna?' Or you can make it alphabetical, so that we're trying to find things that begin with a single letter. There's an upper limit on the number of objects you can collect. Then when you come back, you lay everything out. Everyone must label their objects themselves. You might want to include a flower-press in this: either the home-made kind – placing grasses or flowers between sheets of paper and putting these between two books at the bottom of a pile of heavy books – or a commercial kind. When it's all laid out, you invite visitors in.

ADAPTED CRICKET

Cricket is a great game for families so long as you don't play it to the proper rules and you adapt it so that the youngest can be helped to stay doing the exciting stuff. This means bowling slow underarm full toss; not bothering about six-ball overs; having a rule that the youngest has three 'lives' and can't be out first ball; adults carefully dropping catches and when batting, spooning up catches; playing the 'in' rule, which is that you don't have to run to the opposite end and back so long as you shout 'In!' when you arrive at the opposite end; no lbw; agreeing beforehand on how many innings you play each, so there is a definite end of the game. Otherwise there can be tears.

DENS AND FORTS

These need blankets, sheets, boxes and clothes horses. If you don't want the proper ones being used, you need to have a store of old unusable ones. You also have to be happy to leave them standing for at least a day. Adults have to be prepared to be a big bad wolf, 'the enemy', the Romans, or any marauding force.

INDOOR BALL GAMES FOR WET WEATHER

These are best played with a scrunched-up ball of paper. Possible games are lobbing into waste-paper baskets; knocking small plastic figures off tables; 'saves', i.e. using the sofa as the goal and flicking; kicking, throwing the ball into the sofa-goal; cricket, using a table tennis bat or rounders using a ruler.

WATER FIGHTS

Whenever my children spot me recommending things to do, they always say, 'Tell them, "Water fights".' So I have.

ABROAD

Many adults who go abroad with children have at least one person in the party who speaks the language. This may be because one of you comes from that place or you've learned the language at school and college. This means that when you are there, you can 'read' it. The place names, the signs, the posters, menus, shopping and instructions all make sense. The food, landscape and people are familiar to you.

Sometimes, if the children have been going to the place regularly or if you share that language and culture at home, they have lived something of a dual culture, with bilingualism, different ways to eat, drink, dress or whatever.

For others, abroad means 'strange' and if we want this to be a good and interesting experience, we need to find ways to explore the differences and similarities.

In some ways, this is the opposite approach to what some of us Brits are famous for: going abroad to places which are little Brit-holes, surrounded by other Brits. Again, I think our approach should be 'curiosity, curiosity, curiosity', and my starting point is always that people abroad are not better or worse than me. In many respects their needs and desires are the same as mine. Where they're not the same, they are different. And probably, when it comes to it, the difference is no greater or lesser than the differences I experience between different people at home. More than that, I have no right to go to another country and think of myself as better than the people who live there.

I'm always saddened, if not angry, when I hear adults, say, on the boat back from France talking in front of their children about 'the French' and something they saw or heard as if it were weird or bad or rubbish. It turns one particular experience into something wrong with all French people! It's not as if the people saying this sort of thing have solved the problems of the world, is it? And I think, What kind of message are we giving children, if we go places and rubbish them? That only the place we happen to live in is any good? How can that be?

Children, who often need the safety of being the same and dealing with the familiar, will frequently turn up their noses at different food, different loos, different sounds and smells. I think it's really important that we help them get over that. In fact, I think it's our only hope as a human race that we help them get over that. And if necessary help ourselves to do it too. I've found that looking at places abroad that I've come to think of as familiar – like France – through the eyes of my children has helped me hang on to my ideas about a universal humankind and not let myself lapse into any stuff about some kind of imaginary league table of who's best, who's not so good, who's bad and who's awful. There is no league table, I say to myself.

I don't ignore difference. I explore it. I don't seek out sameness. If it happens, it happens. Otherwise, I hope I show my children curiosity.

For starters, it's interesting to be the foreigner. Sadly, we are living in a time when some political parties in Britain and all over the world use the idea of the 'foreigner' as a threat. Children hear this kind of talk on TV and at school. Maybe our own children are the ones who experience the finger pointing at them. In some respects, I see myself as a 'foreigner' not because I want to be but because the kinds of people I can hear being pointed at are my forebears, Jewish immigrants. So, in my mind there is no 'them and us'. I am both 'them' and 'us'. I live in one country while one of my parents, some of my grandparents and all my great-grandparents come from abroad. Rather than setting me apart or making me different or odd – something I may have thought in the past – I now think of this as the future. This is the way millions of us are. And even more millions in the future. 'Them-and-us-ness' is getting washed away, even as there are political parties who think they can draw up lists and say, on this list are the 'us' people and on another list are the 'them' people.

I think going abroad with our children is a great way to talk about all this. We put ourselves into the shoes of the 'them'. We might even hear hostile things said about 'us' – not nice, not good at the time, but a great reminder that when we're back home, we know what that sort of thing feels like to the people we might think of as 'them'.

Here are some of the things we can explore and be curious about:

LANGUAGE

The best places to start are signs and supermarkets. What this means is going back to how we were when we were two, three, four and five years old, as we were learning to read. Rather than being overwhelmed by the unfamiliar, we can try to find the familiar. Because we're English speakers, a great deal of English is around anyway. The sign up for an exhibition while we're here in France, the week I'm writing this very sentence, is for the 'Glorious Sixties'! I have no idea why the 'glorious sixties' needs to be written in English, especially as I don't think I ever remember anyone calling the sixties 'glorious' during or after that time! My daughter has picked up the supplement to the newspaper I was reading and while she was looking at the fashion pages and horoscopes she found there were swathes of it she could understand just by turning words that looked familiar into the English words they looked or sounded like. There are big ads in the Métro in Paris put up by the Métro people themselves (RATP). They show people standing or sitting in their seats while among them human-sized animals do objectionable things like sit on bucket seats in rush hour when it's preferable that they stand up to make more room, or they leap over the barriers to dodge paying. The children asked me what the words meant. Some of it was pretty slangy French and I didn't quite get it. They guessed it from the picture and they got it more right than I did.

Phrase books get better and better. Many moons ago, they seemed proud to give you the right phrase for things like how to ask for the bath to be run a little hotter please. They also try to put in print ways of getting you to pronounce the words and phrases. It always interests me that these phrase books are nothing like the school books that are given to our children. Why's that? Why aren't lessons in a foreign language mostly made up of reading (and talking about) real magazines, newspapers, comics, books, menus, ads, posters, supermarket signs, road signs and the like? I always find it useful and interesting to read the phrase books that are for the 'foreigner' from the country I'm going to and which are meant to be teaching them how to speak English!

So, when I'm abroad, I try to get hold of printed material written in that country, even if it means just looking at the pictures and guessing the captions underneath.

If 'abroad' is Europe, then it's useful to keep in mind that there are families of languages in Europe. Broadly speaking, most of Europe is made up of two families: Romance and Germanic. The Romance languages are spoken by those people who live in places where most inhabitants spoke the same language as the Roman invaders and settlers – Latin. These are in Portugal, Spain, France, Italy and Romania. These five languages and the dialects in and around those countries (like Catalan) owe most of their way of speaking to Latin, the language of the Romans. The other main family is Germanic which includes languages like German, Dutch, Flemish, Danish, Swedish, Norwegian and Icelandic.

As you can see, I've left out English! English is also a Germanic language in its origin because it arrived in what we now call Britain spoken by such peoples as Angles, Saxons, Jutes, Frisians, Franks and later by peoples from what are now Denmark, Sweden, Norway and Iceland. The big difference with English (as opposed to the other Germanic languages) is that this Germanic language became mixed with a good deal of Romance words coming from the Normans.

Part of the fun of going to the countries I've mentioned here is to look at the signs and ads and newspapers and spot the Germanic or Romance words that we've got in English. We may not always get it dead right – and that's for another interesting reason: Latin. After the fall of the Roman Empire, the language of the Church and a good deal of the law, administration and intellectual life continued to be Latin. This meant that one route of Latin words into English and the other European languages was not from the Romans but from intellectuals and churchmen writing to each other in Latin after the end of the Roman Empire, or, later, by people wanting to sound informed and educated.

Again, if any of this interests you or you manage to help your children get interested in it, google any word with the word 'etymology' next to it, and you'll quickly find out whether it came from, say, 'Old Norse' or 'Old French'. You may have the facility on your computer in the Dictionary app. Though phrases like 'Old French' sound very dusty and dull, just think, you're only reading them because William the Conqueror decided that he had more right to rule England than Harold and won the Battle of Hastings in 1066. One of the world's greatest comic strips – the Bayeux Tapestry – tells the story. And behind that other dusty phrase, 'Old Norse', sits the story of open Viking boats sailing across freezing seas to land on the east coast of Britain, followed by many years of bloodthirsty battles and intermarriage.

Every word we speak and write, and every word we hear and read when we're abroad is a little bundle of archaeology. The history is in the sounds and the letters; the order in which they're said or written; and the sequences we put them in in order to make sense. It's very easy for children and us to get trapped into thinking that the most important thing about language is to 'get it right'. In fact, just as important is to 'understand what other people are saying and writing' and 'to make ourselves understood'. I am a passionate believer in the power of curiosity about language. It's really helpful to follow up children's queries about where words and phrases come from, the similarities and differences between what we say and write in one language and what we say and write in another. This lifts language off the page and connects it to real people. It reminds us that language comes from people and is meant to be for people. And it's people who change language. Being abroad can remind us of all this so long as we let ourselves be interested in the language we hear being spoken and the people saying it.

Of course this links to the languages that children learn in schools. It may not be a direct link, teaching them the exact way to, say, form the past tense but it will help put them in the right frame of mind to feel open to a language, and not feel that it is a battle in the face of strangeness.

FOOD

The story of food and the Brits is fascinating. I was brought up in the London suburbs in the 1940s and 1950s. Because my parents came from an immigrant background, they sought out foods that weren't around in the shops in Pinner and Harrow apart from in one or two delicatessens. Many of the foods and flavours that are now 'normal' were simply not available. It's hard to imagine but hardly anyone outside the small inner London Italian community ate anything made with chopped tomatoes or tomato concentrate. Now, it's hard to think of people of who have *not* eaten these things. Before we went to France for the first time in 1951, I had never seen an aubergine or a baguette. When I was about seven in 1953, my mother took me on a special trip to Rathbone Place off Oxford Street to visit Nam Tings, the only Chinese restaurant outside London's East End that she knew of. There was a time in the 1960s when the greengrocer in Muswell Hill in north London used to pride himself (loudly and often) on not selling 'foreign muck'. He meant courgettes.

Foreign has become us. I think this has made it much easier when we're abroad to give 'foreign' a go. And indeed to have that conversation about how foreign became us, how there was a time when I didn't know what a pizza was, I had never had spag bol, or egg fried rice. Sometimes it means being much more relaxed in cafés and restaurants than we might be at home. So, rather than nagging children to finish what's on their plates, it means swapping and sharing, encouraging them to give something a go and not getting snarled up if they don't like it. I can't think of the number of times we've said, 'Have a bit off my plate, just give it a go, if you like it, you can order it next time . . .'

Along with that, if you order dishes that they haven't seen or tasted, it's great to have conversations about, say, meat that's bloody, or sauces and what's in them. There's a café we go to in France that sells bison steak. What? It comes from a farm where they rear bison. I can't tell the difference between bison steak and steak from cattle and in the chat about cattle, bison, we're soon on to my memories of having eaten ostrich and alligator in the US and their memories of watching *I'm a Celebrity* and eating kangaroo testicles . . . and do we 'eat to live' or 'live to eat'? It's all very well living in a world where we choose what we eat and express strong preferences, but what would we do if we couldn't? This leads on to the chat about 'the one food you could live off' if all you had was one type of food and an unlimited supply of water. I say it's avocado. And the great thing is you wouldn't have to cook it. One of them says it's eggs and you could eat them raw. I say that I have eaten raw egg and also in Germany I've had egg 'spun' into hot soup . . .

These 'chains' of chat about food when we're abroad are very important. They prevent us from being imprisoned by a narrow range of taste. And they can open out into where food comes from, how people earn a living from it, and what happens when there are millions who don't have enough of it. We might be in a place where there are people in the streets or in the countryside who are in that situation.

How has it come about that some people eat more food than is good for them, while others can't get enough?

SCRAPBOOKS

One way to help bring a lot of this together is to encourage children – or indeed to do it ourselves – to make scrapbooks. This can be particularly good fun for children aged about five, six or seven. Having just got used to understanding bus tickets, bills, handouts, museum fliers, food wrappers and the like at home, suddenly there are all these new ones.

What do they say?
What do they mean?
Why are they different colours?

Collecting them and sticking them into a scrapbook 'freezes' them, and gives everyone who was on the holiday a chance to remember the taste of that sweet, the visit to that show or museum, that ride on the bus . . . And people cluster around the scrapbook arguing about them. If it's the five- or six-year-old who has made the scrapbook, it's one of those rare moments when an artefact or object they have made is important enough to be interesting for everyone.

Children a bit older may want to combine the scrapbook with a log book, just jotting down dates, places and a line or two about what they did. I can remember that we made a scrapbook-log book with my mother from a holiday in France in 1953. We collected French bus and train tickets, chocolate wrappers and shop bills with a passion and pored over these trivial and ephemeral things for years afterwards, remembering the strangeness of it all. I'd even be prepared to make the claim that that scrapbook was one important foundation stone in helping my brother to become a collector, classifier and scientist – he's a palaeontologist – and for me to become another kind of collector and classifier: a writer, broadcaster and critic of literature.

My mother did not go to school beyond the age of sixteen, though she trained first as a secretary and then, after the Second World War, did eighteen months of 'Emergency Training' to become a primary school teacher. Somewhere in her personality, background, thought-processes and training, she got into the developing mindset of her two little boys in the 1950s. I love reading and speaking French. I always want to know more and more about French history and culture. All my life I've been going to France. I don't exactly know why. Of course I can remember that my father spoke it very well and would sing funny, rude and sad French songs. But perhaps making that scrapbook has had an important part to play too.

DAYS OUT

OUTINGS
AND
VISITS

The easiest thing to do is to plan outings *without* including the children in the process. We know the reason why. We fear that perhaps the only ideas they'll come up with are Disneyland, theme parks and repeated trips to the movies. And why not? After all, these are the only venues that put on a strong showing in the ads on TV. This means that it takes a bit of effort and propaganda to find other places and sell them to the children too. Not easy, but possible; and always easier if you are away somewhere where the big attractions like Disneyland are too far, too expensive and not practical. My optimistic hunch, though, is that the more we involve children in the looking, finding and planning, the more they'll get out of the day.

MUSEUMS

Museums are a very mixed bag, with some putting in a good deal of time, energy and thought into how to involve and interest children and young people, others less so. That is a story in itself, and quite interesting to get children thinking about.

Is this museum child-friendly?
What else could it do to make it more interesting to children?

Though museums have been around for hundreds of years, the idea of attracting children – even of displaying objects that might interest them at a level they could see – has only been around for just under a hundred years. My mother, who was brought up next to what is now the Bethnal Green Museum of Childhood, often described going to the museum on that site as her 'university'. The museum in the 1920s was a general Victorian museum telling the history of the earth, British history, and natural history in a pretty stuffy sort of a way, but she used to take herself off there all on her own and stare at the exhibits. I found out recently that at the same time as my mother was going there the first-ever experiment in creating a children's gallery inside a museum was being made.

She didn't ever mention that to me; perhaps she didn't really know about it at the time. Even so, I often think of my mother, going there, 'escaping' – as she put it – from her home to discover ideas, knowledge, history all on her own. She used to talk about it with a sense that this was an opportunity that she was lucky to know how to grab. A story like that about how precious it can be to find out things ticked away in my head. I often try to pass on that idea of how exciting it can be to find out something all by yourself.

I guess also this is what fires me up to go to museums with our children, wondering if there'll be something there that will grab them. Quite often, we take a cue from something they say – maybe it's something they tell us they're doing at school, or something they ask a question about. Sometimes it's because there's a special exhibition on. We only have to hear them say the word 'Romans' or 'Tudors' and we're thinking what museum might flesh that out, what display, building or house is there that will show something of how those people lived or what they thought? No matter how hard they try in schools to fit the jigsaw of the past together, it's not until you see objects, buildings and costumes in front of you that you start to get a feeling for the detail and reality of it.

Once you get there, I admit to feeling a bit of a tension between wanting to help children see things that I think they might like and just letting them find things for themselves. I end up with a compromise. First off, it's to encourage them just to find anything that they think looks interesting; and then following that up by getting them to show me what they've found. Then off the back of that, I might suggest one or two things that I've found. This way it's a swap, with them getting the first bite of the cherry. And it's just as likely that they will find something that I've missed, as I might find something that they've missed. That's the principle I hang on to. I'll also do my best to follow up any queries they might have, by saying, 'I wonder if it tells us here' – meaning the labels and commentaries that are by the side of the exhibits.

Sadly, many of these are written in an English that children find quite difficult and I rarely see children reading them on their own. They need translating so that they answer the kinds of questions that children ask. I'll always give that a go, if there's something they're trying to figure out.

With big museums, it's nearly always counter-productive to do too much. For people going to the big London museums, say, there is of course a huge temptation to try to pack in as much as possible in the time available. We're of the strong opinion that the trick is to plan beforehand which of the galleries we're going to visit and do all we can to stick to that plan. If we're going to do the Greeks, let's just stick with the Greeks. The trick then is to slow things down. Depending on the display, one of the things our children have enjoyed is stopping to draw something. So, with the Greek gallery at the British Museum, say, you can easily whip round the sculptures and vases in about ten minutes, without really looking at very much. If you say, Let's draw a favourite picture, and another, and another, and another – by the time you've done about three and looked at each other's pictures, you've spent an hour or so. That's probably enough for the time being; have a drink and a bite to eat and think about what to do next. This keeps the trip pleasurable, light, and makes it a good memory worth repeating. The moment you start to get that aching-feet, aching-shoulder feeling, a sculpture starts turning into a vase which starts turning into a mosaic which turns into a clay tablet, and you know it's going to end up in the memory in the same place as that gorgeous meal that went wrong.

Museums are putting in time and effort to create trails and

guidebooks that are child-friendly. I'm always inclined to give them a go as an alternative to my bite-size approach. It's also handy if the children come with queries from whatever they've just learned at school, seen on TV or read in *Horrible Histories*. It makes the trip part of the 'follow-up principle'. As I say, spending time drawing is a great way to concentrate time and effort: getting more from less. And drawing things sticks them into the memory far more than just looking.

As a general thought, I'd say that when we're with children, if we take it slowly enough, any museum anywhere will be worth at least a one-hour visit, with things to see and spend time looking at, wondering about, drawing and remembering. And not just 'worth it'. They'll be valuable, long-lasting, terrific experiences. I'm a major fan of all museums. Some of our best, most thoughtful conversations have been in a museum or afterwards. Some museums are worth two hours. Occasionally, you can get three hours out of it.

In passing, I've noticed that children will ask:

Where does the stuff in the museum come from?
Who owns it?
Who owns the museum?

These are important questions and because it's not always immediately obvious what the answers are, I've often spent a few moments on them. In their own ways, these are questions about who 'owns' knowledge, or, at least, who's in charge of it. This is all very political and some of the objects we might be looking at – the Elgin Marbles, for example – might be a matter of international dispute. Sitting in the museum café, having drawn some warriors' legs and horses' heads, I've found that we got quite serious about why 'we' have the Elgin Marbles

and the Greeks don't. Or indeed why they're called 'Elgin' and
not 'Parthenon' . . .

It's great to look out for freaky little museums too, the kind
set up and run by an obsessive, or the kind that has just grown
out of the odd place it finds itself in. I found myself once in
what was the world's first operating theatre near London Bridge.
You go through a building and up into an upper floor. The big
room reveals an operating table laid out in a kind of mini-
theatre – so that the students could watch the operation. I had
to pose semi-naked for a photo, while looking out from under
a sheet pretending that I was about to be operated on in order
to demonstrate that I was going to donate my body to science.
In the little shop there are wonderful accounts of early Victorian
medical practices. There are one-off little museums like this
all over the country and in many other countries too. What I
like about these is that the less professional some of them
appear to be, the more likely it is that there'll be an interesting
story to find out about the eccentric benefactor or collector
who put the museum together. And there's nearly always
someone interesting to talk to about it, a person who can start
off a train of thought or a line of enquiry. In a tiny museum
in Limoges, in France, there are the real remains of an RAF
drop into the region in support of the Resistance there during
the Second World War. That was definitely worth a long look
and contemplation.

Who kept that long enough for it to have survived till the
time the museum was created?

Why?

Then the shop. As with swapping favourite 'finds', we tend
to go for giving the children some money to buy what they
want, while we buy what we want. This means that on the
journey back and on tipping out stuff on to the kitchen table,

the conversation goes on between what we've each found. I admit to being a 'hey listen to this' bore. If in the book or booklet that I've brought back I find something that I had missed in the museum, or that explains something that the children or I had asked, then I am likely to blurt it out in front of everybody. I hope that this will be at least a bit infectious, no matter how much others take the mickey out of me for doing it.

GALLERIES

Art galleries and exhibitions can be daunting. Hundreds of pictures, sculptures and installations, people looking very serious and quiet. And surely everyone knows more or better stuff than I do? I always remind myself of that second principle that my parents passed on to me: you are entitled to any of this. I translate this into meaning that I may or may not be 'getting' the painting, I may or may not be getting what someone else is getting, so I will concentrate instead on letting myself see if I can get what I want from it.

This may be reading about the artist.
It may be asking myself, What does this remind me of in real life?
It may be asking myself, What other painting, sculpture, photo, film, play, story does it remind me of?
It may be asking myself, What does this painting make me feel?
How do I feel standing looking at it?

So, rather than worrying myself about, say, 'What does this picture "mean"?', I ask myself questions that I *can* answer and will get me involved in thinking about the painting. In fact, these quite simple questions are linked to some of the big questions that people ask about art to do with artistic movements, or their links to other cultural objects and events. By starting

251

my thinking in an open-ended way, I'm not under any pressure to 'get it right' or to think what I'm supposed to feel rather than think what I do feel.

By mixing up those open-ended questions with some of the commentaries on the walls next to the pictures, I find going to galleries exciting, fun and uplifting. I'm not oppressed or depressed by the experience. I don't ever feel that someone is trying to put one over on me. I don't ever feel that I don't have the right to be there.

So, in light, unobtrusive ways, I try to pass this open-endedness over to children: find your favourites, tell us why they're your favourites.

What ones didn't you like?
Why was that?
Did you have any questions?
I wonder if there are any answers to that in the commentaries on the walls . . . do you want any postcards of any of the paintings?

Again, it's crucial not to spend too long. Of course children might well find spending two hours in a gallery a tough ask. They are used to flicking between moving images on tablets and TV screens. Looking at paintings and sculptures is a slow, static process and a gallery is in some ways a very artificial place for looking at paintings. Many of them were intended to be hung up in positions where people could see them again and again so that interesting details could emerge over time. Zipping round a gallery in an hour is perhaps the wrong timing for a picture. This is an interesting thing to talk about too.

And as with the museum, one way to make the images do their work, and to help make them stick, is to have a go at drawing one or two of them. Or even drawing one part of them – a hand or a tree. Again, less is more.

Booklets and catalogues from galleries and art exhibitions are lovely things to collect. Some of the thoughts and feelings about art that have stayed with me the longest have come in the reading immediately after an exhibition or a visit. I also find that writing poems triggered off by paintings works well both for me personally and when I'm working with children. This can happen in front of the painting itself, looking at a postcard or book afterwards or just by daydreaming about it. I'll come back to this in the next chapter.

This is not a matter of trying to be especially clever or knowledgeable. It's more just letting some thoughts grow. One painting that affected me was a picture by Edvard Munch. He was standing looking out of the picture between a dark grandfather clock and his bed. So, I just wrote that today I saw Mr Munch standing between the clock and the bed . . . between the bed and the clock.

I've found that children can do that very easily. They transfer the images of the painting to images made of words. Sometimes this makes them feel confident to give paintings or people in paintings feelings and thoughts. This is 'interpretation' and all the more valuable for that. You can read more on this in the next chapter.

CASTLES AND COUNTRY HOUSES

I have to say that I'm a sucker for these. Ironic, really, given my beliefs about equality and the like! I think I know why. I like the way each house and castle gives us a line through history of how a famous aristocratic family lived and ruled across several centuries. And – I'll be honest – I do get a kick from reading and hearing the very solemn and respectful words that guides and guidebooks use to describe this 'great' family, along-side what are often quite awful goings-on: episodes where someone was bumped off, a country was invaded, someone died of an unmentionable illness, there was an uprising somewhere that was put down, mistresses were 'disappeared' and so on. Alongside this, there are the 'treasures' ('Where did that come from, Mum?'), huge paintings showing this or that person puffed up and made to look grand, and vast rooms where we can walk and wonder what people did in such vast places. Eavesdropping on the range of comments flying about between the guides and visitors is great too.

Though this story wasn't an official visit to a great house, I often think of it when we're going round a country house. We were camping on the Welsh border, I was about ten and my friend twelve. We told our parents that we wanted to fish in the river – not that we knew how. The farmer (Bert Fidler) who owned the campsite told us that we needed a permit. The person who dished out permits – I think he sold them – was General Bates who lived in the big house on the hill 'over there'. If we wanted a permit we'd have to go and get one from him. I don't think Bert Fidler thought we would go and find General Bates on our own, but he didn't know our parents. So, as Bert had said the house was on top of the hill over there, that was where our parents said we should go. And we went.

We crossed the river on 'the wires'. This meant side-stepping with our feet on a wire below, while holding on to another wire above. The walk up the hill was through a field full of bracken that had grown up above our heads, thick and tight. It took us a good while to climb up through it, and when we got to the top it opened out on to a wide lawn, landscaped with bushes and trees. Across the lawn: the big house. So, now, two boys in shorts, with knees, arms and faces messed up by the bracken, arrived at the door of the house. We knocked and far off from inside we heard a gruff, posh voice, call out to us, 'Who's there, what d'you want?' We said that we were two boys who wanted to fish in the River Monow and that we wanted to have a permit. The door opened and standing in front of us was a man on massive crutches, with a white moustache and fiery little eyes.

He asked us in to a room that I always think of when we're in big country houses. There were tiger rugs and various beasts sticking out of the walls, rows of guns, and tall paintings of people in uniforms. He made us sit down, and he sent someone off to get us some lemonade. He asked us to repeat what we wanted and asked us how we got there. We told him that we had walked up from the campsite, up the hill. 'Ah,' he said, 'you came through Tinker's Bath. No one ever does that. My word,' he said, 'I admire your sporting spirit.' We drank the lemonade and he kept saying, 'I admire your sporting spirit.' At the end of it all, he told us that we didn't need a permit, we could fish as much as we wanted and he told us of a route back that meant that we didn't need to go through Tinker's Bath.

On the way back, my friend Martin kept repeating, 'I admire your sporting spirit' and then he said, 'Did you see his lips? They were quivering.' He said that he had read about people like him and it always said that they had 'quivering lips'. 'And that's what he had: quivering lips.' When we got back to the campsite, Mart told the story, and made a special point of talking about the quivering lips. I kept thinking about the tiger rug and the beasts' heads sticking out of the wall. I think there was an elephant's foot umbrella stand too. Perhaps I've imagined that.

Such adventures don't crop up on every visit to every big house, but there are elements of it, even so: something of the grandeur, the landscaping, the dead animals, the tall paintings and the guns. There are always the guns. I've found that this inevitably links with questions that children ask about the British Empire. Living in twenty-first-century Britain doesn't necessarily get you thinking about the Empire very often, but being in a big house will almost certainly bring us face to face with places all over Africa, India and the Caribbean at the very least; perhaps Canada and Australia too. There aren't many places we visit where this is put in front of us in such an obvious way. And of course many of the objects on display were 'brought back' (the guidebooks sometimes say, euphemistically) from all over the world.

You usually get a sense of the cross-section of society that is needed to keep such establishments going – whether that was three hundred years ago or today. Sometimes there are wonderful Victorian kitchens to explore along with early examples of central heating and refrigeration. I often think that visits that show such contrasts are great for stimulating thinking about how people lived or on occasions still live.

When such places are castles, there's the added dimension of 'knights in armour' which often feeds into various TV series or films doing the rounds. As a child I was captivated by castles. I loved the Tower of London and read up about the great escape of the Earl of Nithsdale who dressed up like a woman to get out. I was gruesomely interested in imprisonments, tortures and beheadings. I loved knowing the names of the different towers and who was imprisoned in which bit for how long. On holidays, I pleaded to go on visits to the smallest pile of stones to see the 'keep', the 'bailey' and the moat. I learned how to say 'crenellation'. I often think that whatever lit me up might also light up my own children. If not, there might be something like it. Either way, it's the 'lighting-up' feeling that is the motor for finding out more.

In some places, these days, castles are fleshed out with tournaments, jesters, guides in costumes and the like. Sometimes, the people doing these make special efforts to connect with children while at the same time trying to avoid prettifying the tough nature of lives and battles of the times. These can be provocative, exciting days with odd curios in corners that the children remember: a special viewing glass for looking at the ceiling, a tiny gold ornament dating from Anglo-Saxon times and so on.

Quite often, castles have played a part in an episode of history that is too detailed to be covered in school, like the three King Edwards' suppression of the Welsh, or the border battles between the Scots and the English. This can make for the day's visit being a bit of a story that may not be fully told while you're there. Sometimes this needs to be unpicked out of the guidebook on the way home. Perhaps our curiosity will be infectious. I find the stories melancholy, as they seem to give accounts of people driven by needs and desires that I don't recognize in myself: battles and wars for control of dukedoms, the perpetuation of dynasties, clashes with aristocrats or monarchs higher up the food chain. It's a leap for children too, I've sensed, to go from the kinds of lives we lead to the lives of these warring barons and dukes. A lot of their questions add up to 'What was it all for?' and it's interesting for me, I can say, to be able to admit that I don't know! I don't really know what drove these people. The facelessness of the suits of armour, the helmets and visors seem to me to have a grim, mechanical look. I often hear people around me on these visits expressing their emotions about the bleakness of the castle walls or how damp they feel. I like this meeting of emotions and facts. It generates questions and wonderings in children.

Many of us have found that Terry Deary's *Horrible Histories* have done a great service in one respect: these places can't be dressed up any more as delightful little fantasies about damsels, jolly tournaments and religious devotion. I suspect he's set more young minds racing and wondering about history than anyone has ever done before.

PREHISTORIC SITES

Some of the best times to be had with children are in places that at first glance don't seem to hold out great prospects. Obviously, Stonehenge or Avebury are incredible and awe-inspiring but there are hundreds of other sites that offer up smaller moments of curiosity: stone circles, prehistoric houses, 'barrows', standing stones, dolmens, earthworks and the like. At first sight, some of these just look like a ditch and a hillock, or a few scattered stones. If you arm yourself with a book or a guide, however, they become full of mystery and a cause for speculation.

Why would people (who had to spend so much time and effort in keeping warm and getting enough food for themselves) also spend so much time building graves and monuments for dead people?
What did they do in stone circles?
What did they do with standing stones?
And what language did they speak?
Is there any part of the language they spoke that we still speak?

You can 'read' the earthworks a bit more easily than the standing stones because they're encampments. With the help of a guide-book with its 'reconstructions' of rows of stakes, you can imagine people inside keeping out people trying to get in. I've mentioned one of these earlier in the book – Loughton Camp in Epping Forest near London, where, some people have said, Boudicca camped, on her way to London when she led the Iceni against the Romans. If you go on a sunny day, the sun streams through the trees and as you walk round the ridge – probably a defensive wall of some kind – you stroll in and out of beams of light coming through the trees. The air is full of birdsong and the earth smells leafy and thick.

In Cornwall and the Orkneys there are prehistoric houses in very good nick, while in places in, say, Northumberland, there are stones with prehistoric patterns on them.

What do the patterns mean?
Who put them there?

Just occasionally, on very early monuments there are 'runes' – this is the writing used by the Anglo-Saxon or Viking settlers. One of our children got quite excited by this as a few are written on some stones in the museum on Lindisfarne (Holy Island) and there are imitation runes written up in Alnwick Castle. They are like a code and he enjoyed matching up these ancient letters with the sounds he could make.

So, if the Anglo-Saxons arrived writing in runes, why did they switch to writing with what was mostly a Roman alphabet?

At one encampment in Cornwall there was a re-enactment of some Arthurian battles. I settled down with my son and at first I thought it was a bit of hooey, knights in armour pretending to bash each other's heads off, and lots of shouting. Then, even as I was thinking just that, the guide stopped the show and said almost what I was thinking: that's probably a load of nonsense, he said, but it's what people have believed about

Arthur. If there is any truth to the Arthur story, it was probably more like this, he said . . . And then he and his burly mates switched costumes and re-enacted something a bit more like an ancient Britons versus Anglo-Saxon battle. I thought that was clever presentation, creating questions and debate even as they were all putting on a bit of a spectacle.

This sort of thing comes under the word 'interpretation' and the museums, National Trust, heritage and ancient sites are all working on this. They know that it is part of their job now to provide us, the public, with some 'interpretation' of their collections, exhibits and sites. I know this because I was asked to do some interpretation at a wonderful place called Grimes Graves. These are ancient flint mines where the peoples who mined for the flints and turned them into scrapers and weapons also seemed to have created flint collections way down below in the mines.

Again the question crops up: Why would people who expended so much effort just to stay alive, also spend all that effort digging out and shaping stone flints and then not use them?

I was briefed by an archaeologist and wrote a set of poems and charms which are imaginary thoughts of the people who made Grimes Graves. For some people, I hope that it triggers off some thoughts about the graves, the miners, the work they did and the look and feel of the flints themselves. I hope also that it will encourage people to write their own poems, paint pictures, make models or whatever; in other words do their own 'interpretations'.

If you want to get all *Horrible History* about these ancient places then the fate of various people – nearly always men – found in bogs can be followed up in some museums. It's becoming clear that at various moments in the lives of some peoples, it seemed appropriate to garrotte a young man with a leather cord and throw him in a well or a bog. Whether this was for punishment, sacrifice or some other purpose is not known. The story of how such bodies have survived and what they've found in them is a wonderful piece of creative science. You can even try going home and eating a home-made version of the dead man's last meal.

ROMANS

All over Britain and Europe there are Roman remains and bit by bit in a family you can piece together quite a lot about how the Romans lived. A bath here, a mosaic there, a bit of tiling in another place, a preserved leather sandal in another. There are some prize sites that you can visit in places like Bath and Hadrian's Wall but it's well worth looking out for the less well-known ones where a villa in the middle of the countryside, the remains of an amphitheatre, or an inscription on a stone in a museum can give you that odd feeling that it wasn't all that long ago that the Romans walked past this spot. Holidays in Italy, on the Mediterranean Islands and Greece are of course quite another matter. To stand in the Colosseum, say, and imagine gladiators and emperors and the ticket-buying public is utterly extraordinary. At the Pompeii exhibition at the British Museum in 2013 we saw what was one of the world's first comic strips done as a mural: three men in a pub, talking dirty. Meanwhile, at Housesteads and Vindolanda you can stand on the Roman wall and imagine what it was like, with you and just a few hundred others, in the freezing weather wondering who was going to appear over the horizon to attack you next. You are, after all, part of an occupying army. In the information nearby, they tell you that this soldier on the wall could have been from Hungary. A Hungarian in

Northumberland looking out for a Pict who doesn't want you to be there . . .

In some of these places they sell card cut-out models of ancient buildings. I admit to becoming quite obsessive and buying several of these and making them with my children. They involve patience, a good sense of humour and good glue. Something about the length of time it takes seems to bring you closer to the shape and purpose of the original building. It's not everyone's cup of tea and I probably only make them because I spent many years watching my brother making such things and feeling that I was too young or too clumsy to make one myself. So maybe it's some absurd, pointless challenge I give myself while drawing my children into this crazy net! Even so, as long as I only impose it on myself and not on them, it's probably only a few moments (hours, actually) of harmless masochism. In fact, though I told myself that all sorts of interesting questions about the Romans would crop up, the most persistent one is: Why are you doing this, Dad?

SPORTS STADIUMS

When one of my children came to his 'gap' year I asked him what he wanted to do. He said he wanted to go to Latin America, Brazil and Argentina. I thought, Wow, that's bold. I would never have thought of that. Good luck to him. What are you going to do when you get there? I asked. He said that he and his friend Ian were going to visit the football stadiums. But it's not the football season, I said. No matter, he said, they just wanted to go where all those amazing players came from and see what it was like.

I admit that I was nonplussed – thrown even. Why would anyone want to spend their precious gap year time going to two huge very special countries only to spend all their time looking at empty football stadiums? I kept my thoughts to myself and wished them well and off they went, sending back photos of themselves standing on the exact spot where Maradona, Zico, Garrincha, Pele and the rest jinked and skipped round defenders. Even as I am writing this, my son and his friend are finalizing plans for their trip to the World Cup 2014.

If, instead of being nonplussed, I had put away my prejudices, I could have seen that my son was doing precisely what I did with my parents, what I did with him when he was a boy: following my nose to find out more about places and things that I was interested in. It just so happens that for him it's the mystique, excitement and logic of football. It doesn't even have to be the game itself. It's the spirit of the sport, which, for him, outlives the games. It's possible I could even take a tiny bit of self-satisfaction from it: that he decided to build on the kind of outing that I had done with him when he was a boy. It's just that it wasn't a history or literature or science visit but a football one. Wakey-wakey, I say to myself, this is how we make sure that life has meaning for us and this is his particular way of doing it. As it happens, now it's also how he earns his money. It all adds up somehow!

Stadiums offer guided visits when they're not being used and you can pay homage to old kits, boots, balls, trophies, badges and walk where your heroes, or your parents' and grandparents' heroes, walked, ran, tackled and scored.

Sometimes I've taken my children to games and matches and it's the kind of 'theatre' where you really don't know what's going to happen next. The more you go, the more the characters reappear – whether that's on the stands or the pitch. They play out their roles going with or against expectations, sometimes responding to our cheers and yells. The goodies are ours, the baddies are theirs. After a few outings, you're rewarded with never-to-be-forgotten cameos. For Arsenal fans, one of the great moments in the modern era was when they went into the last game of the season knowing that if they did the highly unlikely thing of beating Liverpool 2–0 at Anfield, they would win the League. It had to be 2–0. Anything less, Liverpool would win the League. Arsenal were leading 1–0 with a minute to go. So near but so far. Surely, it wouldn't be possible. At this precise moment, one of the Liverpool players was caught on TV holding up his finger and mouthing to his mates, 'One more minute'. That's all Liverpool needed for them to win the League instead of Arsenal. It was a certainty. Arsenal had the ball. The ball was kicked upfield, centred and Arsenal's striker scored. It was 2–0. The whistle blew. League won. Hysteria all over north London and in the Rosen household. Never to be forgotten.

Now scroll forward to a game at Arsenal, a season later: Arsenal versus Liverpool and that same Liverpool player is playing. What does the whole Arsenal stadium do every time he touches the ball? They all hold up their finger and shout, 'One more minute!' That would be the end of it and like a lot of stadium banter it would have faded away, other than that it got to him. The reason why I remember it so clearly is that it got to him at the very moment when he was standing on the touchline just a few yards from where my son and I were standing. Provoked by the crowd, he turned round and started shouting back at us. For the record, you just don't do that. This was a total collapse of concentration and protocol. As a top sportsman, you show your greatness by ignoring the idiots (like me) who are shouting some stupid jibe at you. And you use the jibes to give it back to them by doing something wonderful on the pitch, like scoring. But no. He stood and waved his arms about and shouted at us.

Childish? Crazy? Pointless? Reprehensible?

Possibly so, but utterly, utterly memorable. And from then on it becomes a shared moment of delight, silliness, laughter and imitation in family chat. Sport has that capacity to create legends. I was once on a visit to a museum that had previously been a workhouse. A man standing next to us told us that he used to be the goalkeeper for Halifax. He said his name was Barry Palfreyman. He told us stories of how in the old days a goalkeeper would be kicked and bashed by forwards. He became an instant legend for me and my son. When we played kick-about football together, my son would do 'saves' and shout, 'Barry Palfreyman!'

DAYS OUT, OUTINGS AND VISITS

Big-time professional sport is a matter of wonder and excitement but it can also be an extraordinary thing to investigate.

Who are these shadowy people behind the scenes who run the game, who own the clubs, who own the players?

How can a player be 'owned'?

What happens if a player doesn't want to do what his owners say that he should do?

If a player, say in tennis, has a coach, why would the player sack the coach?

What do managers and coaches say to players and teams to get them to play well or better?

Is there real equality between sexes and races in sport or is there sexism and racism?

Top-flight sport is always full of scandals, people and clubs being fined and suspended. Why's that?

What's the truth behind these or do we never find out?

Thinking of my son and his gap year, stadiums themselves are tributes to the science and technology of stadium-making. A visit to one or two brings you face to face with the immensity of the buildings and the challenges faced by architects and engineers to get tens of thousands of people into them safely. The history of sport is also full of terrible accidents and disasters.

Did they happen because the owners didn't want to spend the money in protecting the fans?

Are these scandals rather than accidents?

How much money do the top-flight clubs and games deliver to owners and backers?

Meanwhile, every sport generates a legalistic jungle in its rule books and arbitration systems. If we're thinking of children and young people, this involves a deep initiation into legal thinking, writing done in a language that is as clear and unambiguous as possible.

So if it is clear and unambiguous, why is everyone on a Saturday arguing about such things as whether 'he was offside' or 'not interfering in play'?!

When children get the bug of a major sport, you can hear them arguing in the line-ups in the playground in the morning. This often happens about the age of nine and more often than not with boys – apologies for the stereotype of present circumstances. Some people find this chat 'nerdy' or infuriating.

Why should it be that these boys are spending so much time and effort on something so pointless as twenty-two men kicking a ball about?

As someone who enjoys the game, I'm prejudiced, but I don't think the nerdiness is an 'instead-of'. The deeper the nerdiness, the more able such children are to amass data, assess it, argue about it. These are transferable skills, if you like.

League tables, form tables, scoring systems in any sport involve complex arithmetic, guesstimates, assessments. Reading sporting programmes is a complex bit of reading with many different genres of writing within the same booklet: stories, biographies, statistics, formal accounts, exhortations, memoirs, crosswords, puzzles, cartoons, poems and so on. One of my children gave up reading books for a while and just pored over football programmes. It was hard work, and he taught himself how to do it.

THEATRE

Some of my most treasured moments from my childhood are being taken to the theatre. I was lucky enough to have been taken to see the great theatre director Joan Littlewood's productions for children: her versions of *Christmas Carol*, *Treasure Island* and a folk-opera called *The Big Rock Candy Mountain* where the American folksong collector Alan Lomax played a hobo taking us on a trip across America singing songs as we went. I've never forgotten these, nor the trips to what I thought was a hysterically funny panto in Norwich or to the Old Vic to see Zeffirelli's *Romeo and Juliet*, productions of *Julius Caesar* and *Midsummer Night's Dream* with Frankie Howerd playing Bottom. My father and mother both produced plays at their schools and it was fantastic fun to go and see the plays they put on. In one of these, the school students in the play told my father that there was a little girl giggling on the front row. 'That's Michael,' he said. Later, I joined a theatre company and spent many hours at university involved in writing, directing and acting in plays.

This means that anything I say about theatre is heavily prejudiced in its favour. I think theatre is great. I love going to see plays and pantos, ancient or modern. Dance, musicals and opera are marginally less appealing for me but if something looks interesting I'll try to get to these too. At various stages in their lives I've been involved in taking my children to the theatre, or helping them join such things as puppet-making and puppet play-making and dance clubs.

What do I make of all this? I ask myself. I think there's something important (of course I do) about watching and making drama. I think it's a way in which we can try out other ways of being a person. We can be nicer or nastier, bigger or smaller, sillier or more sensible, wiser or not so wise, angrier or calmer, and so on. The immediacy and liveness of theatre is that it can feel like we are really with the person going through the experience. It is as if we are there with them. I'm also interested in that complicated stuff to do with whether we are watching a 'character', an actor or a person. And I'm interested in how far we get 'in' to the action, thinking at times that we can stop what's happening or make things better. I've found these questions will link up with the children's questions too.

I have felt and seen the amazement and joy and thought that happen to children in the theatre. In the intervals and afterwards, these can be great times for conversations about motives, reactions, fairness, sadness and whatever. I try very hard to not behave like my dad did, which was to start gabbling away about what he thought without waiting for us to say what we thought. In fact, our children have got so good at talking after a show we can hardly get a word in. All the better, I think. I hardly need yet another opportunity to talk about something!

So, along with everything else it's great to watch out for shows that look as if they'll be suitable. There's obviously not much point in taking children to shows where they'll be sitting next to you nagging to leave after twenty minutes. On the other hand, there might be occasions where you feel that you want them to give it a go . . . it might end up being rewarding further down the line. An example of that, of course, is 'classic theatre' – anything from Shakespeare to Ibsen. I'm a great believer in doing a bit of preparation for these either by telling the story of the play before we get there, or by finding a good telling of the story in a book. So, someone like Geraldine McCaughrean has done excellent re-tellings of the Shakespeare plays and there are really good book versions of the ballet and opera stories. I don't think at all that this is 'cheating' or 'giving the game away' or anything like it. I think it lets the children relax and not worry about missing the story-line and they can get on and see how the production has let the story unfold, how the actors are working, what great 'moments' are made in the play.

It doesn't take long for children to get a sense that theatre comes in many shapes and sizes, many styles, many types.

Why is it that in some plays the actors talk to us, the audience, and in some they don't?
Why is it that we can sometimes hear people thinking aloud, and in others they don't?
Is there a difference between a musical and an opera?
Is there a difference between ballet and contemporary dance?
And what does it actually mean to act? What is acting?
What is theatre directing? What do directors do?

Of course, there is the whole technical side of theatre – lights, sound, costumes, sets, make-up – which can sometimes grab children, particularly if they get to help on a production in or out of school.

If we've ever been involved in any kind of production, at school, in a club, in amateur theatre or professionally, it's great to share stories about this: mistakes, triumphs, disasters. These tell us that putting on a show is about pulling many different strands and activities together. It's always a big co-operative enterprise to get a show on. That's part of the nail-biting fun of it.

Quite often, the 'big' words like 'tragedy' and 'comedy' or 'classic' start appearing when children are at secondary school, and it's great to be able to draw on some theatre experience from when they were younger, when these terms come along. Talking about such things in the abstract doesn't mean very much, which is only another way of saying that these words don't matter a great deal unless they are attached to real experiences of watching or being in plays.

Another side of this is something to do with confidence. For some people, the only way they can feel confident is when they are performing. For some, doing theatre in any role at all, designing, lighting, acting – or whatever – is such an intense co-operative bit of work that they are lifted by that. It's not simply that they feel worthwhile, they really are being worthwhile. Their contribution is crucial. There aren't many activities that a group of people can get involved in co-operatively and fairly equally, with no competitive outcome. This means that theatre can be a rare and especially valuable experience. Again, of course, I say this because I've spent most of my life being involved in various kinds of performance, so I'm bound to say it's important!

That said, please don't read this to mean that I think it's worth pushing children into theatre when it's quite clear that they can't stand it, or the particular form they're being pushed into doesn't interest them. This is a tough and necessary lesson to learn for parents like me who are theatre-addicts. Children have to find their own niches, their own aspects of the game that appeal to them. That's the only thing that matters. When our children said that they had done puppet-club for long enough, that was long enough. When one of them said that they wanted to do one kind of dance rather than another, that was what we had to try to help them do. No argument.

CONCERTS

In the last few years, I've been involved with putting on jazz and classical music concerts for children. The jazz shows were a mix of me reading poems and live jazz; the classical concerts were orchestral shows with me doing such things as telling the story of *Firebird*, *We're Going on a Bear Hunt*, or a made-up story about a time-travelling theme park called the Great Enormo. Some of these were in big symphony halls like the Royal Festival Hall or the Albert Hall. The idea behind all of them was that children would be introduced to jazz, how musical instruments make sounds, how orchestras and classical music work. At one point in one of the shows, we had thousands of children pretending to be alien killer wasps in outer space (yes!) buzzing in time to an orchestra, under the direction of the conductor. So these were concerts tailor-made for young audiences, with participation as well as time just to listen.

I noticed that big concerts with a young audience in mind, with a mix of music from the past along with newly composed pieces, do happen – but not very often. This means that when it comes to ordinary jazz and orchestral music, we have to decide whether our youngsters will enjoy a full-length show that doesn't have them directly in mind. I'll admit to being cautious about this. Is there much point in taking children to concerts that we think may well bore them after half an hour or so, just because we think it's good for them, or that they ought to like it even if they don't? If our children come from homes where they hear jazz and classical music all the time, or play it themselves, then it's much easier. You just pick concerts where favourite musicians and composers will be performing. Even so, perhaps we should be braver in our family about this, do a bit more research of the 'What's On' guides and find concerts that might grab them. A few weeks ago, my son and I had the surreal experience of playing football in a leafy grove on one side of a park while a brass band on the other side of the park ran through a gamut of favourites. The sound of the tunes filtered through the trees, mixed with the birdsong while we congratulated each other on how we 'bent' the ball or made spectacular saves.

Enjoying music gives us a space to be in that helps us think in new ways. It might give us space to daydream, or to come face to face with emotions we hardly knew we had; or for some, it's more mathematical than that, and it's a pleasure in the 'architecture' of the music, its patterns, symmetries and contrasts, how the patterns unfold and develop. Whatever it is, it gives us all, children included of course, another place to be, another space to fill, another way of thinking.

It's usually easier to find concerts suitable for children with music from the charts as it's quite likely that they hear this on the radio and TV or find their way to it online. The sound and feel of the music is firmly in their heads and they may well say that they want to go and see that artist. I can see in my mind's eye the sheepish look on my neighbour's face as he told me that he was going to a Kylie Minogue concert with his nine-year-old daughter during Kylie's 'I Should be so Lucky' phase; and the even more sheepish look on his face – perhaps for different reasons? – when he came home.

CONCERTS

As I write this, we're just about to head off to some big music festivals because I've been booked to do a spot in the family tents. I'm intrigued to know what our children will make of them. I feel I'm about thirty years behind the truck on this one, because I've known of other families who've been taking their children to the festivals for years. Well, I suppose it proves that a person can change habits of a lifetime even when it comes to doing things with children, an area of people's lives where it seems we are often at our most cautious. I wonder, which will be the bigger subject of conversation on the way back, the music or the mud?

VISITORS

One of the most powerful parts of my childhood was going round to other people's houses or people coming over to ours. Perhaps this was because our parents had loosened ties with their parents, more or less cut ties with wider family members and were living in a place some distance away from the people they had known when they were children themselves.

For a few years we had a lodger who spent most of his time in his room, surrounded by books and papers. When he came out, he was happy to ask and answer questions. My brother and I studied his habits and when we went back to our bedroom we would practise doing his way of spreading jam on toast, or closing a door. We would weep with laughter as we competed with each other to see which of us could make our chins look exactly as moist as his. Then one day his ex-wife appeared, looking grey and fraught. We all crept around quietly while our mother wondered out loud if they were going to get back together again. She came in to see us. It turned out that Mum had been to school with her. She had a smile that went right the way round her face. She looked at us as if we were delicious little cakes. Little cakes that she couldn't have. She stroked my head. Then off she went. They didn't get back together. Her name was Fanny Greenspan. 'Fanny Greenspan,' we said to each other. How could someone be called Fanny Greenspan? My father said that 'Greenspan' came from a German word meaning the furry stuff that appears on copper. I've never checked whether this was one of his hoax explanations or if there's any truth in it. 'Call My German Bluff' perhaps.

Brian, the lodger, had a complete set of *Encylopaedia Britannica* sitting on the mantelpiece in his room. If I went to his room, he would take down a volume and look things up for me. I liked him. I was sad that he and Fanny Greenspan didn't get back together.

It turned out later when I was a teenager that I would bump into Brian at meetings. He had grown a little goatee beard on his moist chin and always carried a placard saying something that no one else had thought of. When he saw me, he would nod and smile as if he knew more about me than I did. Or perhaps it was that he knew more about everything than anyone else did.

At the college where my father worked, there was a French 'assistant' who wore incredibly thick green glasses. It looked as if he had the bottoms of two wine bottles over his eyes. He had a little black pointy beard and wavy black hair that he combed forward over his forehead into a fringe. He often came to stay and we all spoke half in French half in English and we taught each other different French and English accents. He taught us a 'Midi' accent while we tried to teach him a Cockney one. He did imitations of his father while we did imitations of ours. The worst telling-off he ever got from his father, he said, was when his father would slowly take off his glasses and say, 'Bertrand, je préfère que tu ne le fasses pas.' (Bertrand, I would prefer it if you didn't do that.') As Bertrand said this, he narrowed his mouth into a professorial pout. We all sat about, miming taking off a pair of glasses, narrowing our mouths and saying, 'Bertrand, je préfère que tu ne le fasses pas.'

It all went wrong when we went with him to the village he came from in France. First, his brother walked all day in the sun, got sunstroke and had to stay in bed for a week. Then it turned out that Bertrand, though a very self-sufficient sort of a bloke in England, reverted to type back at home with Maman. The two men sat on the terrace while Maman waited on them. For some reason this enraged my parents and Bertrand was wiped from the invite book. 'Why doesn't Bertrand come over any more?' we would say. 'Phah!' our father would say, 'Did you see how he was in the summer?' It didn't seem to me to be a sufficiently sinful act to justify him being banned. Our mother later indicated that she hadn't thought his interest in teenage girls at 'La Fête' was entirely a good thing either.

My brother and I spent many hours talking about Brian and Bertrand, their coming and their going. I can see now that these were profound ways of exploring and finding out about other people and, eventually, our own parents. We watched our parents with eagle eyes, trying to figure out what they really thought, whether they said what they really thought to Brian and Bertrand, whether they said what they thought to us. When we chewed it all over in our room, we were building up knowledge about behaviour, personality and motive. Just being put in the company of strangers at close quarters was enough to set off these thoughts.

Just as important for me were the times I stayed with other people – especially if they were friends I wasn't at school with. In a way, I was one person with my school friends and I was three other people with these three out-of-school friends. At one place I was mad about football, in one I was into model trains and in the third I was in a world of foreign, strange and magical sights and tastes. There were the three sets of parents, each with beliefs about when you were allowed to eat biscuits, why plastic was better than china, and why Armenian food was good for you. Each offered up living spaces that were so very different too: a classic suburban house with a lawn and raspberry plants; a first-floor rented flat backing on to a railway line and a brand-new council flat with a lift, a communal playground and a communal laundry. Beyond this was an array of grandparents, one wearing spats, another cooking 'pilaf' and playing solitaire, some speaking other languages: German, Yiddish or Armenian.

At the time, this was all normal. It's just what I did. From the perspective of now, I can see that it filled my head with variety. I was drinking in different ways of living and thinking. I don't know whether to call this 'mind-expanding' or whether it raised an awareness about diversity and the movement of people, migration and settlement. It was also about the kindness of strangers. People welcomed me into their homes. One mystery: I can hardly remember these three boys ever staying with us. They must have done. Our parents would have done swaps. But why can't I remember that?

Meanwhile, a fairly endless flow of friends, colleagues and close relations came through our flat and we visited their homes. Some stopped to question and probe us. We questioned and probed some of them. A woman from New Zealand told us about kiwis and rugby. A man who worked at Sun Engravings talked for hours about a conspiracy at his factory. There was the scandal of the boy who was in trouble for spitting at a policeman but it turned out that the policeman had spat on his own jacket all along. There was a grandmother who kept chickens, and an uncle who worked at Ford's.

It's not just the detail of this kind of thing that's important for children. It's also how we as parents talk about it all, how we listen to our children's questions about the people and stories, how we repeat these, wonder out loud about them, joke about them. Children quite often get half a story right and the other half wrong or they get the wrong end of the stick entirely. Talking and sorting them out is deep. It's how, when I was quite young, I figured out that sometimes the wrong people can be right and the right people can be wrong.

LEARNING HOW TO LEARN

As I'm writing this, my youngest son has started to get interested in football. This means going over to the park and playing it. But it also means, for him, getting involved in all the facts and figures. As it's the World Cup coming up, it also means collecting stickers and cards (with footballers from the different countries on them) and putting them into folders.

Now it's easy to think of this sort of thing as trivial or unimportant. Ultimately, it is. It's just sport and stats.

But if I watch closely what he's doing and how he's doing it, if I make sure that I stick to my 'key words' and 'best intentions', something important is happening for him. And in a way, for me too. And us.

So, rather than think about whether the 'facts' are unimportant, I can think of how he's going about the job of investigating and discovering things. And what he's learning about how to learn.

First off, he took me to the corner shop to buy stickers. We stood in front of the display racks and it wasn't clear to either of us whether you had to choose different packets in order to get different stickers – as you might buy different boxes of chocolate to get different chocolates. Or whether each packet was a kind of lucky dip: you might get different stickers (of pictures of the footballers) or you might sometimes get the same ones. We asked the shopkeeper and he didn't know. He said that new ones were coming in next week. I asked if this was like one of those things where you buy a packet a week – and each week you get new players. The shopkeeper didn't know.

As we stood in the shop, I could see that this was in its own way agonizing for my son. Should he risk spending his pocket money on two packets that looked the same? Or wait till next week? I didn't say anything. I said that I didn't know. I took a step back. I thought that he would learn much more by making up his own mind about it, rather than me putting in my two-pennyworth. And anyway, when it came to it, I didn't know any more about it than him.

He took a long time. Much longer than I would usually spend standing in a newsagent wondering how to spend £2. In the end he decided to go for buying two now – and not wait till next week.

We left the shop, he opened up the packets and the stickers turned out to be mostly different though one or two were the same. I then did stick my oar in. I said that if anyone else at school was collecting the stickers, he could 'do swappses' with them. And I told him about how when I was a boy we used to do swappses with cigarette cards and there was a time once when packets of tea had cards in them and we did swappses with them.

Then I told him how we used to play a game flicking the cards up against a wall and when one card landed on your opponent's card, you won his card.

Meanwhile he started sticking the stickers in his sticker-book.

I don't know if it was this that got him interested in the cards on sale as well as the stickers. These also come in packets and they go into a plastic folder.

The book and the folder together are pretty complicated. The players have to go into their respective countries. There are stickers for stadiums. Some of the cards have to go into a special section at the back divided up into such categories as 'Experts' or 'Double Trouble'. As you don't have all the cards, slotting them into their correct pocket involves a long process of counting off the players on a list, leaving pockets empty for the cards you haven't got yet, and slotting the ones you do have into the right place. This is, as I say, long, fiddly and very easy to get wrong.

I soon saw that this was about patience, care and attention to detail. He said he wanted me to help and I had to force myself to not dive in or take over, when, say, he was slow, or felt that he needed to check something even though it was right. This had to be his thing. My job was to do nothing more than be his assistant.

Meanwhile, we were talking about countries all over the world, the languages they speak, the players' names, why someone with an African name might play for France, why someone with a Slavic name might play for Australia. We talked about why some players who play in Latin countries have their nicknames on their shirts.

Along the way, we also looked at the way in which the names of the countries in the folder are not the same as the ones we use. So, to take one example, we say, 'Holland' but the folder says, 'Nederland'.

We talked about our favourite players. His is the Uruguay player Luis Suarez. Mine is the Ivory Coast player Yaya Toure. In the middle of this, he said, 'How do you get born black?' So then we talked about inheritance and eye colour, hair colour and the like and how skin colour is only one of hundreds of differences that we pass on to each other.

And then there is the code.

In the stickers folder is the coded system they draw up to show the teams' progress through the knockout stage of the tournament. It's a complicated matter of labelling winners and losers as designated by labels like D1 or F2. This meant discussing leagues, points systems, knockouts and the rest. He wasn't sure he got it, so I said, why didn't he get a bit of paper and draw it all up, make his predictions and see what happened. So he followed it through and ended up with a Brazil vs Germany final to be won by Brazil. (As I write this, I don't know if he's right or not.) Doing these predictions and drawing it all up took at least an hour.

Clearly, when all this is put together, it involves many different kinds of skill, learning and discovering. If you wanted to put school words on it, you could say it involves maths, English, foreign languages, geography, 'setting', predictions based on analyses of facts (i.e. 'form') and much more. He pushed himself to overcome irritation with the physical business of getting cards into tight plastic pockets, making errors with where to slot in the cards.

There are also many emotional rewards in it for him. He's someone who loves to get things in order – clothes, books, toys – and doing this satisfies him immensely. When he goes to bed after a session with the folder, I can see him smile to himself that he's got it right. There have been times when he's gone off to sleep in an irritated mood because something wasn't sorted, wasn't in the right place.

I guess there's also something important going on between us. He's in charge of something that he knows I am really interested in. When I'm watching a club game on TV, I ask him which country does this or that player play for and he looks it up in his folder or sticker-book. I couldn't figure out how the classifications at the end of the folder work. He did. He's the expert. What seemed to him like a tangled mess of cards, stickers, folder and sticker-book is now in order. And he knows that he did all that, apart from one or two moments where he asked me to help him hold cards, count empty pockets or some such. As I say, it's been crucial that I haven't taken it over, or expressed any kind of negative judgement of him or the activity.

As I write this, he's looking forward to showing it to his older (much older) brothers, one of whom is going to the World Cup. I can see that even though he is the youngest, he feels he has won himself some status. He's carved out something for himself.

As I say, it's easy to think of this sort of thing as unimportant, 'not very educational', not 'intellectual' or not creative. I think just the opposite. To see his persistence and eagerness, to hear him talking and asking questions and forcing himself to remember and discover more, to see him improving his hand–eye co-ordination, is an absolute treat.

My father once told me when he was studying that he was reading someone who said there is 'perseverance' in general, and there's 'perseverance in the face of difficulty, obstacles and discouragement'. He said that the person he was reading at the time had invented a word for this second kind of perseverance and it was 'perseveration'. He said that one of the key markers for people who really know how to learn, and for people who know how to invent things and be creative is that they have somehow got 'perseveration'. They have learned how to keep going with something.

I think that to get to this, you need to have the feeling inside yourself that you are good enough to keep going, that you can overcome an obstacle, or that you can keep going through the finicky, boring stuff to get to something that looks or feels good.

This isn't acquired from being handed some little slogan like 'Keep right on to the end of the road' or some such. You have to have plenty of experiences like my son is having with the football stickers and cards.

One last thought: let's say he had got fed up halfway through. Let's say he jacked it in and said that he didn't want to do it any more. What then?

I think I would have tried to help him carry on . . . for a bit. I wouldn't have pushed it. I would have told him about something that I had jacked in and something that I had persisted with. I would have asked him if there was anything else I could do. Or if there was anyone else who could. If it was all no, I would have left it. No recriminations, no complaints, no sneers or jeers. That's what I hope I would say.

POSTSCRIPT

The car's broken down. It's a disaster. A car full of children stuck by the side of the road. The AA say it will be two hours before they can get to us. I go off on one about how the car has only just been serviced and hadn't the guy said that there was something wrong with the cooling system but he couldn't figure out what? Well, this is bloody it . . . we won't be home till midnight . . .

Out of the corner of my eye, I notice that the children have moved away from where the car is beached by the side of the road. I look over. They are on the edge of a bit of scrubby grass, standing around randomly picking at bits of things. At least, that's what it looks like.

I go on running through the irritations and anxieties of life, hoping that they won't be added to by children getting fed up. Or bored. Or both. Or worse.

Actually, it was me who was fed up. And bored. Or both. And if I'm honest about it, I had no idea how to fill the next two hours of my life.

But the children weren't bored. Or fed up. They had roamed around this scrubby patch of ground and discovered little reedy plants with bobbles on the top – the kind of plant that grows in wet fields. More than that: they had discovered that if they picked these and did some kind of duel with them, there was a game they could play. A bit like conkers. One of them held out the reed. The other whacked the reed to try to get the bobble off the top. It wasn't easy. You had to get the angle right. And you could lose your own bobble.

It needed rules. They invented rules.

One strike each. A successful hit earned you another go against your opponent's reed. It soon became clear that some reeds were better than others. But should you look for a good attacking reed, or a good defensive one? Tactical decisions needed to be taken. The air was thick with their discussions, shrieks of laughter and passionate activity.

I went on being fed up and bored.

I often think of this story as a reminder of what happens when children have the space, time and confidence to find out things. They were inventive and co-operative. They investigated the world around them and interpreted it. All this delivered them a way of getting through something that could have turned out to be tiresome – stressful even.

And they were happy. Or I should say: they did things that made them happy.

I've tried to learn from this incident. When it comes up in my mind as a memory, I see myself sitting by the side of the road, angry and sulky. I see them twenty or thirty yards away, safe but detached. I'm not chivvying them, they're not chivvying me. I'm not setting them learning objectives, they're not bringing me their work for me to approve. I'm not going to test them and examine them in order to find out if they've achieved the learning objectives that I've set them. I'm not going over to them and streaming them into different abilities at playing the reed game. I'm not going to test them and grade them according to their scores. Yet, plenty of learning is going on here. What's more, some of the learning is the learning I've done in thinking about it. I find myself hoping that at some point in or after the reedy game saga I told them how impressed and amazed I was by what they did. And that I loved them for it. We have to do that every day. Even when we're fed up with them. Or just fed up.

I've mentioned several times in the book that the survival kit my father gave me was 'be curious' and 'be entitled' – meaning 'be entitled to take an interest in anything and everything'. I hope that these words – and the book as a whole – will raise questions as to what kind of words of wisdom you would want to pass on to your children. Storytellers talk of 'wisdom tales': stories that give us wise thoughts that we can carry around with us in the scenes and characters of a story. We went to see Taffy Thomas when he was 'crowned' as storyteller laureate and he told a story that went something like this:

In a town long ago, the old mayor was going to retire. In this town, they left it to the mayor to decide how the next mayor was going to be chosen. His way would be like this: he said that anyone who wanted to be mayor should come to a meeting the next day. At the meeting, he gave everyone a sunflower seed and he said, 'Whoever can make this sunflower seed grow the tallest will be the next mayor.'

So everyone went away and a few months later, after the sun had shone and the rain had rained, the old mayor called everyone together again, asking them to bring their sunflowers. Some were huge, some had many sunflower heads on them. The old mayor walked down the line, looking up and down, looking under the leaves, looking in the soil, making appreciative little noises: 'Hmm . . . yes . . . nice . . .' and so on. There was one sunflower that was clearly taller than the rest. Surely it would be simple to decide who would be the next mayor.

Then he got to a small girl who was holding her pot. There was no sunflower in it at all. 'Hello,' he said, 'what happened here?'

'I planted the seed,' she said, 'but it wouldn't grow.'

The old mayor looked at her.

'And you,' he said, 'are the next mayor.'

Now with 'wisdom tales', you can stop there and just wait to see what people will make of it. To tell the truth, even now, I'm torn as to whether to go on and explain more than I need to. OK, I'll succumb but if you tell the story, you can decide where you will stop and wait. Taffy Thomas told us that the mayor had boiled the sunflower seeds so that they wouldn't and couldn't grow. Now, I really do think I don't need to say any more. My daughter said, 'I like that story.' It may not be as snappy as 'be curious' or 'be entitled' but I guess that there's something worth passing on in this story too. I hope you have others.

Finally, I would like to stress that this is a book that is really nothing more or less than being about 'good ideas'. It's not a book of 'the only ideas' – that would be a curriculum or syllabus to be tested in an exam. We are parents and carers, we really don't need to do any more of that kind of education than the children have to do already.

It's not a book of 'all the ideas we need to know'. I don't think such a book can exist. There are some massive 'books of knowledge' out there already. Maybe somewhere out there there's a 'tiny book of knowledge' that only has about twenty pages, each with something on it that sparks off hundreds of thoughts and lines of enquiry. Or your children and you could write one, perhaps.

This book is not even a book of the 'best ideas'. Everyone

has 'good ideas' and if anyone reading this thinks that an idea in the book is 'not good enough', you can, in the spirit of the book, argue with what I've written. Or, go one step further: you could come up with better ideas. Even better, you could try out these better ideas with your children. This would be the 'test it and see' way, which you can follow up with: 'adapt and change the things you read here so that they'll work in the world you find yourself in'.

As I write these words an image comes into my mind: the shopping trolley has broken. The plastic handle has split in two. I can go round the corner and buy a new one. Or I can grab some duct tape I've got in the drawer and do a lash-up. As I'm doing it, I can hear my wife laughing at me.

'What's the joke?' I ask, with the slightest, slightest edge of rattiness in my voice.

The children watch as this little spectacle takes shape.

'You're doing a Harold,' she says – meaning my father, Harold.

Even as she says it, the duct tape gets a bit wrinkled.

It's a bodge. But it works.

I say it out loud: 'It may be a bodge, but it works.'

Smiles pass round the room.

But I'm proud.

I head off to the shops.

On the way, I remember that I've heard these words about bodging before. Heard, hundreds of times, as my father and mother tried to fix a leak in the roof of the old van, make a bag for our family tent out of an old blanket, or scribble the letters for anagrams in crosswords all down the margins of the newspaper . . .

Come to think of it, this matter of adapting and changing might be the best idea in this book, because in adapting and changing the things we find, we change ourselves.

FOOD FOR THOUGHT

WRITING IDEAS

For the last forty years or so I've worked in schools, libraries, book festivals and book clubs, often helping children to write. Mostly, this has been about helping them write poems, but sometimes it's been helping them write stories, sketches and plays. More often than not, this has been linked to thinking about ways of performing what the children write, sometimes to do with making audio or video versions.

It goes without saying that I think this is important for all sorts of reasons at the same time: all the way from practical things to do with learning how to write and read, through to exploring who we are, how we are with other people, what the world around us is like, and how confident we are at writing and speaking about these things. With writing poems, it often turns out that our attention is drawn to how language itself works, how and why some people speak and write in different ways from each other, how we can play with language so that it makes different sounds, or how different sounds make different meanings. A lot of this may well make it easier or more interesting when it comes to reading. It may well make it more likely that we get to be more curious about what others have written. Sometimes, it's other people's writing that sets us off writing.

Once we write about something, we have a bit of ourselves to look at. It's a bit like looking in the mirror, except we have made the picture ourselves. So in a way, when we read what we've written, we are looking at ourselves from outside ourselves. Impossible, in actual fact, but it's a bit like that. This enables us to be more aware of who we are and what we're like. Then, if we share what we write with others, we are able to compare all this. This is also a way of becoming more aware of who we are and what we're like. If we do this in a generous and constructive way, we learn how to help each other think, write and come up with opinions.

TALK WITH YOUR PEN

So, first off, any single one of the moments I've described throughout this book is a possible moment for writing. As I always say to children, the best place to start – if you're stuck – is to think of talking with your pen. Imagine talking about what you've just seen or heard or thought. Imagine that you're telling your friend or your mum or your dad about what you've just seen or heard or thought. Now, instead of telling it, write it.

DAYDREAMS

The other great source for writing is daydreams. I often say, just give yourself thirty seconds, one minute, five minutes, a half hour . . . Just daydream. Just let your mind range over something or other that you once did, or wanted to do, or was afraid to do or was jealous that someone else could do. Then, talk with your pen about that. I believe that if we help children get into the kinds of places and experiences I've described in this book, plenty of daydreams will arise from them, and then the daydreams will, if we listen to them, be great starting points for writing.

PAINTINGS

More specifically, I've mentioned paintings. If you look at a painting, you may well start to figure out what someone in the painting is thinking, or you may have a feeling that a part or all of the painting is 'giving' you. These are good places to start writing. There should never be any pressure to write a lot or to 'write well'. All you need to do is jot something down. It's just a matter of finding some words in your head to express what that person in the picture is thinking, or what the feelings are in that corner of the painting, or the painting as a whole.

FAVOURITE POEM

A good way to write poems is to find a poem you like and let yourself think either, I could write a poem like that, or, This poem reminds me of something. Either way, the trick is to grab that feeling when it comes and jot something down. If you notice that a poem is a list, then you can try doing a 'list poem'. If you notice that a poem is a question and answer, you can try doing that. If you notice that a poem seems to have a chorus or a refrain, then you can try doing a 'refrain poem'. On the other hand a poem may spark off an idea about, say, 'envy' or 'being lost', or 'being irritated' or a 'mystery in the woods', and you can take off from there with your own version, your own thoughts. The starting point in these cases is a poem, so that just means reading a few poems together.

WORDS AND PHRASES NOTEBOOK

Alongside this, some children may enjoy the idea of having a book (or a digital memo pad) where they can put interesting or moving things they've heard or read. It's just like collecting coins, stamps or old bones. It's just collecting words and phrases instead. It can be from the TV, lines from songs, a few words from a speech in a film, a title of a book, something you heard on a bus – whatever. If you collect these and then occasionally look back at them, they may trigger off words, thoughts and ideas which may then in turn start up something you may want to write about. It's like your own private bank of thoughts expressed in ways that you've found interesting. My parents made scrapbooks on the wall in our kitchen. We all wrote up things on the kitchen tiles and they stayed there till we rubbed them off and started again. It's why I remember that my mother called our broken dishwasher a 'wish-dasher'.

RIDDLES

I go round the world but stay on the corner. What am I? A postage stamp.

Figurative writing is where you use an image of one thing to tell you about something else altogether. We do it when we talk to each other too. If I say, 'every cloud has a silver lining', or 'put your back into it', or 'I'm all over the place today', or 'I sound like a broken record', 'the weather's up to no good again' . . . and thousands more, these are all idioms, metaphors, similes and personification, also called figures of speech. A good deal of poetry does interesting and deep things with these. You can introduce them to children in a mechanical way by getting them, say, to 'make up a simile poem'. I'm not so keen on this as they often sound like exercises.

Here's another way: you start by doing a mixture of telling, researching and thinking about riddles. Riddles are often another kind of figurative language. They express one thing with an image taken from somewhere else. Quite often they express two impossible opposites: like staying in the corner but going round the world – this is called a paradox. Quite often riddles contain a paradox.

So, I suggest to children that they pick any object (a chair, an apple, a fridge), or any idea or feeling (like 'time' or 'happiness') and make a riddle. To help them, I say:

Often – but not always – it works well by getting the object, idea or feeling to talk as 'I', as with 'I go round the world but stay in the corner.'

If it's too hard to work out some things to say, here are some questions that you, as the object, idea or feeling can answer. Put your answers one under the other and it may end up being a riddle. As you write, remember that part of the fun of a riddle is that it shouldn't be obvious. The answer should not be easy to get.

- What can you see?
- What can you hear?
- Is anybody near you saying anything? What are they saying?
- What are you thinking?
- What do you wish for?

- What do you hope for?
- What makes you angry?
- What are you afraid of?
- What are you jealous of?
- Do you have any other feelings?
- Can you think of a paradox about yourself, two opposites about yourself which taken together are impossible – just like the stamp staying in the corner but going round the world?

Now look at your list of answers. Read it through. Does it make sense? Is it possible to give it any kind of rhythm? Perhaps by repeating bits of it? Are there parts that are too ordinary and dull? Try cutting them? Are there bits that could do with a little more detail to make them more interesting? Add something.

Now try it out on an audience. If they get it right away, perhaps together you can think of ways of making it harder?

After all that, you should have an interesting piece of writing about quite ordinary things like a clock or a table or time or sadness or some such. And you've written some of it in figurative ways. You will have imagined, say, what makes a clock sad? Or what can time see?

This is one of the qualities that makes us find poetry interesting.

REPETITION

I've already mentioned this. A good deal of poetry revolves around repeating things. When we talk about 'rhyme' this is a way of saying that a poem repeats sounds. When we talk about 'rhythm' it's a way of saying that a pattern of beats is repeated.

One way to explore this is to see what happens if we repeat a phrase or sentence. Anything at all: 'no smoking', or 'please keep off the grass'. If you repeat phrases like these, you will start making a rhythm. Different words, phrases and sentences make different rhythms. Children will know this without knowing it. They do it, without us pointing it out, when they play games, ask questions again and again, or try to attract our attention.

You can just try making rhythms with things you hear or see written up, song titles, film titles, shop signs, place names or whatever.

Alternatively, if you know anything about drumming or musical rhythms, you can pick one of these and see if you can make up words to fit it. So instead of saying, 'tum-te ta ta', you can say 'happy birthday', or alternate 'happy birthday' with 'tum-te ta ta'. If you know the bars of a particular drum beat, you can make up nonsense phrases or real phrases to fit. In the jazz work I did, I couldn't 'hear' one drum link until the drummer told me that it was 'rinky-tink, tonky-tonk'!

Shakespeare wrote in a rhythm that is like saying 'today' five times in a row. You can have fun pretending to be Shakespeare by saying 'today' five times in a row as if you're saying something first angry, then happy, then nasty, sinister, mysterious, sexy or whatever.

RAP

Most rap starts out with a basic four strong beats in a row or line. Part of what makes it exciting is that the singers squeeze different numbers of syllables between the four strong beats. This makes it seem as if one moment it's speeding up and another moment it's going slow. Then after a few lines, it changes rhythm into maybe a little sequence of two-beat lines, or one-beat lines, and then goes back to the four.

You can have fun trying to make up rap 'couplets' (two lines that rhyme) round a table, while someone keeps the rhythm. Some people can do 'beat box', making a rhythm with their mouths. The easiest things to make up raps about are yourself or the other people in the room: what they look like, what they're wearing, what they do at the weekend, that sort of thing. There is nothing funnier for children to hear than, let's say, a grandparent making up a rap. And very irritating if they're good at it!

Rapping is also good for making up something that really matters to you.

LIMERICKS

Elsewhere in the book I've mentioned limericks. Once you get the hang of these, you can try making them up, the moment you hear someone's name, or a place name that seems to have some good rhyming words that go with it.

IMAGISM

This was the name of a poetic movement. One way to translate it into something fun to do is to give yourself a rule: in this poem, we will only write about things we can see. That means not including anything we know about through any other senses – i.e. nothing that we can hear, touch, smell or taste. We can't include any thoughts, feelings or ideas.

So, you could try writing a series of 'imagist' lines (with or without a rhythm) about anything you're looking at: a beach, a building, a photo, a table. You can then see what happens if you repeat some of the lines. One way to repeat is to do what's called 'framing'. That is, making the only two lines that repeat, the first and the last. Another way is to make the repeating lines a chorus. That is, you repeat a line, every two or every four lines. (Or at any interval you like, as often happens in songs.)

Imagist writing often sounds very bare. That might be interesting or dull! It all depends.

What may make it more interesting is if you give yourself another rule: this bit of imagist writing will be about a feeling, I won't tell you what the feeling is, but you will have to guess the feeling when I read it to you. But whatever happens, I won't include the word for that feeling in the poem because it is strictly 'imagist'. So, let's say you decide that you will write a 'sad' imagist poem about a field or a river, how will you do that? Will you try to make it sound in a certain way, perhaps? Are long vowel sounds like 'oo' and 'ah' sad? Or are consonants like 'm' and 'n' and 'ng' sad too? Will they make it sound sad? Or will there be a way in which if you show that time is passing or things are dying, it will make it sad?

What happens if you repeat words, phrases and sentences? Does this make it sound sadder?

What happens if you try out some other feelings like, say, nasty or triumphant? Is that possible?

Some of the best poems I've ever seen children write have come about this way.

IMPOSSIBLE WRITING

This is how I describe another kind of writing. Let's say you look at a photo of some people sitting, lying and standing under a tree. What happens if you talk about things in the picture in ways that are 'impossible'? So, rather than writing that the people are standing under the tree, you try saying, 'The tree is holding up the woman' or 'The ground stretches out the man', or 'A stool has curved its back under a boy.'

CHORUSES

Sometimes these can be starting points. If you are somewhere like, say, in a car, at the swimming pool, in your room – or remembering it, or daydreaming about it, you can try thinking of a chorus that expresses this. It can be very ordinary, like 'in my room, in my room' or, 'at the pool, at the pool', or you can think of something like, 'sitting-thinking, lying-thinking' or 'splish-splash, splash-splish'.

This is your chorus.

Now you can decide to use this chorus every other line, every two lines, every three lines – or however.

Now what to put in between the chorus?

You can try answering questions you ask yourself like:

What can you see?
What can you hear?
What are you thinking about?
What are people saying?
What are you saying?

What are people doing?
What do you think they are doing?
What do you think they are thinking?

You can then put these answers in between the chorus line.

After you've had a go at doing one of these about a place, you can try doing one about something like 'in my mind', or 'when I felt anxious' or 'when it was raining' or something imaginary like, 'in the cave of the evil one'.

INSIDE A POEM OR STORY

One of the best starting points for any writing is from inside a poem or story. If you know *We're Going on a Bear Hunt*, you'll know that on the last page there is a picture of the bear, walking away, off down a beach. Some people are very affected by this picture. They wonder what the bear is thinking. And why is he thinking whatever it is he's thinking? If people ask me what the bear is thinking, I always say, 'What do *you* think he's thinking?'

That's what I mean by writing from 'inside a poem or story'. In every book, play, film, opera or poem there are moments when the person, creature or being is having thoughts that the piece of writing is not telling us. We guess them, or think them. If you know *Hansel and Gretel*, you'll know that there is the awful moment, the second time that the parents have abandoned the children, when the children realize that they are lost and can't find their way home. So, we can ask, what are Hansel and Gretel thinking at that very moment? Just as in musicals, operas and Shakespeare plays, we can turn these thoughts into a solo piece, monologue, aria or soliloquy – a stream of feelings and thoughts about the state that 'I' am in.

Alternatively, you don't have to write this kind of poem from the point of view of a person. In stories and poems where something happens, there is always an object or place that has 'witnessed' the scene. With Hansel and Gretel in the forest, we might imagine that there is a tree who is witnessing what they're doing. In some scenes in stories, the object itself is the cause of all the bother! Famously, it's a hankie in *Othello*. It could be Odysseus's boat, or Icarus's 'wings'. In ancient Greek plays, a 'chorus' – as in the 'chorus' in a musical – expresses feelings and ideas that a character is having or should be having. So, in *Hansel and Gretel* you could write a 'tree chorus'. They might wish that Hansel and Gretel take this or that course of action. They might also make sounds of the forest as the wind goes through their leaves. They might describe what they see in an *imagist* way, the moon above, the forest floor covered in leaves. These might make a *chorus* (in the other sense of the word, meaning a repeated line). They might warn them of what could happen to them.

If a child is engrossed and interested in a story or play and has got wrapped up in what people are feeling, then usually they find doing this kind of writing easy and interesting.

After they've written it, you can see if doing some repeating, or making up a chorus, or giving it a rhythm makes it better or worse.

AVOID PROPER SENTENCES

Another experiment in language is to make up a rule: no writing in proper sentences. A lot of poems avoid whole sentences. To give the impression of time passing quickly, or of a person having a stream of thoughts, the usual structure of sentences starts to disappear. In the most famous speech of all – 'To be or not to be' – Shakespeare has Hamlet starting to break up his sentences as he begins to wonder about things in complicated ways.

Some subjects are better for non-sentences than others. One of my favourite poems when I was a boy is by one of the climbers on the world's first successful Everest expedition. He wanted to describe the breathlessness of climbing. The whole poem is made up of words like 'foot', 'breath', 'gasp' without ever using full sentences like, 'I took a step to my right.'

With one group of children who were talking about getting lost in the supermarket when they were very young, we had a go at writing like that. I suggested as 'input', things like what could you see, hear and smell, when you were lost? What were your thoughts? Feelings? And the rule was – no sentences!

Other experiences that are good for this kind of writing are being in a race, in any kind of panic, getting worried about something, anything really, really exciting like something in sport that you're watching, or a moment of great emotion. Getting rid of sentences seems to suggest that sentences are too logical for this emotion.

LOOKING CLOSELY

Maybe you've collected something like a pebble or an odd-shaped stick, or you're looking closely at a single object at home like a button or a badge. Maybe there's a reason why you're looking closely beyond the object itself, because, say, it comes from a grandparent.

One way to write is to look very closely at this one single object. To start off with you can try writing about it an *imagist* way. Try to capture every detail of it. Then you can try thinking about it in the *riddle* way, from that object's point of view. What can it see? What is it thinking? You can try writing about it from *inside its story* – in other words from the point of view of what it has seen and heard in the past. Objects have histories. Maybe the object can 'remember' being owned by a grandparent and what that grandparent went through.

LETTER POEMS

Related to this are the letter poems we can write, where we write something 'to' someone without necessarily ever sending it to them. Some of the most interesting of these are ones for someone we know we'll never see again or for someone in the future, or for someone imaginary, who may be in a story or film or just someone we have daydreamed about. We can also write letter poems to our previous or future self, or more particularly to 'me' at a particular moment from the past or future . . . perhaps just as something important is happening – something awful or wonderful.

POEM POSTER

Without writing anything, some children like making a poem poster. This need not involve anything much more than writing out the poem on as big a piece of paper as you can find and thinking up things to draw around it or stick on to the poster. This is a way of interpreting a poem without trying to come up with 'critical' language. It's more about turning feelings and thoughts into colours, shapes, designs and images. When children have done this, you can then sit and chat about why they have done it in that particular way, and you will always find that they now find 'critical' ways of talking about a poem. Drawing, painting, cutting and sticking things inspired by the poem, and *then* talking about this, releases their thoughts and enables them to turn these thoughts into language.

PERFORMANCE

Something similar happens with performance. I think it's less important to start with the idea of learning by heart, than thinking of how to perform a poem. That's me talking from my experience of trying to learn my own poems – which is that though I know about three hours' worth of my own poems, I've never sat down and learned any of them. What I've done is perform them over and over again, until I knew them. The will to learn them off by heart came from the performing. This means that the performance is more important than simply knowing them. It means that what dominates the performance is the need to express something rather than the need to get all the words right.

In home life, it's possible to factor in performances, if people like it. Many Scots' people have the advantage of a Burns Night to focus people's attention on 'getting something up' for the occasion. For those of us who aren't Scots, we have to think of another excuse. Sometimes the performance will arise out of the writing. People will want to perform what they've written. Then when someone else comes over, there's a repeat show. And another. And another.

STORIES

One simple thing to do with stories is to take an old folk-tale, Greek myth, scene from the Bible, Shakespeare play and do an update. Turn all the characters into modern people. Don't write it like a folk-tale. Try to write it as if it's a very modern piece of writing, an event that happened the other day, near you. Try as hard as you can to disguise the characters you've taken from the old story. Add in sub-plots or other characters if you need to.

To make it into a game, each do an update and see if the others can guess where you got the story from.

Something similar is to take any story and change the characters, the time-frame or the setting. So you could take, for instance, a Roald Dahl story and keep the plot, more or less, keep the setting, more or less, keep it in its time-frame but change, say, the age and sex of all the characters.

Next time, you could try changing the setting or the time-frame – so it all happens in, say, Roman times, or the future.

Another time you can try keeping all the characters and write another story for them, so you end up with a sequel or 'back-story' or 'prequel'.

So your four 'variables' are plot, characters, time-frame and setting. You can change one, two or three of them, but not all of them.

And that's the story of Hollywood! Many films that we see are versions of previous stories with one, two or three of its elements turned into something else. What tends to happen is that as we change one or more of the four variables, we have to change the dialogue and we have to introduce more characters and settings to make it work. By the end, it may well feel as if we have written something 'new'.

Story-writing gains a lot from looking at the way people make the stories we read and watch. You can pick one aspect of a story and then look at how different writers do it, like, say, 'openings'. Not just the opening words but, perhaps the opening minute. How do writers create an interest in their first minute? What happens if you try to imitate that, with no intention of writing any more? Who can write the most interesting first minute?

Then after a few goes, is it possible to write any more of the story or play or script?

The writer Morris Gleitzman once told me that his rule was to 'always start any scene at the last possible moment'. He said that he asks himself what is going to be the most interesting point in the scene that he's about to write and starts there. If there is anything that needs to be explained that he's missed out by starting at that spot, then he can always go back and explain it.

It can be fun trying to do this. What you may well finish up with is a very good short story! Interestingly, Shakespeare's *Romeo and Juliet* is mostly written in this way.

Another way of thinking about stories is to imagine that anything you write about represents something else. If I write about an 'ordinary' family, the moment I start to talk about their jobs, or where they live or what their children are like, this family starts to 'stand for' or 'represent' this kind of family in real life. It's rather like the way people who talk about elections invent types like 'pebble-dash subtopia man' or 'Ford Mondeo man'. This is saying that this sort of person who owns or does a certain kind of thing, represents a type.

All stories do this. Even if it's something mythic or imaginary, like a hero fighting a monster or a superhero fighting off the baddies, this 'represents' feelings that many people might have or ways of behaving that many people might have. Meanwhile, the battle or struggle will 'represent' a way of seeing the world, say, that a great and wonderful hero could 'save' us.

So another starting point for stories is to think along these lines. What do I want my characters to 'represent'? A fight for what's right? That friendship is the most important thing we have? Or you can never rely on anyone apart from yourself? Or you know a bit about everyone else and nothing about yourself?

Sometimes, the characters in a story do all the action but something like a river or a city or a boat or the sea is also a character. What this setting or object does, calls on people to behave in response to it.

So, you've put your characters in a boat, perhaps it's a re-make of *Hansel and Gretel*. They've been abandoned. Instead of the forest, there is now the sea. There's a storm. Hansel (who is now called Raffi and is aged eighty-seven) says he can handle it. It turns out he can't. Gretel (who is now called Surya and is aged ninety-one) tells him that he can't. They argue. They remember stuff. From a long, long time ago.

The storm gets worse . . .

SUPPLIES TO HAVE AT HOME

One of the ways to enable our children to learn and to want to learn is to make sure they've got the stuff that will encourage them and help them.

ELECTRONIC AND DIGITAL GEAR

At the most expensive end, of course, there are the smartphones, tablets, Kindles, laptops and various hand-held digital devices. Even as I'm writing this, new devices and new apps are being invented and developed. I've watched children no older than three, possibly younger, playing with these. They're 'reading' screens, choosing icons and images. I have a friend, the artist Hervé Tullet, who has devised a wonderful moving 'blob' app, which has hundreds, possibly thousands of visual combinations that you choose between.

I can see nothing wrong with these. I would only say that we shouldn't use them as dummies, ways of getting children to shut up. We should get involved with them, talk about them, find ways of playing two-hander games with them, so that they contribute to talk, not take away from it.

Perhaps you can't afford some or any of these, in which case, your ally is the library. I fully understand, what with the cuts and the like, that these too may be out of reach. If there is a library sufficiently near, then this is a plea to you to help your child use it – particularly if the electronic and digital stuff is not possible. At the library, you can book time on the computers so that you have access to the internet. If you have a Kindle, you can also get any ebook that the library service has on its stocks, for free. Not many people seem to know about this, so I'll say it again: you can get any book that the whole national library service has on its stocks as a free ebook for your Kindle.

Just as important as these bits of gear are the old hands-on stuff to do with 'making and doing'. For young children, these include:

A DRESSING-UP BOX OR BIN

One of the key ways in which children 'find themselves' is by pretending to be someone else. This is part of the process of building up what I called their 'inner talk'. It is also vital for their learning how to listen and talk. By putting on an old hat, or a pair of shoes, the child tries out being 'the other': the child gets to know what they think it feels like to be a mother, a doctor or Godzilla or a singer and so on. The child gets a chance to invent, investigate and experiment with other identities. Sometimes this can be fun and rewarding to do on their own, sometimes great to do it with others, so that playing can turn into sketches and plays.

These may at first glance seem trivial or silly but quite often what's going on is very serious stuff to do with power and control; or sometimes very serious stuff to do with interpreting some difficult and troubling things that the children have heard and seen at school or at home; and sometimes difficult and troubling things that they've seen on TV. When the children play, they are, in effect, taking these things that they've heard and seen and laying them out in front of each other to investigate through their play. You'll hear them inviting each other to be this or that character. Then you might hear them discuss whether that character would or would not say or do such and such a thing. That's where they are 'investigating' and learning. Then again, one or other of the characters might be in control or in charge. The others might be that powerful person's inferior, obeying orders. Then they may swap over. This involves them experimenting with and investigating the kind of world they're in, where there are people who are in charge and people (like them) who are supposed to do what they're told.

If you listen in on their play, you will hear this sort of thing going on. Believe me, it's important stuff.

BITS

This is the bits and pieces collection that your children can use to make cards, pictures, posters and the like. It's really important to stock up on glitter, coloured tissue paper, several different kinds of glue, scissors, buttons, staplers, stickers, stars, sticky dots, crayons, coloured pencils, felt tips of different sizes and colours, watercolours, 'poster' paint, 'pipe cleaners', straws, ends of cloth, wool, string, cotton and the like, cotton wool, shiny paper, card, sugar paper, paperclips, safety pins, split pins and so on . . .

Quite often we have to help them keep this in good order with folders and boxes and cubby-holes. Same goes with helping them display and show off the things they make so that friends and relatives can see what they've done. By doing that, we show them that they matter and have a rightful place in our world and the world outside.

MAGNIFIERS

Magnifying glass, Creature Peeper, microscope, telescope, binoculars.

These not only magnify things, they also help us 'freeze' and isolate things. This is as much a mental as physical thing. Each of these little bits of apparatus asks of you or your child to pick something out, 'frame' it in the window of the magnifier and think about it. This stops the world going round for a moment. There is just your eye and the creature or thing. This concentrates the mind and sets up all sorts of questions and talk.

Don't squirm at this one, but on one occasion one of my children (all at some time or another, actually) had nits and we were looking for lice. When we found one, it occurred to me that I didn't really know what a head-louse actually looks like. So with a pair of tweezers I put the louse between the slides of a microscope and took a look. Though it had been drenched in anti-nit, anti-lice shampoo, it was still alive – of course – and we looked at it waving its legs. Lice are 'translucent' – that's to say, you can partially see through them, though they are brownish in colour. So you can more or less see into their bodies. We discovered that a louse that has been busy doing what lice do, is full of blood. So in the heart of this translucent, wriggling shape – looking a bit like a tiny lobster – there was a little red cloud: my child's blood.

TREASURES

We all need time and space to discover what are our real treasures. With us all being coaxed into buying more and more stuff for our children at gift-giving times and holidays, it's very easy for us or them to lose sight of the idea of small important things that have value and meaning beyond being expensive, fashionable or big. I have no magic formula for making this happen other than trying to be observant about which way your child is heading. As an idea of what I mean here's something that happened to me. My parents, with the very best of intentions spent many, many hours trying to figure out what my brother and I would like for Christmas. They went to great lengths, going 'up to town' to specialist shops to find something or other that they thought we'd like or, more likely, that we'd benefit from.

On one occasion they got the idea that, what with my interest in animals and birds, I would like to catch butterflies. (This was long before this sort of thing was banned.) So they got me the gear that you needed to catch, kill and display butterflies. It was elaborate and, in its own scientific way, beautiful. Jars, bottles, chemicals, tweezers, pins and the rest. I had never said that I wanted to catch butterflies. I had never said that I wanted to display them. All I had ever done was become quite interested in reading about badgers and – believe it or not – cows. Never mind, my parents were going to be one jump ahead and get me a large slice of expensive gear intended for catching and displaying butterflies.

As it happens I was quite interested but quickly became intimidated by the difficultly of catching butterflies in the net, and the complicated matter of getting them from the net to the jar where the butterflies were killed. And the matter of not mixing up the chemical that killed them with the chemical that relaxed their wings all added to the seemingly over-complicated set-up. All the while in the back of my mind was the idea that this was all cooked up by my parents because they thought that it would be 'good' for me. The intention was honourable, it's just that their method was faulty.

Meanwhile, my real treasured possession was a 'map measurer'. One of the pastimes that my parents did pass on to me directly was the joy of walking. In order to walk in Britain, you needed a 'one inch to the mile' Ordnance Survey map, a very particular kind of map with a whole set of symbols that enabled you to read off the landscape exactly where you were.

I took this very seriously indeed and with various friends, whether it was on holiday or during term-time, went for long walks – anything up to twenty miles in a day. I was doing this without parents, with friends, from about the age of ten onwards. Part of the seriousness and joy of this was calculating and knowing exactly how far we were going to walk, were walking, would walk, or had walked. The most accurate way of figuring this out was with a little pocket-watch-like thing, that had a tiny wheel on the bottom. What you did was put the wheel of the 'measurer' down on the map, and run the wheel over the map along exactly the same roads and paths that were your route. Then, when you had done the trip with the wheel, you lifted it off the map and looked at the dial.

This was my top treasure. This was an enthusiasm that had come from me. This was something that I wanted to do and wanted to do with my friends rather than with my parents. And the map measurer was something that I had longed to have, saved up for, bought and was now using to find out more and more about the very thing I was passionate about. This was many, many times more of a treasure to me than the butterfly collecting set.

Many years later, I got the tremendous satisfaction of having my father ask to borrow it from me so that he could calculate the mileage he claimed from his college for his travels round the south of England, supervising students doing their teaching practice.

SOME BOOKS AND ADVICE ABOUT BOOKS

WARNING: SOME OF THESE ARE OUT OF PRINT SO YOU'LL ONLY BE ABLE TO GET THEM SECOND HAND OR IN A LIBRARY.

I have not included fiction and poetry here.
There are some lists of recommended books to read online.
www.booksforkeeps.co.uk is a site with reviews of children's books and advice on books.
www.booktrust.org.uk is a site dedicated to books and reading of all kinds intended to 'inspire reading'. If you're looking for funny books for your children, search for the books listed under Roald Dahl Funny Prize.
Carousel is a magazine for parents and librarians about all the latest children's books.

The best way to help children read fiction and poetry is to help them browse in libraries and bookshops so they can choose the books they want.

At school, there will be more recommendations, help and guidance.
Schools should be helping children to 'read for pleasure'.
At www.readingrevolution.co.uk you can see my twenty-point

plan to help set up what I've called a 'book-loving' school and community.

There will probably be a school library and visits from a touring bookshop of some sort.

If not, why not help start one with other parents?

Look out in your local newspaper for authors' visits to schools, local festivals and libraries.

These can be the key moments when children's interest in books and reading takes off.

LOOK OUT FOR

Shire Publications: for local interests, crafts.

Letterbox Library, www.letterboxlibrary.com: book club that specializes in books for all cultures and books dealing with human rights.

Catalogues, guides and programmes that go with exhibitions, visits, tours, museums.

Local history guides.

Local dialect publications.

'I-Spy' books for spotting things around us – I loved doing these when I was a boy. They come in and out of print but they're back in print at the moment. They're particularly good for journeys and holidays.

Phoenix: weekly comic with a variety of comic styles.

There is now a good clutch of children's magazines available. These are the ones I've seen: *Stew, National Geographic for Kids, Dodo, Okido, Discovery, Story Box, Anorak, The Caterpillar, Loaf, Adventure Box, The Loop*.

Thames and Hudson – New Horizons: very well-written, brilliantly illustrated series of books covering many themes to do with art and culture. They are small and accessible for older children.

PLEASE USE

Libraries
Independent bookshops
Charity shops – books sections
Second-hand bookshops
www.abebooks.com for millions of second-hand books; just use the 'advanced' search, find the 'pull-down' to search for books starting at 'lowest price'.

BOOKS WITH GREAT ADVICE ON BOOKS FOR CHILDREN – ESPECIALLY FICTION AND POETRY

Eccleshare, Julia, *1001 Children's Books You Must Read Before You Grow Up*
Rough Guides to Children's Books (there are three of these, 0–5, 5–11, teenagers)

NON-FICTION BOOKS FOR ADULTS BUT GOOD FOR SHARING OR TALKING ABOUT WITH CHILDREN

Addis, Ferdie, *Opening Pandora's Box: Phrases We Borrowed from the Classics and the Stories Behind Them*
Augarde, Tony, *Wordplay*

Bono, Edward de (ed.), *Eureka! An Illustrated History of Inventions from the Wheel to the Computer*

Brooks, Helen (ed.), *The Rainy Day Book*

Crystal, David, *Language Play*

Davidson Cragoe, Carol, *How to Read Buildings*

Donaldson, Margaret, *Children's Minds*

Freeman, J.W., *Discovering Surnames*

Hitchings, Henry, *The Secret Life of Words: How English Became English*

Irvine, Robert (ed.), *Ultimate Guide to Google's Hidden Tools: 427 Amazing New Tricks You've Never Tried*

Lancaster, Osbert, *A Cartoon History of Architecture*

Mills, A.D., *A Dictionary of English Place-Names*

Quinion, Michael, *Ballyhoo, Buckaroo, and Spuds: Ingenious Tales of Words and Their Origins*

Quinion, Michael, *Why is Q Always Followed by U: Word-Perfect Answers to the Most-Asked Questions About Language*

Rosen, Michael, *Alphabetical: How Every Letter Tells a Story*

Schwake, Susan, *Art Lab for Kids: 52 Creative Adventures in Drawing, Painting, Printmaking, Paper, and Mixed Media – for Budding Artists of All Ages*

Siegal, Michael, *Marvelous Minds: The Discovery of What Children Know*

Wittich, John, *Discovering London Street Names*

NON-FICTION BOOKS GOOD FOR CHILDREN AND YOUNG PEOPLE

Antram, David, *How to Draw Cartoons*

Ball, Johnny, *Ball of Confusion: Puzzles, Problems and Perplexing Posers*

SOME BOOKS AND ADVICE ABOUT BOOKS

Baxter, Nicola, Galante, Luigi, and Boni, Simone, *Inside Story: Extraordinary Buildings Unfolded*

Body, Wendy, and Palmer, Sue, *Words Borrowed from Other Languages*

Bounty Books, *Cooking with Kids*

Bragg, Melvyn, *On Giants' Shoulders: Great Scientists and Their Discoveries from Archimedes to DNA*

Colombo, Luann, *Uncover the Human Body*

Colson, Rob, *Perplexing Puzzles, Cryptic Challenges, Remarkable Riddles*

Corballis, Paul, *Pub Signs*

Daynes, Katie, and Allen, Peter, *See Inside Space* (an Usborne Flap Book)

Dickins, Rosie, *The Children's Book of Art: An Introduction to Famous Paintings*

Ford, Jason, *The Super Book for Super-Heroes*

Geography Collective and City Farmers, *Mission: Explore Food*

Hart-Davis, Adam, *Inventions: A History of Key Inventions that Changed the World*, illus. Nishant Choksi

Isaacson, Philip M., *Round Buildings, Square Buildings and Buildings that Wriggle like a Fish*

Law, Stephen, *Really, Really Big Questions: About Life, the Universe and Everything*, illus. Nishant Choksi

Lupton, Ellen and Julia, *D.I.Y. Kids*

Micklethwait, Lucy, *Colours: A First Art Book*

Millard, Anne, *A Street Through Time: A 12,000-Year Journey along the Same Street*, illus. Steve Noon

Noon, Steve, *Open House* (a lift-the-flap book)

Pinder, Andrew, *Illustrated Guide to Training Parents*

Rees, Nigel, *As We Say in Our House: A Book of Family Sayings*

Renshaw, Amanda, and Williams Ruggi, Gilda, *The Art Book for Children*

Restak, Richard, and Kim, Scott, *The Playful Brain: The Surprising Science of How Puzzles Improve Your Mind*

Rice, Chris and Melanie, *How Children Lived: A First Book of History*

Robinson, Tony, *Bad Kids: The Worst Behaved Children in History*

Roche, Art, *Art for Kids: Cartooning: The Only Cartooning Book You'll ever Need to be the Artist You've Always Wanted to Be*

Rothenstein, Julian, and Gooding, Mel (eds.), *The Playful Eye: An Album of Visual Delight*

Saulles, Tony de, *How to Draw Horrible Science*

Shannon, George, *Stories to Solve*, illus. Peter Sis

Shannon, George, *More Stories to Solve*

Solarz, Ewa, *Design: Domestic Equipment: Sleek, Ingenious, Groundbreaking, Noteworthy* illus. Aleksandra and Daniel Mizielinski

Sturgis, Alexander, *Magic in Art*

Taylor, Tanis, *Teach Your Granny to Text and Other Ways to Change the World*

Turner, Tracey, *Whitaker's World of Weird*

Vries, Leonard de, *Victorian Inventions*

Wolf, Gita, and Ravishankar, Anushka, *Puppets Unlimited with Everyday Materials*

Woods, Rebecca (ed.), *Easy Cakes and Cookies: Cupcakes, Brownies, Muffins, Loaves and More*

Worley, Peter, and Day, Andrew, *Thoughtings, Puzzles, Problems and Paradoxes in Poetry to Think With*

PUZZLES AND THINGS TO DO

1. THREE CHILDREN ARE IN THE PARK

One of them is called Phil Black, one of them is called Jerome White and the other is called Lulu Green.

Phil said, 'Crazy thing. We've all got names with colours in them, we're all wearing T-shirts that actually are those colours but none of us is wearing the colour that matches our names. Crazy, eh?'

The one in the green T-shirt laughed and said to Phil, 'Yeah? And? So?'

What colour T-shirts was each of them wearing?

ANSWER

Working from the facts that we've been given we know:

The three T-shirts are black, white and green.

Phil Black is not wearing a black T-shirt, Jerome White is not wearing a white T-shirt, Lulu Green is not wearing a green T-shirt.

Phil Black is not wearing a green T-shirt because we know that the person who has 'said something to Phil' is the person 'in the green T-shirt'.

We now know then that Phil is not wearing black or green. So, he must be wearing a white T-shirt.

The one in the green T-shirt cannot be Phil because we now know that he's wearing a white T-shirt. So it must be Jerome or Lulu . . . but hang on, it can't be Lulu Green because no one is wearing a T-shirt the same colour as their name. So Jerome White must be wearing the green T-shirt.

And Lulu Green must be wearing a black one.

2. THIS IS WHAT'S CALLED A 'METAGRAM'

When this is empty it makes a great sound
You can use this for frying, it's usually round
When it's hot you flap this using your hand
The donkeys did this in the race on the sand
This is the male of the human race
You might see her looks in your mum's face
This is what you get when you lie in the sun
If you need to move, you could do with one.

PUZZLES AND THINGS TO DO

ANSWERS

CAN
PAN
FAN
RAN
MAN
GRAN or NAN
TAN
VAN

(You can make up your own versions of these; best to start with just two lines that rhyme. The answers have to rhyme too, but are a different pair of rhyming words!)

3. KIM'S GAME

(I loved this one when I was a boy.)

You can play this in different ways.

You start with a tray and on to the tray you put about thirty different items – things like a key, a button, a pen.

The person holding the tray – let's call him Raj – comes into the room with the tray covered with a cloth.

Raj pulls back the cloth for one minute.

At the end of the minute, Raj covers up the tray.

Now, this is where the game can be played in different ways.

One way is to go round the room one at a time, people saying one thing that they remember. If you can't remember anything more, you drop out. Last person standing wins.

Another way is for people to use pencil and paper and write a list. Whoever has the longest list wins.

Another way is for everyone to play against the tray person. So, you each take it in turns to be the tray person, everyone in the room helps each other get the most possible. Whichever tray person manages to get the room to score the lowest score wins. This system is very good for getting people to know each other!

4. MIRROR-WRITING
(I used to do this with my brother.)

This can just be a fun thing to do, or you can make it a game.

First of all, you try to write words backwards.

Then, you take a hand-mirror and check to see if you've got it right.

What do you need to do to get better at it?

Change hands and write with the opposite hand from the one you usually use?

Do the mirror-writing while looking at what you're doing in the mirror?

How good can you get at reading mirror-writing without a mirror?

How good can you get at doing mirror-writing in the air so that another person can read what you're 'writing'?

Once you've got good at it, you can play games where each takes it in turn to write something that you hope the other person won't be able to read. Whoever succeeds wins. Use the mirror to check that the writer is not fibbing!

5. SPELLING GAME
(This one comes from my father.)

This is a game where you take it in turns to spell a word but you mustn't be the one to say the last letter.

Because a lot of words start the same way but have different endings, it can get very interesting when it comes to wriggling out of saying a last letter or setting up someone else to 'lose'.

Let's say you've taken it in turns to spell out, N, A, M.

Whoever comes next might think that they are going to lose because they will have to say, 'E', making 'name'. But no, if they say, I, – and there are the right number of players – this may mean that the next person has to say, 'N' and the next has to say, 'G'.

6. HARMONY SINGING AND ROUNDS

(From my brother.)

I'm not very good at singing and I find it difficult to sing in harmony or sing rounds. When I get the hang of it though, I feel dead chuffed.

We all know tunes that are rounds even if we don't usually sing them that way. 'Frère Jacques' and 'London's Burning' are the two I know best.

The usual way to do these is for singers to start up their singing one after the other. The first singer starts singing 'London's burning, London's burning'. The moment they start to sing 'Fetch the engines' (on that same beat), the second singer starts at the beginning, while the first carries on. The third singer listens to the second person singing 'London's burning, London's burning', and this third person starts up singing 'London's burning, London's burning' on the first beat of 'Fetch the engines' . . . and so on.

You each agree to sing the whole song, let's say, twice.

Now, there is usually a 'proper' way to do this; that's to say, quite often a round is geared so that it fits perfectly for three or four singers to sing separately and for each singer to sing the whole thing through three times. Or something like that. You can experiment to see which is the best. If there are only two of you, you can split a round in half at the halfway point.

There are guides for doing this online. Just google 'singing rounds'.

If you want to explore this a bit more, in Shakespeare's plays, rounds are known as 'catches'. The one I like best is a rude one in *Twelfth Night*: 'Hold thy peace, thou knave!' and every time I hear it, it reminds me of the time I was going to be Sir Toby Belch in the school production but I had a car accident on the night before the dress rehearsal and missed doing the show. I'm still sad about it, fifty years later!

And of course, apart from 'Frère Jacques' there are plenty more in French and other languages. The one my parents used to sing me is in German, 'O wie wohl ist mir am Abend' and sounds sad and beautiful.

You can find these online, being sung really well.

If you can get the hang of singing rounds, you might be able to sing in harmony. My brother – who can sing very well – struggled to get me to do this. When his voice broke, he wanted to sing the bass line under me singing the melody. Because we sang the same hymns and carols in school, he would get me to sing them while he sang the bass line that he had learned in the school choir. Great idea, but I would hear him singing and start to drift towards his harmony.

Nearly always, bands and duos use harmonies, so one way to get into this is simply to imitate them. Another way is to start with a tune that everyone knows really well like 'Happy Birthday' and experiment with starting 'higher' or 'lower' and sticking with it all the way through.

7. PROBABILITY

My friend Jack has two children; one of them is a boy. Do you think that it's more likely that the other one is a boy or that the other one is a girl?

ANSWER

This is the old conundrum similar to the tossing coin one.
You can do this as an exercise.
Take the coin, say, 'Heads or tails?'
And then you keep doing it, keeping a score.
You can experiment by always placing the coin on your thumb
with the same side up every time. Or you can switch it each time.

What happens?

Back with Jack and his two children.

Here are the possibilities:

Boy Girl
Boy Boy

So, mathematically, the chances are: one in two or, as we say,
fifty, fifty.

So, why in some families do we see, say, three girls and no
boys?
And what about the births as a whole in one country, is it
exactly 50:50?
If not, why not?

8. NEVER-ENDING CIRCLE

Can you make up a phrase or sentence which if you put it in a circle can let you start where you like and finish where you like – it will still make sense?

One way is to do it with two words like, say, 'dream' and 'sweetly'. Then you can repeat these to make a circle as big as you like. You can start on the 'sweetly' or the 'dream' and it will make sense.

'-ing' words work well too as with, say, 'flying' and 'birds'.

The moment you go to three or four or more words it gets much harder!

One obvious one is to write, 'and round and round' many times!

What about 'always eat caterpillars'?

Over to you!

9. PAPER GAME

Cut out two squares.
Lay them side by side.
How can you cut these up so that when you rearrange the pieces they'll make a square?

ANSWER

If you cut each square across from corner to corner – diagonally – you'll now have four 'equilateral triangles'. You can arrange these into a square by making them all point towards each other . . .

10. I ALWAYS LIE

I always lie. Am I telling the truth?

ANSWER

If it's the truth then that means I always lie.
But if I always lie, even saying, 'I always lie' can't be the truth.
That should mean then that I wasn't telling the truth.
I was lying.

If saying, 'I always lie', is a lie, that means even saying, 'I always lie' must also be a lie . . .
So, does that mean it's turned out to be the truth?

How to get out of this?

What if the truth is that I don't always lie – I sometimes lie?

In that case, saying, 'I always lie' is not the truth, because I only lie sometimes, and on this occasion, that's what I was doing: I was lying, by saying, 'I always lie'.

11. LETTERS INTO NUMBERS

ABCD x E = DCBA

ANSWER

2178 x 4 = 8712

This reminds me of that old conundrum: can you think of a sum that works that uses the numbers – digits, actually – in the right order?

12 = 3 x 4

12. THE AMAZING NUMBER 37

Explore the number 37 by multiplying it first by 1, then by 2, then by 3, then by 4 and so on . . . keep going all the way to 27.

See any patterns?

ANSWER

When multiplied by a certain kind of number, you get a rising sequence of three-figure numbers with something similar about them . . . (I don't want to give the game away. Discovery is all!)

13. A TRUE NUMBER

Why is 317 not a true number?

ANSWER

Turn it upside down to see.

(It says 'LIE'.)

14. CAN YOU TALK IN 'KEY-JUG LANGUAGE'?

To do this, all you have to do is talk by saying the letters of each word, and after each letter you say the word, 'key'. At the end of each word, you say, 'key-jug'. You try to do this as fast as you can. The faster you say it, the harder it is for the person listening to get what you're saying.

You can take it in turns to disguise what you're saying, and see who does best at disguising and who does best at deciphering.

I've found it fun to start by saying, 'Hello, my name is Mike.' This comes out as:

H-key, E-key, L-key, L-key, O-key-jug, M-key, Y-key-jug, N-key, A-key, M-key, E-key-jug, I-key, S-key-jug, M-key, I-key, K-key, E-key-jug.

15. THUMBS UP

You need at least two players, and one 'caller'.

The caller shouts any of these:

'Thumbs up!'
'Thumbs down!'

'Thumbs in!'
'Thumbs out!'

The people playing must do the opposite of what they're asked to do.

So, 'Thumbs up!' would normally mean you should hold out your fists with thumbs up, like a Roman Emperor saving a gladiator. In this game, 'Thumbs up!' signals that you must hold your fists with thumbs down. 'Thumbs down!' means you must do thumbs up.

For 'Thumbs in!' where you would normally hold out your fists with your thumbs pointing towards each other, you must hold our your fists with your thumbs pointing outwards.

'Thumbs out!' means you must point your thumbs inwards, towards each other.

If you make a mistake, you're out.

16. THE MIND-READING TRICK

(Thanks to Johnny Ball for this one.)

You take a piece of paper and tear it into nine squares. You must do this by making three columns each way.

Then, you hand out the pieces of paper to nine people (or if you have fewer in the room, doubles and triples to people till you've got rid of all of them).

You tell people that you want them to write a word on the pieces of paper, or a number, or draw a picture or a diagram . . . and you leave the room.

When they're ready, you ask someone to collect up the pieces of paper and then spread them out, with the writing upwards, on the table in front of everyone.

FOOD FOR THOUGHT

You say that you are a mind-reader but not a perfect one. You reckon though that you can read the mind of one person in the room. You pick one piece of paper, you read it out, you think, you think and then you identify the person who wrote it . . .

How do you get it right?

ANSWER

Only one of the pieces of paper will have four torn sides, the middle square. What you have to do is make sure that you remember which person you gave this square to.

If people don't get it, repeat the trick, making up some other phooey to do with mind-reading to distract them from the squares themselves.

17. FOLD-OVERS

The surrealists used to play a game where they wrote a line of poetry on one line, folded over the piece of paper with that line on it and handed it to the next surrealist. Then, when it had done the rounds, they unfolded the piece of paper, and read the lines as if it were one poem.

If you are surrealist-minded, this is a great game to play. You end up with strange poems.

If you are more logical and would like something like a story, you can do fold-over this way:

First-off writes what is obviously a first line of a story. The last bit of the line – the hook, if you like – goes on to the line or space below. It is an unfinished part of a sentence. First-off folds over their line leaving the hook for the next person to finish off and start another line. And so on until you all think it's the end.

Unfold and see what kind of story you've got.

Wide-lined paper is best for this.

So, a story might turn out like this:

I've put a // sign where one person finishes and the next begins:

It was a dark and stormy night when

George walked in // 'Hello,' said George. 'I can't find my trousers. Did I leave them in the car?' // 'No, they've gone to bed. I sang them to sleep,' said Mum . . .

And so on . . .

18. DOUBLE-ACT

Get a joke book. People pick jokes.

Find ways of telling the jokes as a double-act.

Think of for example question and answer, interruptions, getting it wrong, repeating each other, pretending not to hear each other.

Practise talking to each other without looking at each other, but looking at the audience.

Or, practise talking to each other and only looking at the audience at the end, when you say the punch-line.

19. I HAVE TWO SAND-TIMERS

One is a 7-minute timer for boiling an egg very hard.

The other is an 11-minute timer for boiling two eggs very hard. (Ignore that, that's a joke.)

FOOD FOR THOUGHT

However, I do want to time something for 15 minutes. I have no watch. How can I use the two timers to give me 15 minutes?

ANSWER

Start the timers at the same time.

When the 7-minute timer is finished, turn it over.

When the 11-minute timer is finished, turn the 7-minute timer over again.

When the 7-minute timer is finished that will be . . . 15 minutes.

How?

The 11 minutes it takes to empty the 11-minute glass is added to the time that's left in the 7-minute glass before it too is emptied – which was 4 minutes.

This is how:

We 'collected' those 4 minutes of time when we turned the 7-minute glass over while the 11-minute glass ran on (11 – 7 = 4).

Because we turned the 7-minute glass back again when the 11-minute glass ran out, those 4 minutes we had 'collected' could now be added to the 11 minutes (11 + 4 = 15).

The trick in these puzzles – you can do something similar with jugs of water – is to work out how you can use the quantity of one to subtract and add against the quantity of the other to make a grand total.

20. MAKING UP SERIES

(My brother and I used to play this one.)

If I write:

1, 2, 3, 4, 5 and I ask you what the next three numbers are, you'll probably say, 6, 7, 8.

Fine.

If I write, 1, 3, 5, 7, 9, you'll probably write 11, 13, 15.

Fine.

And if I write, Z1, Y2, X3, W4, V5 you'll probably get that I'm doing the alphabet backwards and the numbers going up at the same time . . .

Or you can do more complicated things . . .

1, 99, 2, 198, 3, 297 . . .

or

1, 5, 14, 30, 55

That was 1, 2 x 2 = 4. Add to 1 = 5. 3 x 3 = 9. Add to 5 = 14. 4 x 4 = 16. Add to 14 = 30. 5 x 5 = 25. Add to 30 = 55.

So, the way to play is to take it in turns to make up series for the other one to crack.

ACKNOWLEDGEMENTS

The ideas and stories in the book owe a lot to my parents, Harold and Connie and to my third parent, my brother Brian. Being a parent to Joe, Eddie, Isaac, Elsie and Emile and a step-parent to Naomi and Laura has occupied my thoughts for nearly forty years. A good deal of what we have all learned and are still learning is in this book.

I've worked alongside many teachers who've shown me how children and school students can learn with pleasure – in particular, Geoffrey Summerfield, Richard Andrews, Penny Bentley, Sean McErlaine, John Richmond and Alan Newland.

Love and gratitude to Emma who started coaxing me several years ago to put my thoughts on this matter into a book. She even gave me a phrase as a compass to steer by: 'happy and curious'.

INDEX

INDEX

INDEX

INDEX